Authority, Education
and Emancipation

Authority, Education and Emancipation

A Collection of Papers by

LAWRENCE STENHOUSE

HEINEMANN EDUCATIONAL BOOKS
LONDON

Heinemann Educational Books Ltd
22 Bedford Square, London WC1B 3HH

LONDON EDINBURGH MELBOURNE AUCKLAND
HONG KONG SINGAPORE KUALA LUMPUR NEW DELHI
IBADAN NAIROBI JOHANNESBURG
EXETER (NH) KINGSTON PORT OF SPAIN

British Library CIP Data
Stenhouse, Lawrence
    Authority, education and emancipation.
    1. Education, Secondary—Great Britain
    I. Title
    373.41   LA656

ISBN 0 435 80854 0

Filmset by Eta Services (Typesetters) Ltd, Beccles, Suffolk
Printed and bound in Great Britain by
Biddles Ltd, Guildford and King's Lynn

Contents

Acknowledgements   viii
Foreword: The Story behind the Papers   ix

Part One: 1960-65

Introduction: Thinking it through   3
General Education in the Light of the Crowther Report   7
A Cultural Approach to the Sociology of the Curriculum   20
Social Determinism and Education   34
The Concept of Standards in the Theory of Education   47
The Humanities in the Classroom   55

Part Two: The Humanities Curriculum Project

Introduction: Trying it out   69
The Humanities Curriculum Project   73
Humanities Curriculum Project Consultative Committee
    Working Paper No. 2   89
The Humanities Curriculum Project: an introduction
    for experimental schools   107
The Nature and Interpretation of Evidence   115
The Humanities Project and the Problem of Motivation   119
An Appeal for Evidence of the Effectiveness of an
    Alternative Role to that of Neutral Chairman in
    Promoting Rational Inquiry into Moral Issues 133

Part Three: 1972-82

Introduction: Following it up   143
Teaching through Small-Group Discussion: formality,
    rules and authority   146
The Aims of the Secondary School   153
Curriculum Research and the Art of the Teacher   155
Towards a Vernacular Humanism   163
Research as a Basis for Teaching   177

Index   197

For Jean Rudduck, whom I met
at the beginning of the
Humanities Curriculum Project

Acknowledgements

I wish to make grateful acknowledgement to the following for permission to reprint papers: the editors and publishers of: the *Scandinavian Journal of Educational Research* for 'A cultural approach to the sociology of the curriculum'; the *Journal of Further and Higher Education* (formerly *Education for Teaching*) for 'The concept of standards in the theory of education', and 'An appeal for evidence of the effectiveness of an alternative role to that of neutral chairman . . .' together with the short extract from the paper by John T. Hyland, whom I must also thank; the *Cambridge Journal of Education* for 'Teaching through small-group discussion'; and *Curriculum* for 'Curriculum research and the art of the teacher.' My thanks are also due to Hodder and Stoughton Educational for 'The Humanities Curriculum Project'; to the Schools Council for Consultative Committee Working Paper No. 2 and the introduction for experimental schools; to the Claremont Reading Conference for 'The nature and interpretation of evidence'; to the Dartington Society for 'Towards a vernacular humanism'; and to the University of East Anglia for 'Research as a basis for teaching'.

. . . and an Apology

Each of the papers printed here has its location in the historical development of a set of ideas, and I have thought it important not to revise them given this historical perspective. However, I am sufficiently sensitive to the sexist use of language, particularly blatant in some of the earlier papers, to feel the desire to offer my apologies to all readers who for 'he' must read 'she', and my regrets to readers of whichever sex.

L.S.   Summer 1982

Foreword: The Story behind the Papers

The papers collected in this volume, some of which have not previously been published, are not selected uniformly for their quality, but rather as illustrating the development of a line of thinking which has been one of the main themes of a professional career in education and educational research. In the nature of the case, I find the theme, the relation of authority and emancipation in education, an interesting one; but I hope that the collection has an added significance because I was fortunate enough to be given an opportunity which chimed with my interest: the directorship of the Humanities Curriculum Project, which I held from 1967 to 1972. This enabled me to pursue ideas into practice with generous resources and able and like-minded colleagues.

The theme started in my thinking in the period 1951 to 1956, when I studied for the M.Ed. in Glasgow University under Stanley Nisbet – who wrote one of the earliest books on curriculum published in Britain[1] – and Kenneth Richmond – who wrote a later one at the time of the fruition of the curriculum movement.[2] In a series of student essays I struggled with the problem of general and moral education and of indoctrination. In an examination answer I found insoluble the problems of moral education, given that teachers' qualifications were academic, not moral.

Work in sociology and social psychology, undertaken for the same degree under Zevedei Barbu, led to a fairly systematic reading of Marx, Pareto, Weber and Durkheim, which sharpened my sense that social theory was fertile for my problem. At this point, in the summer of 1954, I discovered and read very carefully the work of George Herbert Mead, not then very fashionable, and from him was led to Sapir, Whorf and Vygotsky. I also began to read anthropology, turning again and again to one particular study, *The Realm of a Rain Queen* by E. J. and J. D. Krige,[3] which I still find one of the most fascinating accounts of growing up and learning in a preliterate society.

An interest in culture led naturally to an interest in mass

communication and mass culture, which introduced me to
Blumer through his work on cinema (1933).[4] By the time I
graduated in 1956, my problem was formulated as the relationship of culture to the development of individuality and of the
individual's powers, to the creation of new meanings, cultural
innovations. It was seen from a perspective that was broadly
symbolic interactionist.

The origins of the problem which obsessed me lay firmly in
practice. As a pupil at Manchester Grammar School I had been
fortunate in my sixth-form experience to meet three teachers –
Bunn, Mason and Lingard – who had opened ideas to me in a
way that emancipated me by enhancing my sense of my own
powers. When I came to teach, I discovered that though the
school system valued achievement narrowly defined, it did not for
the most part value the emancipation of pupils through knowledge. Nor could I satisfactorily do within the system what had
been done for me.

To put the matter in up-to-date terms, education was involved
in reproduction of the distribution of knowledge: I had attended
a privileged school, where knowledge and the power associated
with it were represented to me as my right; and now I taught in
schools where the message was that many are called but few are
chosen. I became particularly interested in the plight of 3T2, the
bottom leavers' class in the multilateral in which I taught in
Glasgow. And I related their situation to that of the trade
unionists I met in my evening classes for the extra-mural
department and through the Scottish Socialist Teachers. It was
my head of department, Jimmie Christie, whose care for the same
things as myself had brought me into that group. In the 1950s the
thesis of reproduction was in essence familiar among its members,
though the term was not.

I left Glasgow for Dunfermline because Fife was offering houses
to teachers; and there I finished my largely irrelevant dissertation, which by its insistence on statistical procedures turned my
eyes away from the classroom rather than towards it. When I
graduated with my M.Ed. I applied for a Simon Fellowship in
Manchester University to undertake a comparative case study of
education in Macclesfield and Dunfermline. At the same time I
applied for a staff tutorship in psychology and secondary
education in the Institute of Education of the University of
Durham, which was located in Newcastle-upon-Tyne. The latter
came up first. I was offered the post and accepted it.

The papers printed here were all published after that move in 1957.

Durham Institute was firmly dedicated to the improvement of practice in schools. Brian Stanley, the professor, had started the Institute's in-service programme with a Froebel course and with it he had established the precedent of visiting the schools and classrooms of the experienced teachers who enrolled in courses for the Institute's diplomas. I found myself sharing with the late Ronnie Morris courses for secondary teachers in Newcastle, Middlesbrough and Carlisle, and visiting a great variety of schools ranging from unreorganized elementaries to newly built secondary moderns. There was a lot to learn and every opportunity to learn it.

Not least from colleagues. Ronnie Morris encouraged me to concentrate on curriculum as a focus of study and used his shrewdness to set me conundrums; Winifred Fawcus taught me about the English primary tradition at its best, my own experience being entirely secondary. Quite specific was what I learned from Dorothy Heathcote, who was the drama tutor. I watched her working with approved school boys in that form of improvised drama which she has subsequently made famous, and I discovered that she could face and use the experience of young delinquents because her transmutation of lawlessness into the laws of drama allowed her to take a neutral stance. It was her art to help people to examine problems through acting, and she had no need to adopt the judgemental stance.

Newcastle is neighbour to Norway and this brought me the opportunity at 32 to make my first trip abroad. Captivated by the country, by resemblances to Scotland and by the friendship of a Norwegian colleague, Per Rand, I learned the language – thereby getting also a working knowledge of Swedish and Danish – and set about a doctoral study on the history of the comprehensive idea in Norway. Its interest is partly that it dates back into the nineteenth century when a famous Norwegian educator, Hartvig Nissen, succeeded in setting up a comprehensive elementary school, the *Folkeskole*. Subsequent extensions of compulsory schooling were then assimilated to the comprehensive tradition.

Nissen also wrote about the education in Scotland, and my first academic publication was an account of his work, which constitutes a source for Scottish educational history. In 1852 Nissen received a government stipend to visit Scotland and study the Scottish educational system in the time of David Stow and

John Wood. He reported on his visit in a book, *Beskrivelse over Skotlands Almueskolevaesen.*[5]

The paper I wrote on Nissen[6] is not worth reprinting here since most of it is not relevant to my theme, but one aspect of it is worth mentioning as an influence on my later thinking, including the Humanities Project.

Nissen was greatly interested in the encyclopaedic readers which were then widely used in Scottish schools. The character of these is sufficiently revealed in his account of one of the volumes of 'The Moral and Intellectual Series':

> The fourth volume is composed of 324 pages and contains 16 pieces on English history, 42 pieces on general world history, 14 pieces of mixed content, 6 pieces on physical geography, 5 pieces of mechanical content, 7 referring to pneumatics and hydrostatics, 3 to hydraulics, 3 to optics, 1 to acoustics, 1 concerning magnetism, 2 concerning electricity, 9 referring to astronomy, 1 to geology, 2 to mineralogy, 8 to chemistry, 6 to animal physiology, 4 to plant physiology, and 14 to natural history. In addition there are some geographical and chronological tables, scientific definitions, geometric and astronomical definitions, and finally, as is customary in reading books, some pages which contain a catalogue of the roots of many English words of Latin and Greek derivation.

The elementary school of those days was mainly concerned with the teaching of reading, but the teachers wished to give the children not just reading skills but also knowledge. Hence the reading book was not, as were the books I had been given for use with 'non-academic' pupils of 13, 14 and 15 in a Scottish school, drained of significance in the pursuit of motivation and vocabulary control. On the contrary the nineteenth-century reading book aimed to be important for what it said.

Seen from one point of view, the Humanities Project materials were a loose-leaf, twentieth-century adaptation of the old encyclopaedic reader. And they were also caught in an aspiration prefigured by Nissen in an odd setting. He described and commented on an examination of reading in a school he visited.

> In English some pieces were read from the reading book. All, without exception, read well, some remarkably finely. Thus, there was a lively thirteen-year-old boy, who had to read a short rhetorical piece, whose opening was: 'Liberty is commensurate with and inseparable from British soil; British law proclaims even to the stranger and the sojourner, the moment that he sets his foot upon British earth, that the ground on which he treads is holy, and

consecrated by the genius of Universal Emàncipation!' He read with absolute certainty, with strong and true intonation and with an expression in which deep and noble British self-esteem proclaimed itself, and he carried away all the people who were present to such an extent that an involuntary burst of applause broke out.

And Nissen comments:

... when the simplest working man's son in the common school is thus through the employment of the materials of instruction which are prescribed for him, in a position to strike the very heartstrings of his superiors and carry them with him in the stream of emotion, then one not only understands, but feels, that this people is one and that education, though its levels be different, yet is similar and common for all sections of the people.

No doubt Nissen's enthusiasm for the comprehensive primary school has led him into wishful thinking.

And yet . . . how to reinterpret in the contemporary school that aspiration towards a democratic intellect which might increase the powers and independence of the pupil? There was, it seemed to me, a need to increase the seriousness of the content of reading materials in schools if this content were to be seen neither as the occasion for an exercise nor as matter to be mastered, but rather as the cultural basis of interaction within the learning group.

This focus on the relation between the culture available in our society and the micro-culture of the interacting group – and especially the learning group – became central to my interest, the problem being to interpret the sociology of knowledge and culture in a sufficiently flexible sense. And circumstances responded to my interest: there was no sociologist on the staff of the Institute in Newcastle and I was able to move to teach sociology rather than psychology. There were in those days few formally qualified sociologists about and with Bernstein, Peters and Wiseman urging the teacher educators to abandon their integrated courses for a collection code based on the contributory disciplines, there was a demand for adaptation or retraining. Bill Taylor, then a lecturer at Bede College Durham, and I organized a sociology reading group for the college lecturers of the Institute area.

For me it was not to last for long. I responded to an approach from Jordanhill College and, tempted by a return to Scotland at a professorial salary, applied for the principal lectureship in education and got the job.

It was, I suppose, in many ways a mistake, and certainly it was an uncomfortable move at first. Whereas I had enjoyed a room of my own in Newcastle, I found myself sharing a crowded departmental staff room where it was impossible to work. In a college of some three thousand students the administrative load was heavy. Most oppressive of all was the absence of a research tradition. Fortunately, Henry Wood, the Principal of the College, wished to move in the direction that would remedy these discomforts. We made progress, but I did not stay long enough to see the individual rooms, and I stayed six years.

There I wrote *Culture and Education*,[7] which was, so the review said, the first application of the sociology of knowledge to curriculum. There too I edited *Discipline in Schools*,[8] written by colleagues in the education department; and they were good colleagues. The meetings of the Scottish branch of the British Sociological Association were important to me; but though I gave a paper on cultural sociology and the curriculum and another on Parsons' pattern variables as tools for the classification of classroom climate, these were the times before the interests of sociologists turned generally to school and classroom. I felt isolated and outside the main stream. Thelma Bristow, the research librarian at the London Institute, helped to keep intellectual contacts going. Jean Floud gave important encouragement.

During my time at Jordanhill I had to teach more widely than sociology and secondary education, and I had to teach in a philosophic tradition. That brought some reading of existentialism and of phenomenology, which I had not met in my philosophy course at university. And of course it brought also a reading of and personal acquaintance with Richard Peters. *Authority, Responsibility and Education*[9] made its contribution to the process model; *Ethics and Education*,[10] among other contributions, provided the distinction between the teacher as in authority and as an authority, which was crucial to the teacher role in the Humanities Project.

In 1966, while *Culture and Education* was still in press, I visited the United States for the first time to attend a conference, and there I met Joslyn Owen, then one of the joint secretaries of the Schools Council. We talked over the ideas I had been writing about, and I sent him a typescript copy of the book. In the autumn term of that year I was invited to a one-day conference at Nuffield Lodge, which was chaired by Tony Becher. Its purpose was to discuss a report which later became Schools Council Working Paper No. 11: *Society and the Young School Leaver*.[11] My reaction to the report was rather hostile, and I made this plain, arguing the need for much richer curriculum content, for the integration of 'young school leavers' with other pupils who stayed on – as the 'early leavers' soon would – until the examination year, and for much clearer help for teachers with the kind of methods that might be developed in the classroom.

I had not long returned to Scotland when I had a telephone call to say that the conference I had attended was set up to look over likely candidates for the directorship of a curriculum project, and that they had decided to make the offer to me. The project, which was already virtually secure of its funds, was to be called 'The Humanities Curriculum Project'. One chapter in *Culture and Education* had been titled 'The Humanities in the Classroom'. It seemed that I was being given the chance to develop and discipline through a major curriculum project the set of ideas I had been working on over the years.

It was much later that I discovered that nobody in the Nuffield Foundation or the Schools Council – the joint sponsors of the Project – had in fact read the typescript I had sent them.

My situation, when I came to London to run the Project, was a strange one in many ways. Although I had grown up in Manchester and had had four years in Newcastle, I had never taught in an English school, and for the past six years I had been training teachers in Scotland. My first university, St Andrews, had had a chair in Humanity – there it meant Latin. So my notion of humanities was humane letters. I knew little of the English move to integration in the curriculum; and, as I found out about it, I did not find it immediately congenial. I taught English, but regarded history as my first love and my home subject, and my loyalty to historical modes of thinking was rather strong.

At the same time, the situation that I came into was a heady one. I soon found myself giving interviews to the press and being dined by publishers! Not an easy climate in which to find one's feet. And we had to move quickly.

However, the Humanities Project had a strong team. Maurice Plaskow, who joined us from the BBC, started first, and shortly after we recruited John Elliott as a result of a round of interviews. Ann Cook, an American, who later went on to write the Monster books among other achievements, came to us for a year on the recommendation of Halsey. Gillian Drayson (now Pugh) joined us as publisher and office manager. Jean Rudduck came around Easter of 1968 on recommendation from the Schools Council where she had worked on the research team: her task was to administer the experiment in schools and organize conferences. Everyone worked extremely hard. We had to set up experimental schools, work out our logics and produce materials within a year.

Many of those who worked on the Project became researchers, but the Project recruited none. By temperament I am research orientated, but I lacked experience. And the Project, designed on the Nuffield model, was uncomfortably developmental. We needed extra research strength and the way to get it seemed to be to set up an evaluation. I wrote a proposal, had it accepted and then found difficulty in recruiting researchers. Such was the view of curriculum projects that researchers were not attracted to work on them. In the end it was Barry MacDonald, who had worked with me in Jordanhill, who joined us as Schools Study Officer with a commission to study the Project in classrooms and design an evaluation. He was later joined by Gajendra Verma, Helen Simons and Stephen Humble. On the project side of the operation, we recruited John Hipkin, Patricia Haikin, and later Alan Dale, an HCP teacher, and Ron Bland, who was seconded to us by Bishop Lonsdale College.

At first one had to feel one's way, both in achieving enough common ground in the working group, and in validating the ideas we were exploring and the stances we took. Working Paper No. 2 of the Schools Council: *Raising the School Leaving Age*[12] was a considerable support. One of its authors, John Witherington, HMI, visited the project, expressed the view that what we were attempting was consonant with the spirit of the working paper, but warned us that it was likely to take sixty years!

The other author of the working paper was the charismatic and formidable Derek Morrell. A distinguished civil servant, he had for some time been concerned about the idea of the neutral civil servant – the stance did not in his view leave sufficient room for the commitment needed in creative administration – and he consequently reacted unfavourably to our exploring the neutral role of the teacher. A debate by correspondence was followed by a meeting at which I played him audiotapes of classrooms. I remember a long silence and then from him: 'You have there a true rationality of feeling.' His experience of the tape had, I think, been something like Nissen's of the Scottish classroom. By then in the Home Office, Morrell brought four approved schools into the project trials and initiated the Catholic Schools Humanities Project to examine the relevance of the HCP to the confessional school and to produce supplementary materials. Tony Higgins directed it.

We had immense and highly intelligent support from Tony Becher of the Nuffield Foundation and from the staff of the Schools Council. Joslyn Owen, John Banks, and later Geoffrey Caston and Paul Fordham were supportive as joint secretaries and project officers. Jack Wrigley, who understood what I was trying to say about objectives, rescued me by explaining my position and supporting me at a number of conferences.

In the end the Project was extended from 1970 to 1972, moved from London to the University of East Anglia in Norwich, and fell foul of the programme committee of the Schools Council by virtue of including race relations in its topics, and perhaps for other reasons which only a historian of their proceedings could disinter. From 1972 the dissemination hobbled on petty cash. The remains of the team scrambled aboard the rafts of other projects.

There remain a lot of heritables. The Humanities Project was the first to publish loose-leaf resources and substantially influenced publishing formats, even when printing costs dictated book forms. Its materials are still used though often in sixth-form general studies. They are also used in teaching English as a foreign language. In Austria, the Humanities Project teaching strategy has been the basis of a project in trades union education. The influence was also felt in higher education through Jean Rudduck's subsequent project in that area. *Learning to Teach through Discussion* (1979)[13] is a publication by a group of HCP teachers. And because it struggled against its own central authority for teacher autonomy based on teacher research and self-monitoring it founded a strong tradition of the teacher as researcher. Finally, it supported an evaluation which has become extensively influential in its own right.

For myself, I returned to the theme in different ways. In a project on the problems and effects of teaching about race relations, supported by the Social Science Research Council and the Gulbenkian Foundation, I tried – with shortcomings and consequent learning – to mount an approach to a very difficult set of teaching problems in which teachers carried heavy research responsibilities. Now, in a British Library Project on Library Access and Sixth-form Studies, I am looking at emancipation again: this time in the form of the development of the capacity for independent study in the sixth form.

Nevertheless, I have spent a good deal of time thinking through the old theme in the light of reflection on the experience of that particular opportunity, the Humanities Project. It was my share of a decade of opportunities that looks distant – but not I think irrelevant – now.

References

1. Stanley Nisbet, *Purpose in the Curriculum* (London: University of London Press, 1957).
2. W. Kenneth Richmond, *The School Curriculum* (London: Methuen, 1971).
3. E. J. Krige and J. D. Krige, *The Realm of a Rain Queen* (London: Oxford University Press for the International African Institute, 1943).
4. Herbert Blumer, *Movies and Conduct* and *Movies, Delinquency and Crime* (Motion Pictures and Youth: the Payne Fund Series) (New York: Macmillan, 1933).
5. Hartvig Nissen, *Beskrivelse over Skotlands Almueskolevaesen tilligmed forslag till forskjellige Foranstaltninger til en videre Udvikling af det norske Almueskolevaesen* (Christiania: Malling, 1854).
6. Lawrence Stenhouse, 'Hartvig Nissen's impressions of the Scottish educational system in the mid-nineteenth century'. *British Journal of Educational Studies* May (1961), pp. 143–54.
7. Lawrence Stenhouse, *Culture and Education* (London: Nelson, 1967a).
8. Lawrence Stenhouse (Editor), *Discipline in Schools* (Oxford: Pergamon, 1967b).
9. R. S. Peters, *Authority, Responsibility and Education* (London: Allen and Unwin, 1959).
10. R. S. Peters, *Ethics and Education* (London: Allen and Unwin, 1966).
11. Schools Council, *Society and the Young School Leaver* (Working Paper No. 11) (London: Her Majesty's Stationery Office, 1967).
12. Schools Council, *Raising the School Leaving Age* (Working Paper No. 2) (London: Her Majesty's Stationery Office, 1965).
13. Jean Rudduck (Editor), *Learning to Teach through Discussion* (Norwich: CARE, University of East Anglia, 1979).

Part One: 1960–65

Introduction: Thinking it through

The papers in this first section were written between 1960 and 1965. They sketch an aspiration towards a common element in the curriculum which could provide a basis for the development of discourse and understanding among pupils of different social groups and of differing academic achievement. They also try to set that aspiration within a broad view of society and to develop a theory which will support the analysis and understanding of classroom interaction in terms of culture as its product and its medium.

The first paper, 'General Education in the Light of the Crowther Report', was the basis of a public lecture given in the Department of Education of King's College, Newcastle-upon-Tyne. The Report itself had been published in 1959, the work of a committee of enquiry set up in 1956 under the chairmanship of Geoffrey Crowther, at that time editor of the *Economist*. The committee had a particular concern with the balance of general and specialized studies offered to the 15–18 age group. My paper is shaped by this focus.

The context is worth recalling. The Report advocated the raising of the school-leaving age to sixteen, but this did not happen until 1972. At the time of Crowther there was concern that the majority of young people received no education between fifteen and eighteen, and the feeling that an expanding economy demanded and could support more extended education. At the same time, the system remained selective, with grammar and modern schools and indeed a good number of unreorganized elementary schools. In 1960 only 4·7 per cent of pupils in the state system attended comprehensive schools, and many of them were multilaterals.

Crowther accepted the differentiated system of schools which I derided in the lecture by comparison with the road system, picking up the metaphor from the Report's recommendation of an 'alternative road' through schooling with a more practical bias. I also tried to highlight the peculiar British principle that, where there are alternatives available in schooling, the pupils should be selected for them rather than choose them. Clearly, it is difficult within such a system to distribute general education equitably.

At the time most radicals were calling for comprehensive education in terms that suggested that it might bring equality of opportunity and also curricular gains. I still feel, as I did at the time of this lecture, that our society will adapt any system of school organization to the transmission of social privilege. It is the task of the teacher to do what can be done to emancipate each pupil; but it does seem true that certain forms of school organization constitute greater barriers than others to such a programme of emancipation. On the whole I think that comprehensivization has been advantageous to emancipation, but of itself it does not take us very far.

The aims and aspirations expressed at the end of the lecture appear to me to remain valid. Progress towards their achievement has been made, but it has naturally been slow progress, and there are now pressures pushing back toward the curriculum of the all-age elementary school.

If the piece on the Crowther Report sets the ideas to be developed in these papers in the educational context in which they were originally conceived, the second paper on 'A Cultural Approach to the Sociology of the Curriculum' tries to present those ideas within a framework of theory. It is theory developed from a reading of anthropology and symbolic interactionist sociology. In many ways it anticipates the 'new sociology of education', and I still believe that the theoretical stance here outlined is a powerful one for an understanding of curriculum and teaching, particularly in its linking of culture in society with the small-group culture of the classroom.

There was no interest, in British sociology at that time, in the sociology of curriculum or schooling. The paper, given in the University of Oslo, was published in the *Scandinavian Journal of Educational Research* (then *Pedagogisk Forskning*).

The following year I was excited to receive an invitation to lecture in the University of Uppsala. I knew that the Rektor of the University was Torgny Segerstedt, a symbolic interactionist sociologist. I assumed that the sociological bent of the education faculty would be sympathetic, and I guessed that my paper in the *Scandinavian Journal of Educational Research* had attracted their attention.

This seemed the opportunity to present a problem with which I had been wrestling. Just as the current perception of curriculum and schooling as 'reproduction' encounters difficulties in accommodating the observable phenomena of individuation through education, so my theory based upon the concept of culture might seem to lock education within a conceptual framework dedicated by anthropologists to explaining the regularities of human behaviour. The Marxist response is the idea of reproduction being contested through resistance. My attempt to do justice to the observed phenomena of education serving as a means of personal development and emancipation involved detaching 'culture' from behaviourism and from numerable groups and reinterpreting the concept in symbolic interactionist terms. As a medium of interaction it became also a medium of individuation.

I gave two lectures on the theme in Uppsala. The first is summarized here, the second reproduced in full. They were in the style of the first draft of *Culture and Education*, addressed primarily to an academic audience. After I had given the lectures I discovered that there was at that time no notion of the sociology of education among the education faculty of Uppsala, and my lectures came to them rather as from another world. I had been invited because of a mistaken impression that I was an opponent of the comprehensive school.

Another problem in the development of my cultural theory was its relation to philosophical conceptions and particularly to the aims of education. The idea of aims had been translated by American psychometricians and curriculum developers into the behavioural objectives model. This conjoined the propositions that education is an intentional activity and that intentionality involves having a specific goal, with the behaviourist definition of learning as change in behaviour. It thus demanded that the aims of education be analysed into intended learning outcomes which should be conceived as student behaviours capable of being tested. It was not just the crudity of this formulation that repelled me: it was its powerful support of the sort of social determinism through education I had tried to fight first in practice in the classroom and subsequently in my theoretical work. In my own thinking, 'standards', located in the culture as social norms of quality and quantity of school work, took the place of objectives as underpinning the assessment of the outcomes and the process of education. The paper printed here is the first statement of that position.

The final piece in this section is a chapter taken from *Culture and Education*,[1] now out of print. In its first draft this book was much closer to the formal statement of the Uppsala paper than it later became. Val Judges, the series editor, insisted that I rewrite it much more lightly. What had been a tome became a slim volume. The chapter reprinted here is that which most closely fore-shadows the work of the Humanities Curriculum Project. It follows closely from:

Language represents an organization of culture in a symbol system, and this organization depends upon linguistic rather than upon logical or sociological principles. It is not an organization correspond-ing to the analysis of culture presented by the sociologist. Its principles are independent, for language is a kind of calculus of culture, or a conceptual system dictated by human needs and purposes. Those words are best which serve us best, and our purposes require at some times precision and at others ambiguity.

Now the basic purpose which language serves is that of communi-cation; and initially the individual learns language in and for communication. We learn words from the tongues of others and we find that within a more or less extended circle of people the words which stand for our ideas evoke an echo. Thus we enter a world of public meanings.

Once we have learned language, we have command of an instrument which can be used not only for communicating with others but also for communing with ourselves. Language supports our solitary reflection. Given life in communication, it becomes the possession of the individual, who can, as it were, carry it with him into his inner privacy and use it as an instrument of thought. True individuality derives from such reflection. Paradoxically, therefore, the capacity for individualizing experience depends upon a tool forged in common experience. Language is a sort of bridge between the world of socially defined universals and the world of unique individual experience. Used in communication, it implies a con-formity; used in reflection, it liberates individuality. Thought commandeers language and uses it as its instrument.

Hence the attempt to produce and feed within a classroom group a subculture supporting discourse of a kind likely to favour the development of an individuality of understanding.

Reference

1. Lawrence Stenhouse, *Culture and Education* (London: Nelson, 1967).

General Education in the Light of the Crowther Report

A lecture given in 1960 within the University Department of Education, Newcastle-upon-Tyne, and later reworked as Chapter 9 of Culture and Education.[1]

In the inevitable expansion of education during the next generation the emphasis will be on provision for the older age ranges. New universities are to be founded, and technical and vocational education will be developed; but there appears to be a general agreement that no education should be narrowly vocational. Rather a 'general' or a 'liberal' education should be offered. Just what this implies remains vague, but the issues involved are so important that it seems worthwhile to clarify the difficulties. Perhaps the best way to do this is to look closely at the state of the problem in the Crowther Report,[2] the report of the Central Advisory Council for Education on the education of boys and girls between 15 and 18 (1959). It would be wrong to regard any report of this sort as a blueprint – there is no sort of assurance that its recommendations will be carried out, especially where they involve increased financial provision – but it represents a current approach to the problems of the education of the adolescent by a well-informed official committee, and is therefore an appropriate starting point.

The problem of general and specialized education is raised in the original and principal remit to the Council which asked it 'to consider, in relation to the changing social and industrial needs of our society, and the needs of its individual citizens, the education of boys and girls between 15 and 18, and in particular to consider the balance at various levels of general and specialized studies between these ages and to examine the inter-relationship of the various stages of education'. To understand the context in which the Council saw this problem, it is as well to explore at the outset some of the premises underlying the Report, premises which are often accepted implicitly rather than argued, and which are sometimes indeed written into the remit.

The first group of premises concerns the relation of education to social structure. The present class structure of English education is broadly accepted. Although there is an occasional allusion to the independent and public schools, there is no examination of the problems raised by the existence of this private educational system or by the predominantly working-class and lower-middle-class character of the modern school. Yet these are the features of the English system which most forcibly strike the foreign observer. Moreover, the competitive system, which is peculiarly prominent in English education and which has been variously described as 'equality of opportunity', 'merit-ocracy' or 'the rat race' is apparently acceptable to the Council, at least in its broad characteristics. Both these features – education differentiated according to social class, and competit-ive access to opportunity – tend to produce selection, streaming and differentiation in all branches of education and to diminish the common core shared by all. This tendency is reflected even in the experiments with comprehensives. As the Report says, 'All the variants try to provide a common social life, none tries to provide a uniform curriculum.'

The second group of premises adopted in the Report concerns the relation of education to economic life. It is assumed that we live in an expanding economy, based on technology and capable of absorbing more technologists and technicians than it is likely to get. This being so, the acceptance of the proposition that it is a function of education to support the economic life of the community – and few would care to dispute this – leads to a justification of educational expenditure as investment spending.

There is a further premise, however, that education is of and for itself a 'good thing'. This is a faith which appears to be accepted emotionally even when the nature of education is left unexplored. The very word evokes approval. Thus there is a conviction that education must not be seen merely as an investment but also as a social service to be judged by the contribution it makes to the well-being of the individual.

Now the premises regarding the relation of education to social structure and economic life depend ultimately on a highly developed pattern of division of labour in society and a con-sequent hierarchy of specialists. Such a pattern of society implies the existence of a developed vocational and specialist education. By contrast, the idea of an education serving the needs of the individual, unless those needs be construed narrowly as an ability to compete, seems to imply an ideal of general education. I think it is fair to say that a distinction between vocational and general education is drawn in both the remit and the report, but that there is a faith that there is no inherent opposition between the vocational and the general. The Council's position makes this faith inevitable for them; to fail to hold it would be to abandon hope of a general education. One need not quarrel with them in this except to suggest that the whole problem has perhaps been insufficiently analysed.

It has been neatly formulated elsewhere by Ralph Perry.[3] 'There is a familiar distinction between that vocational or professional education by which the individual is fitted for a place in the social division of labour, and that "general education" which conduces to self-development and association with his fellows on common ground. This distinction tends to obscure the fact that by becoming a specialist the individual does not cease to be a man among men, and the fact that there can be no special education which does not affect a man's personality and fit or unfit him for human association.' Here three themes – vocational effectiveness, self-development and common culture – are seen as central, but these three are inextricably and subtly interwoven.

Now, vocational education and some aspects of what is commonly called 'education for leisure' can be taken to be part of a general education. A specialized executive ability is clearly necessary both as a means of earning a livelihood and as a means of recreation. A man lacking such specialized knowledge, understanding and skills is unthinkable; and if we could think of him, we should scarcely regard him as generally educated. Moreover, it is doubtful whether education for self-development can be conceived apart from vocational education and education for association with one's fellows on common ground. Self-development surely depends upon the individualizing of common experience, and the materials on which an education for self-development rests are the skills, knowledge and understandings derived from vocational education and from education in a common culture.

Bearing in mind, therefore, that the fundamental problem of general education is probably that of developing a common ground on which a man can associate with his fellows, we may examine the Advisory Council's approach to the problem more closely.

The Council believes that there is no academic monopoly of

general education. It cannot afford to take any other position, since it accepts streaming in education as a means of curricular differentiation. To suggest that only an academic education is a satisfactory general education and then to deny an academic education to the lower streams of ability would be to countenance for them, the majority of the population who are denied access to the grammar school, a vocational education of rude mechanicals.

Accordingly, in addition to academic education, there is an alternative road – not yet open to traffic – a full time practical education from 15 to 18 which 'should not be regarded as wholly, or even mainly, technical and still less confined to the special needs of a narrow range of occupations'.

This alternative road, like the academic road, is, however, a narrow and selective one. Only the few in the modern school will be able to travel it; and so the middle of the modern school range of ability, the largest element of our population, must have its road too. It appears that they will steer by landmarks rather than by maps, for the Report says of them: 'These too long neglected middle streams have a future, and an exciting one, if they can attract teachers who will take at face value the fact that their pupils will nearly always prefer "I see" to "I understand".'

It can hardly be denied that there are more weaknesses in this prescription than the unacceptability of the psychology in which it is couched, but at least we are on firm ground with the lowest streams of all. Here there is no choice of road to confuse us: we are still trying to make these pupils roadworthy.

Let us examine this educational road system more closely.

In the first place there is the A road, the academic route which leads through grammar school selection and the sixth form to the university. Here the Council accepts the present system of university education for the purposes of its report, though it is critical of selection pressures at entry to university, and also hints that university courses might profitably be lengthened. Specialization in advanced studies is accepted from the sixth form onwards and this specialization is not merely in two or three subjects but in *cognate* subjects. The pattern accepted by the Council is apparently admitted to have some shortcomings as a general education, and this because it fails to provide common ground. Hence, the notorious problem of numeracy and literacy and the separation of the two cultures of science and arts. Hence, too, the difficulty of motivating minority time.

The B road is the route through grammar, technical or modern school to a full-time education up to the age of eighteen based on technology. There is an assumption behind the Council's thinking here that there is a practical sort of mind and that people with this sort of mind have been neglected but should be neglected no longer. The attribution of a particular quality of mind to those who follow this course suggests the possibility of selecting pupils rather than allowing them to choose. The road to be followed leads through a broadly technical education, but it is clear once more that this sort of education, like academic education, has its shortcomings as a general education. 'We would, however, feel that it is essential that some time and care should be devoted to aspects of education other than the technical. In Chapter 25 we gave a good deal of attention to what we have called the "minority time" of the Sixth Form specialist. What we have in mind here is a special case of the same principle, and it is not necessary to develop the argument in detail twice over.'

The unclassified road through modern school and county college carries the heaviest traffic, though perhaps the most slow-moving. Those who follow this road will be given a vocational training which is neither academic nor technical, but is based on general skills. 'General education' looms large in their course, but there is a slight suspicion that this is because we cannot think exactly what to do with them. However, as we have seen, there is confidence in their exciting future if they can attract the right teachers. Though bleak enough, this prospect is not quite so bleak as it sounds, for in our system educational problems are solved by teachers rather than by government committee or research institutes, and one might argue plausibly that this should be so.

Certainly, the general education of these pupils, as the Advisory Council sees it, offers plenty of scope. In the county college, and presumably in the top of the modern school, there are four main strands: 'An appreciation of the adult world in which young workers suddenly find themselves; guidance for them in working out their problems of human relations and moral standards; development of their physical and aesthetic skills; and a continuance of their basic education, with a vocational bias where appropriate.'

Finally, there is the garage and workshop. Here one finds a group of extremely backward pupils who have difficulty in getting on the road at all and a group of devoted teachers serving them so well that in many ways they are better off than those on the unclassified road. The Council is impressed by these teachers and feels that they ought to have a due share of responsibility allowances. Taking everything into consideration, this is perhaps the most satisfactory branch of education. It is interesting to speculate whether this is because we are not embarrassed here by fluent literacy or an insistent demand for meaning and understanding.

Two explicit ideas of a general education emerge. On the A and B roads general education is seen as breadth, or at any rate as not being too narrow. Hence the ideas of numeracy and literacy and the need for a counterbalance to specialized studies which, be they academic or technical, are vocational in motivation. For the other travellers general education seems to consist of learning a sensible practicality in the affairs of this world, moral standards and the ability to use leisure time wisely. Oddly enough, little is made of these qualities on the A and B roads. There seems spare evidence that those who have passed through grammar schools are conspicuously practical, moral and wise; but it may be that society is more tolerant of their shortcomings.

A third idea is perhaps implied. If you can get the pupil on to the motorway, the private or public school system, whether he understands or merely sees, his general education will be looked after. Here general education consists of a socialization into a class culture which involves high ideals of conduct and effective ways of facing the world.

Sociologically, one might interpret the school system in relation to general education as follows. The private school system inculcates moral standards, practical adjustments to living and a general complex of values whose motivation derives from a web of sanctions effective for members of the upper and upper middle classes. On the whole the culture pattern of these groups is adapting fairly adequately to the problems posed by social change. The modern school is faced with the problem of performing a similar task for the lower middle and working classes, but it encounters difficulties, partly because in the past the school has not been important to these groups as an agent of cultural transmission. Thus both the standards to be adopted and their motivation are in doubt. A healthy tradition is lacking. The grammar school is, and the new technical colleges no doubt will be, an avenue of organized social mobility. This mobility is achieved through vocational success, and the school therefore places great emphasis on academic achievement. There is an attempt to reflect the ethos of the public schools, but the most important factor in the general education of the grammar school boy is the pressure exerted upon him by his upward social mobility. His defences against insecurity are to embrace a professional ethic or to assimilate his behaviour to that of the upper middle class which becomes for him a reference group, through whose eyes he values himself.

The Advisory Council, taking what might be called a 'social realist' point of view, expresses the demands of society as it sees them, and these tend to be the demands of parents. It recognizes implicitly a class-structured society in which mobility is accessible primarily through education. Broadly, parents desire upward mobility for their children. Since our society also needs trained manpower, it is prepared to an extent to finance parents in their demand for mobility for their children. The importance of training and the importance of qualifications are recognized by parents and by the Council, and are reflected in a stress on vocational education and on examinations. Viewed against this background, the needs of the individual are to equip himself to make his way in a competitive society.

But the Council cannot accept this as it stands: it believes that education exists for the individual in a much fuller sense than the development of his competitive power. It is not quite sure, however, what this implies, though it does feel sure that 'general education' is not inherently irreconcilable with specialist or vocational education.

It does not seem to me that the problem which emerges is of the Council's making. Rather, I have tried to show that it arises from the very nature of our society in a much fuller sense than the Report itself explores. In any modern society with a highly developed pattern of the division of labour, the relationship between education for specialized vocation and education for consensus and common ground is perhaps the most important of all educational problems. In our own society it is complicated by the peculiar status of our upper middle classes, and the impoverishment of our working class tradition in the long experience of the bleak age of uncontrolled industrial development and board schooling. There is no easy and ready solution to this problem at hand.

A change in the structure of our social system – which is scarcely a ready and easy solution – would merely modulate the problem. Even though it might change the conditions of social action, such action would still have to concern itself with an identical problem of consensus. Revolutions are not solutions to problems but responses to problems for all that they may change the distribution of power and sometimes the principles which govern its exercise.

A change in the state educational system appears to me equally irrelevant here. The problem is one of the classroom and the content and flavour of teaching. I do not believe that the comprehensive school meets the central problem of consensus any better – or any worse – than a bipartite system. Indeed, the extraordinary fact about the comprehensive school is that, other factors equal, it makes so little difference. British comprehensives are more like British grammar schools and secondary modern schools than they are like American high schools or Scandinavian comprehensives. The comprehensive idea seems to me more symbolic than efficacious in this context. Its true source is less a desire for a common culture than an aspiration to equality of status and opportunity, which cannot really be attained in our society. It is a response to competition in education which is more likely to favour the middle-class child who might have been trapped in the modern school than the working-class pupil.

Even the abolition of the public schools would be of dubious significance. It could well lead to an upper middle class domination of the grammar schools or the development in exclusive districts of neighbourhood schools in which parents supported their children in discriminating against the minority in the school who could be regarded as social inferiors. This happens in many American cities. Certainly, abolition of the public schools would increase opposition to comprehensives.

The problem, then, is one of curriculum and teaching rather than of the organization of education. Accordingly, we shall narrow our sights and attempt an analysis of the difficulties as they appear in the schools.

It is first necessary to clarify further our distinction between general and vocational education. We have already suggested that vocational education is an aspect of general education, but we have also distinguished another aspect, education to establish common ground with one's fellows. Now vocational education is an education for a specialist function, and such a function implies a developed executive and active ability. By contrast, the attempt to establish common ground appears to depend, not on executive ability, but on understanding. Of course, such a dichotomy cannot be maintained rigorously, but it is perhaps reasonable to claim that there is one sort of education which stresses ability to act and another which stresses ability to understand. Both sorts of education involve knowledge, understanding, attitudes and skills, but the emphasis is distinctly different. Vocational and specialist education is directed to producing a universe of action; this other aspect of general education is directed to producing a universe of understanding, a universe of discourse. Here professional standards may not be appropriate: they are the foundation of specialist education.

In our society, we resign ourselves to the disadvantage that a developed system of the division of labour produces universes of action which are insulated from one another, but we maintain the desire that people in different spheres of action should be able in most of the matters of everyday living 'to talk the same language', that is, that they should have some measure of common culture. Until we find a better name for it, let us call this education which aims at producing culture shared in social intercourse 'social education'.

Such a distinction as we have now drawn seems to fit the facts. The vocational training, formal or informal, of plumber or artist, doctor or critic, engineer or librarian, narrows the field of competence in order to develop it. 'Social education' by contrast creates extensive groups able to communicate easily with one another on the basis of a common understanding. The private school system produces just such a group, sharing understandings and values. You can say in conversation 'a cosy evening with a bottle of South African sherry' without any fear that your listeners may think you enjoyed yourself; and of course more serious understandings are shared in the same way. There are many such universes of discourse or understanding, which may be thought of as concentric circles. Thus an individual may be located within western culture, the English language group, the British culture, the public school culture, even a family culture. In such a complex situation, simplification is necessary for discussion, but we are perhaps on safe ground in suggesting that a distinction between an upper and upper middle class group, a socially mobile group and a working class group can be maintained. The upper class group and the working class group do not accept each other's values. The socially mobile group is in process of changing its values, and in this process accepts the upper class as a reference group and actively learns its understandings from the gossip columns and profiles of the quality dailies, the fashionable criticism and winemanship of the equivalent Sundays, and the one-upmanship of the *Tatler* and *Country Life*.

Now the commonly accepted point of view is that the culture of the upper group is adequate, that of the lower group impoverished, and with the reservation that the culture of the upper group is being sapped and weakened for want of vigorous development in relation to the conditions of life, this judgement may be accepted. Clearly, it is the basis of the Advisory Council's concern for the morals and practical understanding of the modern school pupil, and their comparative unconcern about this problem in the grammar schools and public schools. The culture of the upper group is powerful enough to enforce conformity to its moral standards, though it should be noted that these are not necessarily those generally accepted in moral discussion.

The comparative adequacy of the upper culture does not imply that the grammar and public schools are succeeding in giving a 'social education'. It would of course be too much to suggest that they do not make a substantial contribution, but the fundamental basis of understanding in the upper group is much more distinctively to be found in the dynamics of that group itself as an association of adults. The public school accepts broadly the values and understandings of the group for which it caters. It may broaden them and deepen them but it accepts them as a framework. One cannot say that the culture of the upper group is produced by the schools. On the contrary the schools survive because they foster the values of the group.

By contrast, the modern schools do not generally accept the culture their pupils derive from their home life and their social life outside the school. They are thus faced with the problem of producing a culture in opposition to the background culture against which they must work.

We have suggested that 'the education of a gentleman' depends as much or more on the pressure of the group 'gentlemen' as upon the influence of school education. But there remains a faith that an academic education can be a general education. There is an academic culture which is as adequate as a gentlemanly culture. Many would feel that Dr Bronowski and Mr Alan Bullock have a social education as adequate as that of Sir Winston Churchill or the Duke of Kent. I believe this to be true, and it is therefore worth examining the claim of academic disciplines to produce a culture.

The education of an historian or a scientist would appear at first sight to be vocational, and indeed it very often is. But academic education can claim a cultural relevance too. This claim is based upon the idea that there are certain subjects or 'disciplines' which constitute syntheses of experience articulated on different bases, that history or science can aspire to give a world view. Since the historian or the scientist can aspire to organize his impressions of the world through his subject on a broad scale, he is able to translate and illuminate experience and achieve a broad understanding from the perspective of a key viewpoint. I believe that this claim can be maintained under fuller analysis.

The problem with this sort of education is that it is essentially an education for the few, since it demands very high ability. It is not until one penetrates to the highest level that specialist disciplines begin to yield general understandings. Thus most honours graduates fail to achieve such a synthesis based on their discipline. The man who is an historian when he reads about the Tudors, but who fails to be a historian when he approaches painting, relations between the sexes, or the shape of prize chrysanthemums has not derived a general education from his studies.

It was a discontent with the cultural and social results of an academic education which prompted the 'progressive movement' in education; and it is perhaps fair when making a quick distinction to say that where academic education finds its ideal in the scholar, progressive education finds its ideal in the artist. 'Free expression' implies the right of the child to grapple with his problems of understanding through the exercise of sensory and sensitive intuition. The ability of children to respond to such an approach does seem in practice to be more widespread than the ability to profit from an academic approach. At the same time, it appears that progressive practice has been more successful in the primary than in the secondary schools. Some would attribute this to the more conservative attitude of the secondary teacher, but it is at least arguable that an education based on imagination can provide a means of synthesizing the experience of the young child, but that it fails to meet the range of needs felt by the adolescent who must seek to understand, not just the experience of his own living, but the wider social reality of which he is now becoming aware. Here one might compare the synthesis achieved by the great artist with the academic synthesis already discussed. Again it seems likely that the final broadening which gives the education its general validity eludes the majority.

Let us now take stock. We have distinguished a specialist education which relies on professional standards, and a social education where standards are in doubt. Both are aspects of general education. Two of the theories which suggest standards in social education, the gentlemanly and the academic, appear to be ill-adapted to universal education because the education based on them is only accessible to élites. A third theory, 'progressive education', offers more prospects but, as it has been interpreted in this country at any rate, seems most effective in the primary school. In its extreme forms it is perhaps too individualistic to answer the needs of older children, for whom society has become a reality. It is possible, too, that it demands an artistic élite.

We require a form of social education which offers an access to a living culture such as can provide a common basis of meanings and understandings, capable of supporting a rich communication between person and person and of supplying a currency for intimate and solitary reflection. In other words, we require a cultural education which impacts on life and quickens the quality of living.

Arnold Toynbee appears to have diagnosed the ill from which our education is suffering:

> One consequence [of the introduction of formal education] is to make education become a burden on the mind. In the act of making it formal we make it cumulative. The successive cultural achievements of successive generations are recorded and handed on, while the capacity of a single human mind in a single lifetime remains within constant natural limits. How is a limited human mind to cope with a cultural heritage that is perpetually increasing in bulk? This problem is aggravated when people begin deliberately to extend the range of human knowledge by systematic research. There will be a temptation to try to facilitate the acquisition of the growing heritage by simplifying its content at the cost of impoverishing it. For educational purposes the culture may be reduced to a conventional form in which it will tend to become impersonal, secular and abstract; and in this process the living essence of the culture may slip out of the meshes of the educational net. The apprenticeship for life may be ousted by a course of instruction set by syllabus. Ordeals that are initiations into

successive stages of life may shrivel into examinations in arbitrarily selected bodies of cut and dried knowledge.[4]

What is the remedy for such an ailment? Where is that principle or standard by which we can select living culture from inert culture?

It would be presumptuous here to prescribe some magical patent medicine. Rather a regimen will require to be worked out on the classroom floor. But some suggestions can be offered.

We must, I think, stop trying to mass-produce gentlemen, academics or artists, and try to produce audiences, publics which are not bound by professional standards. We do not want passive publics accepting and admiring Shakespeare, Picasso, Darwin or Freud, but active publics using and criticizing their cultural experiences. This means stressing content and letting form fall into place as the inseparable realization of content. Our literature, history, science and art should be selected for its relevance to the fundamental human problems which concern pre-adolescents and adolescents, not for its illustration of form or technique or for its importance in the history of a subject. Our procedure should be to stimulate interest in moral and human problems and then to feed discussion.

In the fact that four lines of Burns are quoted in a pub discussion, the teaching of a poem is justified; in a grammar-school man's shock when someone points out to him the relevance of *Antony and Cleopatra* to extra-marital relations is a proof that that particular exercise made no contribution to his social education.

When we have taught our class for a year we shall be satisfied in so far as they can argue a little more deeply over a wider range, and have a greater store of words and ideas that they can apply to a consideration of their own felt experience. As John Dewey remarked in *Democracy and Education*[5], society not only exists *by* transmission and *by* communication, it exists *in* transmission, *in* communication.

References

1. Lawrence Stenhouse, *Culture and Education* (London: Nelson, 1967).
2. Central Advisory Council for Education, England, *15 to 18* Vol I: Report (London: HMSO, 1959) (The Crowther Report).

3. Ralph Perry, 'Academic freedom', *Harvard Educational Review* 13.2.1953.
4. Arnold J. Toynbee, 'Conclusions', in *Education in the Perspective of History* by Edward D. Myers (London: Longmans Green, 1963).
5. John Dewey, *Democracy and Education* (New York: The Macmillan Co, 1916) p. 4.

A Cultural Approach to the Sociology of the Curriculum

A lecture delivered in the University of Oslo, 1962, and printed in Pedagogisk Forskning, *1963 (3, pp. 120–34).*

The purpose of this paper is to outline a conceptual framework which relates the sociology of the classroom to the sociology of the content of the curriculum, and to analyse within this framework the problem of general and specialist education. The tenor of the discussion will be somewhat speculative and the analysis will be broad rather than detailed.

Such an approach can only be justified when breaking new ground. I am encouraged to think it a useful one by a judgement of Floud and Halsey: 'It is regrettable that this whole question of the fate of the content of education should have been relatively so neglected by sociologists. Many questions suggest themselves, to which no answers can as yet be attempted.'[1] If this assessment of the situation be just, there is perhaps some place for even tentative approaches through sociology to problems of curriculum content.

Our point of departure here will be a functional definition of culture. Culture is the medium through which human minds interact in communication. The concept may be compared broadly with that of light in physics. Hoffmann writes: 'Realizing that there must be something bridging the distance between our eyes, the things we see, and the lamps illuminating them, the Greeks gave it objective reality and set about studying it and inventing theories about it. When the modern scientist talks about light, he has in mind just this something.'[2] We assert that there must be a medium bridging the subjective experiences of minds which communicate with one another and we identify this as culture. In doing so, we have not suggested what culture is, but merely suggested its function or location in social interaction.

It is important to notice that this approach detaches culture from numerable groups, as in the phrase, 'the culture of the Bantu', and attaches it instead to interaction situations. Our present concept can be related to social structure, but its immediate location by definition is in the social process.

If we carry our dubious but helpful analogy with light a stage further, we may say that, although we have an immediate physical perception of light, as when we observe light rays, yet the physicist's analysis of light takes us into a conceptual world beyond this immediate one of physical impression, and quite different from it. He speaks, for instance, of waves and particles which are not visible. The immediate perceptual representation of culture as a medium of communicative interaction is to be found in language, and in other symbol systems such as mathematical symbols, chemical symbols or pictures. Music may also be regarded as a highly abstracted symbolic system. All these 'languages' are anchored in culture.

The effective use of language implies a degree of consensus among those who communicate. Culture is precisely this consensus. The relation between language and culture is reciprocal. Language is developed on the basis of culture, but again language determines culture. To an extent we find a name for what we see: to an extent we see what we have a name for.

This is not the place for an extended analysis of culture. Many of the analyses which have been offered are consonant with the definition of culture adopted here. Quite a crude one will serve our present purposes.

Let us say, then, that culture consists of values, understandings and meanings.

Values represent consensus in evaluation, in judgements of good or bad, better or worse. They are socially approved ends in the broadest sense. To say this is, of course, not a statement about the justification of values, but about the dynamics of values. Values are points of consensus created and reinforced in social interaction. Christian values, for example, are created and reinforced in the social interaction of the Church. The problem of the justification of values is not for sociology, but for theology or ethics.

Understandings are understandings between minds. The concept is adopted as a blanket term to cover a range of consensus susceptible to complex analysis, which we shall not attempt here. Information, techniques and interpretations of situations, when shared, are understandings. They are the non-evaluative elements in culture, or rather they are elements not evaluated as ends.

In short, values represent motivational consensus, understandings, perceptual or informational consensus or consensus regarding resources. Values may be regarded as understandings energized by motivation.

Meanings are simply complexes of values and understandings articulated on symbols. They are the echoes which the symbol evokes in the common experience of two or more people. The definition of a word together with all its associative and emotional overtones constitutes a meaning. Most words have complex meanings which are differentiated within the language group. Examples are 'church', 'family', 'fabulous'. Within the group of English speakers, these words have many different meanings. 'Fabulous', for example, may evoke Aesop or Cecil B. de Mille, the fables of the ancient world or of modern Hollywood.

Groups which can interact without misunderstanding do so on the basis of a consensus of meanings manifested in linguistic usage and dependent upon a deeper consensus of values and understandings.

Such a description of the content of culture will suffice in this context. Two other characteristics of culture must, however, be noticed. Culture is learnt and shared.

The assertion that culture is learnt implies that it is a function of individual minds, when the mind is regarded as the locus of subjective experience. The use of the term *culture* to denote objects such as houses, institutions such as churches, behaviour such as gambling, or symbolic objects such as paintings or books, is incompatible with the definition we have adopted. However, culture in the present sense does denote the consensus of values, understandings and meanings which underlie these objects and institutions.

The assertion that culture is shared implies that it is also a function of groups. Theoretically the minimum group is two, but the size criterion of the group is dependent upon the scale of our study. The essential point is that most of what we learn is not unique to ourselves, but shared with others. The process of learning therefore serves to associate us with one group and dissociate us from others. To undertake the learning involved in taking a medical degree associates us with the group, doctors, and dissociates us from groups such as teachers, dustmen and game-keepers. This implication of the idea that culture is shared lies behind those effects of education which are generally described by sociologists as 'differentiation'.

In the context of this view of culture we face the traditional assertion of sociologists that education is concerned with the transmission of culture. If this be true, then on our account, the teacher's task is to transmit values, understandings and meanings articulated upon symbol systems. In doing so, he provides a medium of communicative interaction.

In the normal teaching situation the teacher teaches a group, the class. If he teaches them subtraction by decomposition or laboratory procedure or *Hamlet* or Ibsen, he gives them something in common as a group. As he does so, he cuts them off from other groups and associates them with yet other groups whose classroom experience is close to their own.

Since culture is normally sustained by groups, the question arises whether there is a dynamic principle at work in the group which is being taught. The findings of social psychology suggest that there is, and we can turn to the social psychologist to find the conceptual framework we need to analyse this group dynamic.

Groups achieve communicative interaction through that consensus we have called culture. Communicative interaction is a basic requirement of satisfactory group life, and therefore the group naturally seeks to maintain its culture. The whole system of interaction depends upon the general prediction of the lines of consensus within the group. All members of the group will expect other members to converge in these areas of consensus, which represent the cultural basis of the group.

This culture behind communication and action is not explicit and externalized. Accordingly, it must be inferred from behaviour; and consequently the group can only control and sustain its culture by reacting to the behaviour of individual members. These individuals act within the group and the group reacts, exerting pressures on the individual in an effort to shape his behaviour.

The general picture which emerges from this view of group dynamics is as follows. Culture is represented in a group by a climate of expectation. All action takes place within this climate. The breach of expectation which threatens the culture of the group evokes a hostile group reaction, conformity evokes a general approval, a breach of expectation which is seen as a development consonant with the culture and enriching it evokes emphatic approval.

We have drawn attention to the pressure towards consensus in groups. The socially mediated rewards and punishments which constitute the potency of such pressures are generally called sanctions. Sanctions are quite simply rewards and punishments which are deployed by groups rather than by individuals.

The essential dynamic principle behind culture in groups is, therefore, as follows. In any group in sustained communicative interaction pressures are exerted through the deployment of sanctions. Culture depends upon these pressures, which serve to sustain it.

Thus, to say that a teacher transmits culture in the classroom is to say not only that values, understandings and meanings are learnt and shared, but that they are adequately reinforced by group pressures. Any classroom group will generate pressures and these pressures must be organized in such a way as to support the culture which the teacher is concerned for.

Since this group process in the classroom is powerful, it is potentially the teacher's greatest enemy or his greatest ally. His job is to see that it is his ally. In detail this is perhaps more a matter of generating, feeding and criticizing the culture of the classroom than one of mere transmission.

A number of practical examples may illustrate our interpretation. A simple consensus is that which concerns classroom behaviour. Let us say that the teacher will from time to time wish to talk to the class as a whole. All must then listen quietly. If the culture of the class is against him, talking will recur and the pressures in the class will support it rather than tend to eradicate it. If the teacher succeeds in inducing the group to accept fully the kind of behaviour he wants, then his principal task is accomplished. Inevitably, as in any group, there will be those who fall out of line, either because of lack of self-control or because of that studied defiance of the group which may perhaps be called 'norm blasphemy'. But now the group and the teacher will exert parallel pressures. The class themselves will try to silence the talker. In such a case the teacher commonly says that he has succeeded in carrying the class along with him.

Social pressures may be observed continually in classroom groups. Children express horror at one boy's untidy exercise, believe that poetry is for sissies, agree in the error that the Roman occupation of Britain dates from 55 BC. The teacher's job is to generate in the group a normed, that is a self-sustaining, culture, which he is prepared to endorse and defend.

Little empirical study of this process in the classroom has been undertaken, but a persuasive analogy can be found in industrial psychology where norms of productivity and quality have been studied. By its nature, the 'work culture' of a factory group is rather 'thin', but the principle remains the same.

A further concept must be set into our analysis if we are to relate our somewhat abstract theory to everyday educational observation. The pressures within a group are exerted, not randomly, but according to a systematic pattern. Social pressures applied to behaviour imply a judgement of that behaviour and judgement implies criteria. These criteria on which pressures are organized we shall call standards. We may now summarize our theoretical account of classroom process, and then translate it into the everyday language of education.

The job of the teacher, we have claimed, is to generate in his class a culture based on standards he approves. That culture forms the medium of the group life of the class. We may add that the quality of the group life depends on the quality of the medium of interaction. A rich culture is one which sustains a rich group life.

In common parlance, the job of the teacher is to get the class working self-critically as a group. True educational standards are those which develop and articulate the pupils' capacity for self-criticism. Such standards of self-criticism can only be securely maintained by most individuals through their association with a like-minded group.

So far we have spoken of culture as if it were a mere flat consensus in which any creative innovation would be impossible. This is far from the truth. Creative innovation is only possible through culture.

The reason for this is as follows. The consensus which underlies culture crystallizes into meanings represented by symbols. These symbols, which are learnt by individuals in communication, serve to objectify culture in manipulable form. The language which is learnt culturally in communication can be taken into solitary reflection where the symbols can be re-ordered and can interact so that it is possible to establish new relationships and new concepts. The public language of religion, for example, can be taken into private thinking and used to create a unique subjective experience of the idea of God. Thus individuality grows from culture. Men forge in the dialectic of social interaction the tools which serve the inner dialectic of thought and imagination. And perhaps the most vital criterion of the richness of a culture is the degree to which it feeds individuality and creative innovation.

If this principle is true of the small group, it is true also of public culture. The arts, humanities and sciences are modes of creative innovation which feed on culture. The arts and humanities through their symbol systems offer creative outlets, through which men can develop their resources in handling and enriching the quality of their own subjective experience. The symbol systems of the sciences and their methodology are adapted to the creative extension of man's understanding of and control of his objective environment. The social sciences seek to bridge the gap between the humanities and the physical sciences, attempting on the one hand to study man as object, and on the other to get a purchase on the study of subjective experience. The critical apparatus which is built into the methodology of science and the critical climate which surrounds the arts and the humanities represent the cultural assessment of innovation. All scientific and artistic innovations offer to change the public culture. The critical framework of scientific method filters the innovations of scientists. In the arts and humanities, the role of the critic is to represent the tradition against the innovating individual. In both cases the result is a dialectic interchange between innovator and critic which serves to assess, assimilate and discipline cultural innovations.

We now see a clear line of argument on which we can justify the inclusion of both the arts and the sciences in the curriculum, irrespective of their immediate vocational relevance. The culture of the class, which the teacher supervises, is a sub-culture through which young people enter the cultures of the adult and public worlds. Were the teacher to teach not subjects but, as it were, himself, he would, if he were successful, merely trap the pupils in his own culture. Accordingly, he has to base the experience of the classroom on some objective curriculum material. Because the arts and sciences are primarily modes of innovation, they offer two marked advantages as curriculum. First, they present cultural elements as if they were innovations, and to the individual pupil who is learning they are just that. Thus, Plato's *Republic* is a good basis for education precisely because it presents perennial ideas as if they were new, just what is required in the teaching situation, where that which is familiar in the culture must be discovered anew by the individual. The second strength of these traditional elements in the curriculum is that they introduce the pupil not only to a content of ideas, but also to the arts and sciences as modes of innovation which he can in his turn learn to use creatively. In these subjects the creative and conservative functions of education are most intimately fused.

We are, of course, not concerned to argue that other subjects are not useful, but merely to justify the wisdom behind the traditional focus of the school curriculum.

In the light of the foregoing analysis of the teaching process and its content, we can perhaps make an approach to the problem of general and specialist education.

We may say that the core of the teaching process lies in the teacher's judgement of the standards adopted by the pupils. According to his own standards, the teacher deploys his rewards and punishments, encouragement and discouragement in order to influence the standards of the group. These group standards form the basis of the social pressures which in turn influence the individual standards of the group members. The question of the sources of the teacher's standards arises, and we shall expect to find these standards accepted in the groups from which the teacher draws his cultural support.

Let us take a simple example. In the nineteenth century, it could be argued, the elementary school was largely concerned with educating for clerical and similar occupations. The most powerful critic of the elementary school teacher was the employer. For the teacher, employers tended to become a reference group for standards. Rapid calculation, neat handwriting and so forth were at a premium. The teacher might even say to the pupil: 'What do you think your employer will say to work like that?'

Nowadays, the primary school hands the children on to the secondary school and often to higher education. For primary teachers, the reference group for standards tends to become secondary teachers and academics. Now the primary teacher tends to ask whether her approach to the teaching of number is a good basis for later mathematics teaching. Primary education thus becomes a kind of general educational groundwork, leading to secondary and higher education which tends to become specialized. The specialized standards of the secondary school are underwritten by reference to specialized vocational and academic groups. Thus standards in science derive from academic and research scientists, in literature from university teachers or the more approved professional critics, in mathematics from professional mathematicians. At a more specialized level still, professional standards are formed and developed in specialized professional groups, such as the medical profession and the legal profession.

It is in the secondary school and the university that the problem of the balance between specialization and general education has been most acutely felt. We shall focus our attention on the secondary school and accept as our point of departure the treatment of the situation in the Crowther Report, the most recent English government report on secondary education.[3]

The Crowther Committee felt that specialization in academic and technical forms of education was necessary if high academic, vocational and professional standards were to be obtained, but expressed reserve about the effects of this on the general educational impact of pupils' courses. Their solution was to advocate minority time in which there should be an attempt to counterbalance specialist work by contrasting but complementary studies. We should attempt to make every academic or technologist both literate and numerate, or in a phrase which has become popular in Britain we should try to marry 'the two cultures' of science and the arts. It is fair to say that the idea of general education implied here is that of balance. The aspiration is to produce all-rounders.

This prescription is offered only to the intellectual élite. The general education of the majority of the population in the non-academic secondary schools is not seen as a balance of academic subjects but as a building out of basic literacy and numeracy and the attempt to instil or develop moral standards, good citizenship and a sensible practicality in everyday affairs. Little stress is laid on these qualities in the discussion of academic and technical education.

Here, then, are two standards in general education, and there is yet a third which lies implicit behind most British thinking about education. If the parents can afford to send the child to a public school, he will receive a good general education, whether he has marked academic ability or not.

Behind these notions of general education, there are two distinct ideas. On the one hand, 'general' is taken to mean broad, and is opposed to narrow specialist education. On the other, 'general' implies an education for the general experience of social intercourse and of the human lot.

We may now apply our conceptual framework to the problem outlined.

The prime function of academic education is to transmit specialist cultures which support creative and original work in particular fields. Groups such as chemists, archaeologists, geographers and lawyers adopt professional standards as a basis for action. Through its education each group comes to share a culture of its own, and it is on the groundwork of this common culture that professional activities are carried on. Thus, academic education as it advances, becomes more and more specialized, acting as a means of cultural differentiation in societies where the complication of human knowledge has made it necessary to narrow one's field of attention in the interests of efficiency. Moreover, by distributing knowledge in this way to its beneficiaries academic education secures for them the place in the division of labour for which it prepares them. It not only prepares them to be doctors, but entitles them to be doctors, and most professions based on academic training have a relatively high status in our society.

In addition to this specialist and differentiating tendency, academic education has been held to provide a kind of general education. Here, the argument is that academic disciplines pursued far enough provide a world view. Through them, very wide ranges of experience can be organized by the individual. Thus, an historian, when he reaches a certain level of study, begins to be able to focus human experience historically, a scientist achieves a scientist's view of human life and the universe. The discipline provides a point of view from which experience can be ordered and given meaning. This general effect is achieved, however, only if the study is pursued to a very high level. It is essentially for the few, perhaps even for a small élite among the academic professions themselves.

It may be that at the very highest levels of study men can go out from their own specialist subject to meet others in other fields. Perhaps Einstein and Toynbee and Bertrand Russell could speak constructively together, though each from his own point of view. In general, however, the increase in specialization has tended to lead to a difficulty of communication between the students of different academic disciplines, and it is basically the desire to maintain the unity of the academic world which lies behind the demand for breadth of study.

For the very few who can ascend through knowledge to wisdom, men whom Plato would have chosen to rule his ideal state, an academic discipline provides a general education in the sense of a coherent and unified attitude towards life. For those who cannot aspire so high, a broadening of subjects may at least allow them to communicate with fellow academics about common problems.

This scarcely accounts for the fact that an academic education is reputed to help people to handle the problems of common human experience and the social and moral issues of everyday life. Yet I believe this reputation is not entirely false. The fact is that the social groups to which an academic education gives entry hold understandings and values of far wider significance than those which support professional competence. They have their own manners and morals, their own political and social attitudes. If what we ask of a general education is moral and social standards and ways of coping with life, then these groups can be accepted as sources of such standards – but only for those of like social situation. The position appears to be that academic schools endorse the cultural standards of those social groups which their successful pupils will enter. In a sense, general education is not a matter of curriculum, which is specialist, but of underlying assumptions, and these assumptions do not have to be driven home very forcibly, because the social pressures to which the pupil will be subjected when he finishes his formal education will reinforce the assumptions of the school. In Britain, students often escape punishment for breaches of the law which would certainly be punished in apprentices. I suspect that this is because there is a recognition that, once they have become doctors or teachers or priests, social pressures will ensure that they offend no more.

Thus it is in a sense the selective function of academic education which produces its general effects. The general education of the academic school prepares the pupil for the social destination to which it assigns him.

Let us now consider the high reputation of the English public schools as providers of a general education. Again, it seems that the source of their most general effect is not the curriculum, which is usually much the same as that of the academic grammar school. Indeed, the ethos of the schools themselves emphasizes something other than curriculum content. Most public schools are boarding institutions and they feel that their community life with its emphasis on personal discipline, leadership and so forth is the firmest basis of their influence. In fact, they instil into their pupils in somewhat idealized form the standards normed in the English upper classes and upper middle classes. Because of class influences in the structure of English society most public schoolboys will emerge with a certain status in society and will associate with groups of similar status. In other words, the public school prepares pupils to take their places in the social group which is their destination. Its success is largely due to the fact that adult life confirms the relevance of its teaching.

Teachers in public schools and teachers in academic grammar schools can both find reference groups in society at large to underwrite and confirm the standards they seek to persuade their classes to accept; and they can also feel that when a pupil leaves the school through which he has been inducted into adult culture, he will most often join adult groups which will afford at least general support for the standards he has accepted in school.

In both types of school the curriculum will tend to be academic. At first it will contain a large number of subjects, but these will be taught less for a relevance to life than for a relevance to higher studies. Such a curriculum allows a pupil to choose his specialization. Later, he will narrow his field of study according to this choice, and train himself for a vocation through his mastery of his subject. His teachers will be those who have succeeded on the course which he now follows. They will reflect both the specialist and the general standards of the group with whom the pupil will come to identify himself as an adult.

In such a teaching situation the teacher can enter the classroom confident in the standards of conduct and attainment he intends to demand of his class. Before the process of teaching begins, the end of teaching is defined. The relation of teacher to pupil is that of master to disciple, for the teacher represents the adult world which the pupil will have to enter. This is the traditional view of teaching. Exponents of it have something to learn from other views, but basically their attitude appears quite valid in the academic schools in which they teach. In England, however, such schools, or courses (for it makes no difference to the issue at stake whether the school be comprehensive or not), contain only a minority of the pupils. The majority are to be found in non-academic secondary schools or courses.

A commitment to the idea of secondary education for all implies that we give our pupils something more than the basic literacy dispensed by the old elementary school. But where do we find our standards?

We cannot merely base the curriculum on vocational preparation, though we may offer some vocational training. In the first place it is felt that the knowledge and skills appropriate to the vocations into which the children will enter do not offer the broad educational influences which the academic disciplines do. Secondly, the pupils will enter a diversity of occupations which make different demands and in some cases require very little educational background.

Moreover, we find that the general standards of the social groups to which these pupils will belong are not held in high repute in society, and are sometimes regarded as a social problem. The situation is complicated because the teachers' own standards are usually quite unlike those which hold in the pupils' future background.

It is primarily in such situations, where standards are insecure, that a radical progressive approach to teaching and to the curriculum is appropriate.

There appear to be two other possibilities. The first is to attempt to instil into the non-academic child a respect for the specialist academic cultures he cannot enter. This is to place him in the position of Plato's men with souls of brass or iron, looking up to others with souls of more precious metals. The second is to try to make the children accept the teacher's general standards though they cannot reach his academic standards. This is to attempt to win the working-class child to middle-class standards in moral and social attitudes. Neither of these courses appears to me to be desirable.

A radical progressive approach to education does not prescribe the curriculum to be followed. Curriculum content is determined by the interest of the pupil. This principle is perhaps too vague, laying a responsibility on the teacher too heavy for all but the most talented and sensitive to bear.

We may perhaps arrive at a more precise idea if we begin by asking, not what should be the content of the curriculum, but how worthwhile standards can be achieved in classroom work.

The progressive will tend to urge us, not to bring our standards into the classroom and inflict them on the children, but rather to take our standards from the children or, better perhaps, to generate our standards in the social interchange of the classroom. There are obvious dangers in such a suggestion, and we must be more particular in distinguishing good standards from bad.

Good 'child-centred' standards are attained when the teacher is able to make the pupils accept their work as a challenge. On this basis the class can work together, refining and disciplining their standards through self-criticism in the classroom discussion.

The problem of curriculum can now be expressed as follows: what worthwhile curriculum content can we find as a focus for a classroom experience which will provide this challenge and which will stimulate the pupils to an attempt to find for themselves standards which are worthwhile and viable in terms of their own experience of life?

We noticed earlier an interpretation of a general education as one concerned with those problems which arise from the general experience of social intercourse and of the human lot. These problems may perhaps serve as the basis for a secondary school curriculum for the non-academic child.

We are helped here by the fact that the secondary school pupil is already looking forward to adult society. He is capable of being interested in adult problems such as war, race relations, propaganda, human cruelty, or relations between the sexes. A curriculum such as we have just proposed could consist, not of subjects, but of problems of this sort.

The class are to study and discuss, let us say, war, but how are they to arrive at values, understandings and meanings which support a rich cultural attitude to this problem – surely, because there is fed into their discussion as need seems to demand, man's knowledge and experience of the issues at stake. In other words, they read about war, they consider the technology of war, they look at pictures about war and listen to music relevant to war. They are out to discover for themselves the attraction of war as adventure and then to go on to understand why this is an outlet for adventure which mankind can no longer afford to indulge.

Thus, the subjects of the curriculum are still the arts and sciences, but, while the academic child tends to learn about these as disciplines which he may master by further study, the non-academic child learns about them simply as contributions to man's thinking.

In this way the classroom becomes a kind of cultural laboratory in which new face-to-face culture is generated at a humble level. The pupils are in fact not making a transition from one culture to another, but rather being provided with the opportunity to feed their own culture on the arts and sciences, and thus to build for themselves an enriched medium of communication and thinking. Whereas in the academic school the teacher is, as it were, a servant of this subject, and is training pupils to make a contribution to it, in the non-academic school, the teacher ought to be a servant of his pupils, asking himself how his subject can make a contribution to the quality of their living. It might be that many academic teachers could learn from such classrooms something more of the relevance of their subjects to life.

References

1. A. H. Halsey, Jean Floud and C. Arnold Anderson (Editors), *Education, Economy and Society* (Glencoe, Ill.: The Free Press, 1961).
2. Banesh Hoffman, *The Strange Story of the Quantum* (London: Pelican, 1963, First edition 1947).
3. Central Advisory Council for Education, England, *15 to 18* Vol I: Report (London: HMSO, 1959) (The Crowther Report).

Social Determinism and Education

Two lectures given in the University of Uppsala, 1964.

Summary of the first lecture:

The function of education is the transmission of culture.

Culture consists of common understandings shared with a group of people. It is transmitted, learned and shared.

All culture involves norms or standards which are enforced by social pressures or sanctions. Society with its culture precedes an existing individual, and it is part of the business of education to socialize the individual by inducting him into culture. The individual is socialized through the face-to-face culture of the school and the school class.

A theoretical problem arises since this formulation suggests that the school as a transmitter of culture is simply a creator of conformity; yet we know that schools may also give access to culture in a way that favours creativity and individuality.

The problem is basically a theoretical one, as is apparent from the conflict between theory and observation. The concept of culture has been evolved within a conceptual framework dedicated to the analysis of the social determinants of individual behaviour, and it bears the stamp of its origin. As it stands it is a concept designed to explain conformity rather than creativity. This leads to an unsatisfactory treatment of creativity:

1. creativity may be treated as deviance;
2. culture may be held to lay down limits within which freedom is exercised;
3. action may be regarded as always in part socially determined, but we are then left with the problem of analysing the intensity of determination.

We may distinguish two major frameworks in social science for the explanation of human action, both deterministic in implications:

1. that of psychology, a species of individual determinism founded in the last analysis in biological concepts and in the primary psychological concepts of motivation, intelligence and learning;
2. that of sociology, a species of social determinism, founded in the sociological concepts of culture and of norms and roles.

The problem is to relate these two frameworks, each of which qualifies the other, in such a way as to take account of the wilfulness and creativity of human action. This is a crucial problem for education, which relates the individual to the social.

Social Determinism and Education: the second lecture

Although some aspects of the sociology of education – for example the relation of education to social structure and social mobility – have developed rapidly in recent years, there is still a pressing need for work to be done on the sociology of the school and the classroom. Here only fragmentary and sporadic progress has been made since Willard Waller's classic *Sociology of Teaching*.[1] I believe that the analysis and interpretation of the idea of the school as an institution concerned with the transmission of culture is the most promising foundation for the sociological study of the educational process.

Our theoretical problem arose when it became clear that the adoption of the idea of education as transmission of culture tends to lead us to a view of education which stresses conformity and which sees educational institutions as part of the mechanism of social control. Within this frame of reference, there is difficulty in accounting for innovation, creativity and freedom, all of which are highly valued in our western society. I argued that this difficulty arose from our adoption, with the term *culture*, of certain theoretical assumptions which have become associated with it. The term was shaped within a tradition of inquiry which was concerned to examine the social determinants of customary behaviour. Creativity or freedom was seen as intensely individual, and hence it eluded this system of social determinism.

We now face the problem of handling the idea of creativity within the conceptual scheme of sociology. If I am right in thinking that this problem arises rather from our use of concepts than from any intractable empirical evidence, then we should be able to point a way of overcoming it by revising our theory.

The key question is: does it make sense and prove helpful to speak of the social conditions that favour individuality and creativity? I hope to show that it does, and my interpretation of the situation will be broadly within the academic tradition which is known as cultural sociology or symbolic interactionist sociology.

Culture, comprising complexes of understandings shared among minds, is primarily learned through communication. It is assimilated in this way because it underlies all communication and indeed supports it. Without the common understandings of culture there could be no communication. 'We know, and we can effectively communicate with, other minds because behind us all there is the common life which holds us together as a unity in diversity . . .'[2] The ideational aspect of this common life is what we call *culture*, and it is this fund of common ideas which is passed on in communication and which supports communication. Normally we communicate through symbols – most commonly language, but on occasion mathematical symbols, the symbolic forms of visual art and so forth – and all these symbols represent and grow out of common understandings in the culture.

Thus the child absorbs the culture as he learns the language, for the language is loaded with the values and understandings of the social group which uses it. This experience of adopting values as we learn language is familiar to those adults who are interested in languages other than their own. It is also part of the experience of anthropological field work, as the following passage testifies.

> General behaviour, attitudes, and values are not taught by any formal training. These are inextricably bound up with life in the society and become unconsciously adopted by any one fully partaking in social life. Even a European, when speaking the language and trying to enter into their social activities, finds himself unconsciously taking for granted values that he never had before and which are certainly not to be found in European life. They seem to follow naturally from the social situation and to be bound up with language itself.[3]

From the very earliest then children learn language for and in communication with others. Such a view of language development is scarcely novel, but it needs to be emphasized because it points a paradox in Piaget's account of the linguistic development of children. Piaget claims that egocentric speech precedes social speech, that though they learn words from others, children use them to speak as it were for themselves, before they begin to communicate with others. This seems an uneconomic and slightly illogical theory which is not really forced on us by the empirical evidence, and Vygotsky differs fundamentally from Piaget in his account of the genesis of speech and language. Moreover, Piaget has conceded many of Vygotsky's points.

Vygotsky, having taken the position that 'Speech for oneself originates through differentiation from speech for others',[4] comments:

> Our results must seem paradoxical from the point of view of Piaget's theory: The weaker the child's contact is with the group – the less the social situation forces him to adjust his thoughts to others and to use social speech – the more freely should the egocentrism of his thinking and speech manifest itself. But from the point of view of our hypothesis, the meaning of these findings is clear: egocentric speech, springing from the lack of differentiation of speech for oneself from speech for others, disappears when the feeling of being understood, essential for social speech, is absent.[5]

Writing of the experiments which lie at the centre of his book, Vygotsky says, 'The purpose of all three series of experiments was to eliminate those characteristics of egocentric speech which bring it close to social speech. We found that this always led to the dwindling of egocentric speech. It is logical, then, to assume that egocentric speech is a form developing out of social speech.'[6]

Now, since egocentric speech is for Vygotsky social speech being adapted as inner speech, it follows that those forms of thinking which make any use of language or other forms of symbol grow out of the culture. To say that social speech precedes inner speech is to say that cultural speech precedes symbolic thinking, which is indeed created from it. This suggests that culture may determine our thinking because it provides us with the tools of thought. We do not clothe our ideas in symbols, but rather learn our ideas through symbols, a point which Cooley puts rather well.

> A word is a vehicle, a boat floating down from the past, laden with the thought of men we never saw; and in coming to understand it we enter not only into the minds of our contemporaries, but into the general mind of humanity continuous through time. The popular notion of learning to speak is that the child first has the idea and then gets from others a sound to use in communicating it; but a closer study shows that this is hardly true even of the simplest ideas, and is nearly the reverse of truth as regards developed thought. In that the word usually goes before, leading and kindling the idea – we should not have the latter if we did not have the word first.[7]

In a broad sense we may say that language is a symbolic representation of culture, and this might lead us to the conclusion that the learning of language is merely a mechanism by which we are indoctrinated into culture, a means of inducing mental conformity. We may maintain our view of education as a form of social control and suggest that the development of language is the moulding of the mind. Cultural understandings would then dominate our behaviour, largely because they dominate our language.

Starting from Vygotsky's observation that 'the meaning of every word is a generalization or a concept', we might suggest that the learning of language is a process not merely of acquiring means of communication, but also of concept formation. Our behavioural environment and the entire cast of our thinking would then be determined, or at least deeply influenced, by our language. Such a view is sympathetic to the theories of Sapir and

Whorf in linguistics, and to the line of thinking in psychology which has studied the social determinants of perception.

To assess how far language determines thought, we must consider the development of egocentric speech from social speech, for in egocentric speech we have the stem from which thought grows. Here I shall follow and comment on Vygotsky. In his view vocal egocentric speech becomes the inner speech of thought.

> Inner speech is for oneself; external speech is for others. It would indeed be surprising if such a basic difference in function did not affect the structure of the two kinds of speech. Absence of vocalization *per se* is only a consequence of the specific nature of inner speech, which is neither an antecedent of external speech nor its reproduction in memory but is, in a sense, the opposite of external speech. The latter is the turning of thought into words, its materialization and objectification. With inner speech, the process is reversed: speech turns into inward thought. Consequently, their structures must differ.[8]

It is not possible in the time available to probe Vygotsky's position as deeply as it deserves. Basically, however, it is this: egocentric speech is a stage in the process of the development of inner speech, of the 'inward aspect of language, the side turned toward the person, not toward the outer world'.[9] This inner language is the language of thinking, and it is constructed out of the language of communication. But it is not structurally the same as the language of communication. We forge in communication the tools we use in reflection, but the process is one of improvisation. It may be compared to a problem which we solve by using a chair as a step ladder and a bicycle pump to reach out with. A chair is not designed for this purpose nor is a bicycle pump designed as an extensible reaching stick. In the same way, the language we use in thinking strains the language of communication to serve our own needs. We build a new structure from the elements of the old.

This difference of structure between the language of thought and that of communication is a vital point. Vygotsky treats it as follows:

> Inner speech is not the interior aspect of external speech – it is a function in itself. It still remains speech, i.e. thought connected with words. But while in external speech thought is embodied in words, in inner speech words die as they bring forth thought. Inner speech is to

a large extent thinking in pure meanings. It is a dynamic, shifting, unstable thing, fluttering between word and thought, the two more or less stable, more or less firmly delineated components of verbal thought. Its true nature and place can be understood only after examining the next plane of verbal thought, the one still more inward than inner speech.

That plane is thought itself. As we have said, every thought creates a connection, fulfils a function, solves a problem. The flow of thought is not accompanied by a simultaneous unfolding of speech. The two processes are not identical, and there is no rigid correspondence between the units of thought and speech. This is especially obvious when a thought process miscarries – when, as Dostoevsky put it, a thought 'will not enter words'. Thought has its own structure, and the transition from it to speech is no easy matter.[10]

I am not entirely happy with Vygotsky's distinction between thought and word here, but my final analysis will not depend upon it. What seems to be important is the principle of differentiating structures. Following Vygotsky for the moment, we may distinguish three planes, each with its own structure:

1. Thought
2. Inner speech
3. The speech of communication

To these we may add a fourth structure, that of culture. We are dubious about the relationship proposed between thought and inner speech, but this is not of vital importance to us since it is the relationships between culture and communication and inner speech which primarily concern us.

Here we find first a complex of common understandings which we have called culture. Culture has a structure of its own. It is not composed of discrete understandings but of patternings of understandings. These complexes cluster round cultural values and institutions. Thus, for example, in our own society we have the institution of Christmas, and round it there clusters a complex of Christmas understandings. One might say that the structure of culture is psychological in principle, and not unlike the complexes of depth psychology.

Now, when these understandings are translated into the language of communication, their structure is changed, for language has its own structure, a logic or syntax. Thus, even in the language of communication, we may think. Indeed, literature may be regarded as a species of thinking in the language of communication. Within the discipline and order of languages, we may establish new relationships. For example, adjectives may be attached to unusual nouns, predicates to unaccustomed subjects. We are able to talk of a golden mountain, not because we have experienced one, but because the adjective golden may be attached to the noun mountain according to the structural principles of language, and being so attached it is capable of raising in our minds a new image.

In short, the grammatical structure of language makes it capable of forging relationships not implied in the culture. Much literature achieves its effects in this way. One may say that art depends upon the use of a medium which has structural principles of its own, independent of those of the culture and capable of interacting with these. Thus language can be used as a calculus of thinking.

Now, the inner language of personal thinking seems to me to differ from the language of communication principally in achieving a compromise between psychological, cultural and grammatical structures. Words can be used in personal and cultural connotations, and the grammar of language can be adopted or abandoned at will. Whether it is possible to distinguish between inner language and thought, as Vygotsky does, I am doubtful, but the problem is not one which we need to resolve here.

For our purposes, it is enough to suggest that in the language of communication and in the inner language, it is possible to establish relationships which are not already found in the culture. Language, though created from culture and emerging from common understandings, comes to be a thing in itself with a potentiality as a calculus. Thus, it allows us to handle the ideas of our culture in an active way, and makes culture a resource rather than a determinant. Culture becomes a medium in which we work. Of course, it is clear that the possibilities it offers us cannot be unlimited. A sculptor must come to terms with his block of marble. But we cannot say that the image he will fashion is already implicit in the stone. Because of symbols, culture confronts man as the medium confronts the artist, providing him with the possibility of being creative.

Where does education enter into this picture? Well, of course, education helps to elaborate language and gives us a greater command of the structures of thinking we have just now distinguished. But the matter goes far deeper than that, for education has generally been concerned with a particular kind of tradition, the academic or scientific.

The academic disciplines are a kind of institutionalized public thinking. In mathematics, the sciences, history and philosophy we create highly artificial structures which are from the outset designed for their effectiveness as tools of thought rather than as media of communication. These structures offer disciplined paradigms of ideal thinking. We do not think logically, rather we submit our thoughts to the discipline of logical analysis. Trial and error may be natural, but scientific experiment guided by hypotheses is an exquisite refinement of trial and error. If the arts represent one pinnacle of the creative achievement of men, the academic disciplines, properly understood, represent the other. Barzun has called the academic tradition 'intellect', and has characterized it thus:

> Intellect is the capitalized and communal form of live intelligence; it is intelligence stored up and made into habits of discipline, signs and symbols of meaning, chains of reasoning and spurs to emotion – a shorthand and a wireless by which the mind can skip connectives, recognize ability, and communicate truth. Intellect is at once a body of knowledge and the channels through which the right particle of it can be brought to bear quickly, without the effort of redemonstration, on the matter in hand . . . intelligence wherever found is an individual and private possession; it dies with the owner unless he embodies it in more or less lasting form. Intellect on the contrary is a product of social effort and an acquirement.[11]

Within the culture itself there have been developed institutionalized modes of creativity, of which the most important are the arts and the sciences. Creativity is possible in these modes because they provide flexible conceptual frameworks, calculuses and logics which are not inert but on the contrary highly volatile and suggestive of innovation. That such structures are the means of enhanced freedom and individuality, Durkheim has hinted.

> The pressure exercised by the social group upon each of its members does not permit individuals to judge freely the concepts that the society itself has elaborated and where it has put something of its character. Such constructions are sacred to the citizen. Furthermore, the history of scientific classification is, in the last analysis, the very history of the steps through which this element of social affect has progressively weakened, leaving more and more room for the reflective thinking of individuals.[12]

This reflective thinking of individuals is the key to innovation and creativity; and in reflective thinking the individual and the cultural come to terms. If I am right in seeing academic disciplines as important modes of reflective thinking then it is clear that education has much to do with ensuring that individual and culture meet in a way favourable to creativeness. Before we examine the role of education in detail, however, we must return to the theoretical problem posed by the separation of the two conceptual frameworks, one of individual determination and the other of social determination.

Within the conceptual framework of social determination, the two principal factors in human behaviour are culture, that is the shared understandings and ideas which come to the individual as a member of the social group, and symbolic systems, which are aspects of culture with logics of their own. The symbolic systems provide calculuses of reflective thinking, and present themselves as resources for the individual.

If we now construct a model for individual behaviour, we shall find that symbolic systems enter into it and mediate between the culture as a body of ideas and the action system of the individual actor.

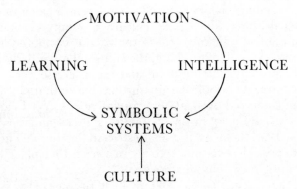

In this individual action system, the concept of motivation is fundamental. As Vygotsky says, 'Thought itself is engendered by motivation, i.e. by our desires and needs, our interests and emotions. Behind every thought there is an affective-volitional tendency, which holds the answer to the last "why" in the analysis of thinking.'[13] Of course, motivation in the mature individual can no longer be accounted for in purely individual terms since it involves cultural values. These values, however, have themselves been filtered through symbolic systems, so that our model is preserved.

By learning is implied here the capacity to acquire information, skills, etc., the store element in the performance of the individual. By intelligence I mean primarily the capacity to adduce relationships and to make imaginative projections. This imaginative aspect of intelligence corresponds in a broad way to the creative or divergent intelligence studied by Getzels and Jackson,[14] and is implied in the final stage of development noted in Inhelder and Piaget's *Growth of Logical Thinking*,[15] a stage at which the thinker can handle the hypothetical as well as the actually existent.

In the individual action system, then, learning and intelligence work in the service of motivation upon the behavioural environment, and in developed cultures a highly significant, or even dominant, element in the behavioural environment consists of symbols and symbol systems. Many of these symbolic systems can be used creatively as calculuses of thinking. They serve the individual as resources in learning and as media for the creative use of intelligence.

In the social action system the shared ideas or conformities of culture crystallize into symbolic systems. In so far as these symbolic systems achieve the effectiveness as a calculus we have mentioned above, they make culture a resource rather than a determinant of thinking. In so far as the symbol systems are inadequate as tools of thinking, the culture they embody will tend to work more as a determinant and less as a resource.

Of course, any tool of thinking has its limitations, and the freedom conferred by symbols is a relative one. Yet I cannot feel that it is helpful to speak of symbol systems and the cultures embodied in them as if they restricted freedom. They make freedom possible – to some extent. In a sense they place limits on us, but only in the sense that an aeroplane limits where we can fly. Although it is true that we can only fly in the part of the sky where our aeroplane happens to be, yet without it we could not fly at all. The relation of symbolic systems to creative thinking is analogous to the relationship of aeroplanes to flying. It does not seem helpful to regard them as placing restrictions on thinking.

It is now possible to marry our two schemes, the determinism of psychology and the determinism of sociology. Sociology is concerned with the social determination of behaviour, and by implication with the social determination of conformity. Conformity gives rise to symbolic systems. Thus culture may be observed in two modes, as patterns of behaviour and as systems of symbols. These systems of symbols constitute matrices or fields, which may be relatively inert or relatively dynamic. A dynamic symbolic field is one which readily produces creative innovation when an individual, directed by motivation, enters into the system equipped with a capacity for learning, and intelligence. The existence of such individuals can be studied within the framework of psychology. In the present state of knowledge at least, we must regard the interaction of individual intelligence with symbol system as constituting an area of freedom or indeterminacy.

Indeed, it is doubtful whether we can ever predict creative response in any normal sense. If we are able to predict what Einstein will think before he thinks it, then we have created it, not Einstein, and he will go on from our position, rather than start afresh. To predict the creative is to make it happen.

The time has now come to apply our findings to the practice of education. It is not possible in the time we have to follow out in detail the implications of our conceptual framework for the sociological analysis of the school and classroom, and I believe that the best way to approach the general problem of application is to present to you a series of questions.

Key questions:

A Questions involving value judgements:

   (i) How far do we wish education to stimulate creativity rather than to produce conformity?

   (ii) Are we prepared to face the idea of an educational system which produces a creative élite and a conforming majority?

B Questions for psychology:

   (i) What is the nature of creative intelligence?

   (ii) What conditions of motivation and learning render latent creativity manifest?

C Questions for social psychology and sociology:

   (i) What kinds of small group structure are favourable to creativity?

   (ii) What kinds of cultural symbolic systems favour creativity?

   (iii) What kinds of social traditions favour creativity?

D Questions affecting educational practice:

  (i) How can academic disciplines be taught for creativity?
  (ii) How can examinations be designed to reward creative responses?
  (iii) What basis for individual creativity can we offer to children of limited academic ability?

References

1. Willard Waller, *The Sociology of Teaching* (New York: John Wiley, 1932, reprinted 1965).
2. Werner Stark, *The Fundamental Forms of Social Thought* (London: Routledge and Kegan Paul, 1962), p. 228.
3. E. J. Krige and J. D. Krige, *The Realm of a Rain Queen* (London: Oxford University Press for the International African Institute, 1943), pp. 109–10.
4. Lev Semenovich Vygotsky, *Thought and Language*, edited and translated by Eugenia Hanfmann and Gertrude Vakar (Boston and New York: Massachusetts Institute of Technology and John Wiley, 1962), p. 133.
5. Ibid., p. 137.
6. Ibid., p. 138.
7. Charles H. Cooley (1909), *Social Organisation*, reprinted in *The Two Major Works of Charles H. Cooley* (Glencoe, Ill.: The Free Press, 1956), p. 69.
8. Lev Semenovich Vygotsky, *Thought and Language*, edited and translated by Eugenia Hanfmann and Gertrude Vakar (Boston and New York: Massachusetts Institute of Technology and John Wiley, 1962), p. 131.
9. Ibid., p. 152.
10. Ibid., p. 149.
11. Jacques Barzun, *The House of Intellect* (London: Secker and Warburg, 1962), pp. 4–5.
12. Émile Durkheim and Marcel Mauss, 'Social structure and the structure of thought', translated by Jesse Pitts from 'Quelques formes de classification primitives'. *Année Sociologique*, 4, 1901–2, 66–72, and printed in *Theories of Society*, edited Parsons *et al.* (Glencoe, Ill.: The Free Press, 1961), Vol II, 1065–1068.
13. Lev Semenovich Vygotsky, *Thought and Language*, edited and translated by Eugenia Hanfmann and Gertrude Vakar (Boston and New York: Massachusetts Institute of Technology and John Wiley, 1962), p. 150.
14. Jacob W. Getzels and Philip W. Jackson, *Creativity and Intelligence* (New York: John Wiley, 1962).
15. Bärbel Inhelder and Jean Piaget, *The Growth of Logical Thinking* (London: Routledge and Kegan Paul, 1958).

The Concept of Standards in the Theory of Education

Printed as 'Aims or Standards?' in Education for Teaching, *64, 1964.*

> 'I suppose the conviction that an educator must
> have aims is generated by the concept of
> "education" itself; for it is a concept that
> has a standard or norm, as it were, built into it.'
>   R. S. Peters, *Authority, Responsibility and Education*[1]

It is a commonplace that educational practice implies problems of value, and most training courses include some study of the value judgement. The central importance of values once admitted, there arises the problem of bridging the gap between the critical study of values and the practice of teaching. The theory of education, as distinct from the study of philosophy by teachers, faces this as its central problem, and upon its solution depends the relevance of educational theory in educational practice. Teachers who enter classrooms for the first time meet the situations which face them partly by recourse to 'methods', partly by modelling themselves on other teachers within the tradition and partly by reacting spontaneously to the life of the classroom. It is the business of theory to help the teacher to gain a thoughtful control of his practice.

The relation of theory to practice is difficult to analyse, but it seems clear that a key to the problem is the development of concepts which imply values and at the same time offer a grip on the practical situation and make it accessible to thought and reflection. To isolate and name an effective concept is the first step in establishing critical control. For example, the naming of top-spin and back-spin in tennis awakes the recognition which must precede a critical consideration of the place of spin in tactics.

The concept most commonly used in educational discussion to link values with practice is that of aims. R. S. Peters has argued cogently that aims, when regarded as 'objectives to be arrived at by taking appropriate means',[2] are not sufficiently helpful in educational discussion, because the model of ends and means is not applicable in many important educational situations. Thus he suggests that:

> ... most of the important things in education are passed on. . . . by example and explanation. An attitude, a skill, is caught; sensitivity, a critical mind, respect for people and facts develop where an articulate and intelligent exponent is on the job. Yet the model of means to ends is not remotely applicable to the transaction that is taking place. Values, of course, are involved in the transaction; if they were not it would not be called 'education'. Yet they are not end-products or terminating points of the process. They reside both in the skills and cultural traditions that are passed on and in the procedure for passing them on.[3]

This philosophic objection to the concept of aims seems to be supported by practical experience. The idea which lies behind thinking in terms of aims is that we can gain control of our actions by planning ahead and that we can criticize our forward plans in terms of their ends. In other words, when we deal in aims, we seek to gain control of the future and shape it so that it develops towards some outcome which we accept as good. Expressed at high levels of generality, aims give little guidance in planning; expressed in detail, they tend to bind the future and to set limits to the possibilities of the developing situation. Controlled development towards a specific goal is implied in aims. And one finds that teachers who conceive and plan their teaching in terms of aims too often imprison themselves.

A further disadvantage is that aims are difficult to relate to any concepts which can be studied empirically and a bridge between theory and practice would clearly be strengthened if we could found one pier on the social sciences.

The final difficulty with aims is that they readily become rationalizations of practice rather than bases for a critique; but this is in truth merely the obverse of their principal advantage as a tool of thinking in education: namely, that they are easy to verbalize. This means that the student can readily formulate aims in lesson preparation. The fact that a student does this exposes his thinking to discussion and criticism. Unfortunately, however, formal verbalization tends to make the link between aim and practice the more tenuous. It becomes possible for the student to learn to say acceptable things without allowing this to affect his practice. In other words, aims are convenient because they lend themselves to verbal expression, but for the same reason they can easily become a matter of lip service.

The concept of standards has much to commend it as an alternative to aims. Standards can be studied empirically, related to practice and analysed philosophically.

By 'standards' I understand the criteria adopted in the criticism of classrooms, and not *levels* of attainment in class work. When classroom behaviour or classroom work is judged standards are always implied. And within the classroom there are two distinct standards operative, that of the class and that of the teacher.

We may consider first the standards of the class. We observe that while the teacher is reading a poem a boy in the back row talks to his friend. Three boys on the row in front turn round and say: 'Sh!' We conclude that the class behaves according to a standard which may be expressed verbally as a principle: 'No member of the class should talk while the teacher is talking to the class as a whole.' This is a standard or convention of classroom behaviour in action. We might further notice that when the class is writing up a scientific experiment, one boy turns to another and says: 'You've forgotten to describe the apparatus.' Here a standard of work is implied. A more difficult standard to verbalize is implied when a pupil judges that he has written a good composition.

Because of the power conferred upon him by his position, the teacher's standards are master standards. It is his task to develop standards of criticism appropriate to the work of the class he is teaching and to make these standards explicit and compelling so that the class can adopt them as their own. He wishes to make his pupils self-critical and thus autonomous in their work, and their self-criticism must be based upon standards which he recognizes as appropriate in a given teaching situation.

The experience of standards may be described from the class's point of view as follows. 'We enter a situation in which a teacher has a power over us. In order to act securely, we must be able to predict his reactions to our behaviour and our work. Sometimes we may want to resist the teacher's power and then we must stick together. When we have a good teacher we accept many of his standards and make them our own; when we have a bad teacher we prefer our own standards and conspire to restrict his influence over us, and to reject it entirely when we leave his class.'

Of course, such an attitude is not usually self-conscious and

explicit. The point to be made is that the class can only interpret
the situation in which they are placed through the recognition of
consistent standards. 'You'd better not talk in Smith's class.'
'Jones likes lots of facts.' 'Robinson likes flowery descriptions.'

Now, standards of this sort are clearly social norms holding for
the class as a group; and there is a considerable body of research
on the dynamics of social norms which can be brought to bear on
classroom standards. (e.g. Cartwright and Zander 1960;[4] Hare,
Borgotta and Bales 1955;[5] Merrill 1961;[6] Johnson 1961;[7]
Rommetveit 1955.[8]) It becomes possible to consider problems of
morale and classroom 'tone' in relation to standards of work. The
predicament of the isolate in the classroom is vividly exposed.
Industrial psychologists have studied standards of output in
factory groups, and their methods could be adapted to the
classroom. (A particularly good account may be found in
Homans' *Human Group*, chapters III–VI.[9])

The teacher's standards are also social norms, but they are
norms deriving from outside the classroom. Sometimes, as in the
case of moral standards, these norms will be endorsed by large
and comparatively undifferentiated social groups, but some
norms will be sustained by more specialized and restricted
groups: teachers or academics or members of the New Education
Fellowship. Because the teacher's standards are seldom idiosyncratic and usually reinforced by groups of this kind, we may
consider them through an examination of the articulate traditions
of the groups with which he associates himself (e.g. Barzun
1959;[10] Barber and Hirsch 1962;[11] Stevens 1960.[12])
Occasionally, we shall find that societies contain groups which
find it difficult to understand one another, for example, middle-
class and working-class or European and Asian. A special
problem obviously arises where the teacher and the class have
disparate loyalties deriving from 'hostile' groups (see Jackson
and Marsden 1962.[13])

If we conceptualize values in practice as standards, we see the
dynamic of the classroom as an interaction between teachers'
standards and pupils' standards. The idea of aims by contrast
seems to suggest that the pupils are passive and obscures the
polarity of forces in the teaching situation.

The focusing of attention upon standards, then, brings to bear
on the classroom a substantial corpus of work in the social
sciences. It also suggests a kind of empirical work which might
play a part in the education of teachers. It would seem profitable

for groups of students or teachers to examine varied examples of children's work and to discuss their judgements of them. Compositions or science notebooks drawn from the classrooms of teachers whose standards diverge would offer an excellent demonstration of the practical expression of underlying values and an opportunity to explore the implications of these as they are projected into classroom work. There seems much to commend this: at least it would give students a chance to clarify their views of what is within the range of possibilities with a 1A or a 3C.

I have claimed that standards can be approached analytically through social psychology and sociology and that children's work can be discussed profitably on the basis of the understanding gained. It remains to demonstrate that the concept of standards leads to a fruitful discussion of values.

Certainly, the basic contemporary conflict in educational thinking can be thought of in terms of standards. The 'traditionalist' can readily express his standards as ideal ends or aims. This is to say that his critical reactions to children's work are implicitly based upon a comparison with an ideal, and thus tend towards 'correctness'. The 'progressive' cannot readily verbalize his standards. He sees himself rather in the position of a critic in the arts. He will not say what children's work ought to be like any more than a critic will say what an unpainted picture ought to be like. He must react critically to the work which comes from the children, refining and developing their standards as he goes. Thus he stresses a 'sense of quality' and 'creativeness'.

One sees clearly why the philosophic approach of the traditionalist will tend towards ethics while that of the progressive will tend towards aesthetics. The traditionalist seeks to outline a philosophy of life, the progressive to articulate a critique of children's work.

I have implied that 'traditionalists' and 'progressives' are groups with their own norms and values which they support by exerting social pressures. So long as the word 'group' is not used too narrowly I think this analysis is valid. A rough and ready test is to enter a group whose ideas are antithetical to one's own. In most cases one becomes aware of pressures being deployed to bring the outsider into line.

An observation of this kind is an observation of the dynamics of standards in action; but it provides no justification of the standards themselves. To examine these critically is to move over into territory which has traditionally been that of the philosopher. But in order to make standards accessible to philosophic criticism one must translate them into some kind of verbal formulation.

It has been suggested that to formulate standards as aims is less profitable than might be hoped; and it is therefore necessary to consider what concept we may employ.

Now within any group of pupils or teachers we may observe standards operating at two levels. In the first place, we may observe behaviourally the social pressures which express the critical reaction of the group to the behaviour and work of its members; and within the classroom we may observe the teacher's criticism of the behaviour and work of the pupils. We can examine which compositions gain high marks and which low marks, which suggestions from pupils are followed up and which rejected. Our observations can be expressed in verbal forms, for example, 'X praises logical paragraph construction, correct spelling, use of wide vocabulary', while 'Y praises imaginative qualities, flexible paragraphing and economical use of vocabulary'. Such verbal expressions of standards may be called critical principles.

In addition to principles which have been derived from an observation of behaviour in the classroom, we can also study teachers' attempts to propose their own principles. Much educational literature is concerned to formulate principles which are recognized by some group of teachers as adequate expressions of the rationale of their critical responses to the classroom.

The comparison of behaviourally derived principles with expressed principles should allow more and more adequate formulations of the bases of critical standards.

Principles derived in this way are necessarily kept in close relationship to behaviour. One might reasonably call them 'principles of procedure' applicable in situations where critical judgements are called for. Such principles are apparently broadly acceptable to the philosopher, for the concept R. S. Peters favours as a substitute for aims is 'principles of procedure'.

> To illustrate more clearly the distinction which I am drawing between 'aims' and 'principles of procedure', let me take a parallel from politics. A man who believes in equality, might, like Godwin, be lured by a positive picture of a society in which differences between people would be minimised. He might want to get rid of differences in wealth and rank, even to breed people in the attempt to iron out

innate differences. He might even go so far as to advocate the abolition of institutions like the army or the Church in which some men were given opportunities of lording it over others. Another social reformer, however, might employ the principle of equality in a much more negative sense without any concrete picture to lure him on his journey. He might insist, merely, that whatever social changes were introduced, no one should be treated differently from anyone else unless a good reason could be produced to justify such unequal treatment. The Godwin type of man would rightly be regarded as pursuing equality as a very general aim; the more cautious liberal would have no particular aim connected with equality. He would merely insist that whatever schemes were put forward must not be introduced in a way which would infringe his procedural principle.

I think this is an illuminating parallel to the point I am trying to make about the aims of education. For, in my view, most disputes about the aims of education are disputes about principles of procedure rather than about 'aims' in the sense of objectives to be arrived at by taking appropriate means. The so-called 'aims' are ways of referring to the different valuations which are built into the different procedures like training, conditioning, the use of authority, teaching by example and rational explanation, all of which fall under the general concept of 'education'.[14]

It is argued that consistent critical judgements can be expressed as 'standards' and observed in action in the classroom. These empirical observations can be expressed verbally as principles of criticism. They then have many of the advantages of Peters' 'principles of procedure', indeed, they are in a sense 'principles of criticism of principles of procedure'. In terms of Peters' analysis these critical principles should offer an acceptable alternative to 'aims' in 'referring to the different valuations which are built into the different procedures'.

Summary

The concept of standards can be usefully employed in educational theory as a bridge between values and practice. It allows us to focus our attention on the critical appraisal by pupils and teachers of classroom behaviour and work.

The idea of standards has the advantage of a firm anchoring in classroom practice, in the social sciences and philosophy. 'Standards' can be studied empirically by the observation of teachers' judgements of children's work; and teachers can become more sensitive to their own standards by discussing children's work. 'Standards' can be assimilated to social psychology and sociology by identifying them as social norms, and thus a considerable body of experimental and theoretical work can be brought to bear on the classrooms. 'Standards' can be identified with principles of criticism, and this leads to a philosophic approach which can readily draw on work in both ethics and aesthetics.

References

1. R. S. Peters, *Authority, Responsibility and Education* (London: Allen and Unwin, 1959), p. 84.
2. Ibid., p. 90.
3. Ibid., p. 92.
4. Dorwin Cartwright and Alvin Zander, *Group Dynamics: Research and Theory*, 2nd edition (London: Tavistock, 1960).
5. Paul Hare, Edgar F. Borgotta and Robert F. Bales, *Small Groups* (New York: Knopf, 1955).
6. Francis Merrill, *Society and Culture* (Englewood Cliffs, N.J.: Prentice Hall, 1961).
7. Harry M. Johnson, *Sociology: a Systematic Introduction* (London: Routledge and Kegan Paul, 1961).
8. Ragnar Rommetveit, *Social Norms and Roles* (Oslo and Minneapolis: Akademisk Forlag and University of Minnesota Press, 1955).
9. George Homans, *The Human Group* (London: Routledge and Kegan Paul, 1951).
10. Jacques Barzun, *The House of Intellect* (London: Secker and Warburg, 1959).
11. Bernard Barber and Walter Hirsch, *The Sociology of Science* (Glencoe, Ill.: The Free Press, 1962).
12. Frances Stevens, *The Living Tradition* (London: Hutchinson, 1960).
13. Brian Jackson and Dennis Marsden, *Education and the Working Class* (London: Routledge and Kegan Paul, 1962).
14. R. S. Peters, *Authority, Responsibility and Education* (London: Allen and Unwin, 1959), pp. 89–90.

The Humanities in the Classroom

From Culture and Education (*1967*)[1]

Does a definition of the curriculum necessarily tend to weaken its relation to the interests and experience of the child? I believe that in the primary school it does, because the young child is lightly socialized and thus a product of his variable immediate environment rather than of a public culture. His curiosity ranges round his intimate experience and his interests follow patterns unnatural to the adult. Thus his response is difficult to predict. In the secondary school, however, we find pupils who are socialized into the general cultures of adult society, and accordingly their values and interests can be predicted with reasonable accuracy. Upon these their culture is integrated, and to feed their culture with the resources of the humanities we must take cognizance of their interests.

What sort of interests seem central to the average adolescent? If one asks adolescents, and if one studies the experiences they pursue through mass communication, one can obtain a reasonably reliable answer. I believe that my own experience of the secondary-school adolescent will be reasonably typical. They are interested in sex, in everyday ethics, in war and peace, in race relations, and in problems of violence and social inequality. They are also interested in sport, pop records, dancing and travel, but when pushed, they concede that these interests seem less important. Some will go so far as to say that this is because they present few problems to them. Two prominent interests of adults are perhaps not generally keenly felt by adolescents, namely, the problems of power and death, though these too can evoke a surprisingly mature response.

Let us be bold, therefore, and say that the curriculum for a general education in the secondary school should, when difficulties of motivation are met, concentrate on the problems involved in sex, war, race, violence, social justice and the general issues of right and wrong. We have chosen the curriculum of the *News of the World*. Some would say that such issues should not be brought into the school. They fear for the school's ability to handle them. Yet to banish them is to delegate to mass communication the task of building out our pupils' values and interpretations in these areas. This seems still more dangerous. If mass communication handles these acutely interesting topics badly, it is no remedy that the school should handle less living and less important issues well. To aspire to a school curriculum which eschews controversial issues is to hanker after the minimal education of the nineteenth-century elementary school.

Nevertheless, one can sympathize with the school-teachers' hesitation. It becomes them. Not only are these topics uncomfortable to handle at times. More than that, the conscientious teacher recognizes the fearful responsibility which is involved in teaching in controversial areas. It is difficult indeed to maintain an unbiased point of view. Or should one in practice be prejudiced in favour of the good? But what is the good? A yawning gulf opens beneath the teacher. It is surely right that he should not go into the classroom and give lessons or lectures or sermons about these matters which cut to the quick of his own and his pupils' values and sensibilities.

Yet he does allow into his classroom the humanities: literature and history and art; and not surprisingly, these very issues are the central stuff of the humanities. Shakespeare alone will demonstrate this. For a consideration of the problems of relations between the sexes, we may turn not only to *Romeo and Juliet* and *Antony and Cleopatra*, but also to Macbeth and his wife, to Brutus and Portia, to Hotspur and Kate. For the problem of war we can turn to the histories, to *Coriolanus*, to the Roman plays in general. Even race problems are represented in the *Merchant of Venice* and *Othello*. *Lear* or *Othello* or *Hamlet* expose the springs of violence. And there is a view of social justice in *The Tempest* or *As You Like It*. And of course Shakespeare is merely one example, helpful because he straddles the interests of mankind.

It would almost appear that the traditional curriculum covers the fundamental interests of the adolescent adequately; and indeed it does. This is its prime educational justification. Its relevance makes it of serious importance.

Unfortunately, however, the situation is not as satisfactory as this would imply. In the non-academic school, the curriculum has too often been simplified in such a way that its content has tended to become trivial. In the academic school the critical and disciplined techniques of study have often been used to push the content to arm's length – or beyond. Ask many a good sixth form what they make of Hamlet's relations with Ophelia, and they will respond with second-hand Bradley. You must push them before they relate it to their own feelings about the commitment of a boy to a girl, the pull of duty, the paradoxical ruthlessness which can invade a close personal relationship. Generally, they will be excited to see the relevance, but surprised too. Dorothy L. Sayers shrewdly observed the effects of a certain type of criticism when she wrote:

> She flicked the pages over hurriedly. 'When I am from him, I am dead till I be with him. United souls are not satisfied with embraces, but desire to be truly each other; which being impossible, these desires are infinite, and must proceed without possibility of satisfaction.' That was a most uncomfortable passage, whichever way you looked at it. She turned back to the first page and began to read steadily, *with critical attention to grammar and style, so as to occupy the upper current of her mind without prying too closely into what might be going on beneath the surface* [italics mine].[2]

Of course, the academic tradition in the teaching of the humanities is not an absurd one. At times this kind of self-protection is necessary, though sensibility more often needs quickening than protecting. One may argue too that the relevance of literature will be made later if people have been trained to read critically for pleasure, though the condition here is not easy to meet, and experience of students with honours degrees in English literature suggests that the argument is a somewhat precarious one.

There is, however, a more substantial grain of sense in the extreme academic procedure. A legitimate principle has been pushed too far; and this principle is one of vital importance in the consideration of an education in the humanities. A major function of the curriculum content is to protect the pupil from the teacher.

It protects him in two ways. In the first place, when he explores sex or violence or war in literature or art or history, he brings his experience to bear on the material, but he does not expose himself personally. Rather, he projects himself into the situations of others. There is all the difference in the world between discussing with·strangers one's relationship with one's wife and discussing Macbeth's relationship with his wife. Discussion of the humanities allows one to handle personal experience through the experience of others, and thus to protect oneself from intrusion.

The second protective role of the humanities is to defend the pupil against the bias of the teacher. If the teacher were to teach, as it were, himself, he would run the risk of imprisoning the pupil in his ideas. But in teaching the humanities he exposes the pupil to a dialectic of ideas. Properly handled, the curriculum helps the conscientious teacher to avoid indoctrinating the pupil with his own personal prejudice.

Such an attitude as I have advocated to the teaching of the humanities may be found in the better sixth forms and in the more lively university departments. Here we find teachers who can produce an atmosphere which leads to student discussion of fundamental issues over midnight coffee. But the principle is valid for the average as well as for the brilliant pupil. The intellectual sharpness may not be there, but scratch the surface and the earnest moral inquiry most certainly is. Nor is sincerity alloyed by the temptation to cleverness which sometimes threatens the academically gifted. Engagement and sincerity emerge in response to a curriculum centred on the vital controversial issues which confront the individual as he tries to manage his experience in our society.

In order that the humanities should pull their weight in the education of the average secondary-school pupil, it is necessary for their relevance to life to be made more explicit. I believe that the best approach to this problem is to organize one's curriculum on a topic basis, and to study not bodies of factual knowledge but the quality of human experience. One should read thematically, rather than in terms of subject discipline, the object being to awaken readers rather than to train critics or scholars. Discussion should be centred on a theme and reading experiences should be assessed by their contribution to the discussion. The important objective is to give an experience of the humanities which produces and feeds a universe of discourse, a face-to-face culture, in the classroom. This culture should then improve and enrich both discussion and individual creativity. The real test of such teaching is whether the pupils discuss and create more sensitively and more maturely when they have passed through it.

In a classroom where teaching is based upon these principles the curriculum may be organized under such categories as 'war' or 'relations between the sexes' or 'cruelty' rather than under such categories as 'the sonnet' or 'the romantic movement' or 'narrative poetry'. The only adequate way to illustrate such an approach to curriculum is by examples.

In studying war an important point of departure seems to be an understanding of the attraction which war has held for men. Paintings of heroic war pictures, recordings of martial music or music dedicated to *la gloire*, and films, particularly those from the last war, can readily be used to supplement reading here. Shakespeare, Victor Hugo, Dumas, Campbell or Scott can capture the sense of glory and adventure which has grown round war. Chaucer's knight and squire show the tradition of soldierly manliness and hint at the experience of travel implicit in warfare. Films and newspapers and novels can also illustrate the way in which this emotion is exploited when a country goes to war. Many of the war books dealing with the Second World War, which are so popular today, have been written by people who discovered themselves in a war, who, whether they condemned war or not, found fulfilment in their personal experience of it. This suggests a bias in many of our sources of information. On all grounds, therefore, we must face squarely and honestly the fact that war can have this attraction. Only thus can we subject the experience to criticism.

But there is also an underlying tragedy in war. A picture of the retreat from Moscow, the 'Battle of Malden', 'Sohrab and Rustum', and the 'Flours o' the Forest' can express it for us, as can much modern war poetry. This tragedy is, in its way, noble, the other side of the glory, the comradeship and the excitement.

The pattern of glory and tragedy in war is, however, based on the idea of individual, or at least personal, combat between men of equal prowess and valour, a combat in which skill and courage must be the determinants of victory. Even then it may be folly. But one must go beyond this picture of combat to ask about the misery of war, the suffering in which man's humanity is so violated that it can no longer be regarded as noble tragedy.

Here one can document the plague and famine of the Thirty Years' War, and the agony of open cities. In this context, quite average pupils can begin to tell you why Picasso's 'Guernica' demanded a technique different from that of the traditional military artist. Wilfred Owen and Siegfried Sassoon lead us by way of Henry Moore to John Hersey's documentation of *Hiroshima*. It is easy to illustrate why in the experience of most men war has become intolerable, so that we no longer have war parties and anti-war parties, but rather a disagreement as to how war may best be prevented.

If we wish to go further, we may explore the genesis of

dehumanized brutality in war. Macaulay's 'Black Hole of Calcutta' and Belsen will serve as examples.

Finally, we may consider substitutes for war, such as mountaineering, sailing small boats across wide oceans, sport in all its forms. Through such means men can follow glory, adventure and comradeship, can even court tragedy, without producing misery for mankind.

This is a mere sketch, round which much improvisation might be done. My main purpose is to suggest that there is no shortage of material, and that, handled in the right way, it bristles with lively speculation. Of course, discretion must be exercised in its use, but we cannot let our pupils into the adult world without demanding some discretion from our teachers. Retreat from life is a poor sort of discretion, certainly not that discretion which is the better part of valour.

The theme of relations between the sexes is perhaps the most sensitive of all. It may well be avoided. A teacher who has handled some living problems candidly and honestly will have gained enough respect from his pupils to tell them openly that, because of the embarrassments which society has set between them, he is not able to see his way through to discussing sex. It is my experience that a class will respect so honest an approach.

For the teacher who does feel able to approach this subject with his class – and one hopes that such teachers will become more numerous – the principal point to grasp is that one is not concerned with biology but with human relations. One can well start from a study of broad character portrayals of unsatisfactory marriages, and ask what human foundations underlie satisfactory relationships. The main theme is the history of humanity's attempts to make possible more human and more rewarding relationships between man and woman. Christianity and the chivalric tradition come into our story, as do Jane Austen, with her pictures of women trapped in a social system where all depended upon matrimony and matrimony upon slender acquaintance and romantic illusion, and Cobbett, with his sober advice to young men and young women. There is a wide range of material in the arts which can help to bring adolescent experience into perspective.

I hope that I have said enough to convince the practical teacher that the approach to the humanities which I have been advocating offers at least some chance of success with bored, or even difficult, adolescent classes. Yet any conviction I can convey in this argument must depend largely on the practicality with which I am able to argue it; for I am seeking a pattern which is workable in the ordinary conditions of the state school system when followed by teachers of professional competence but not necessarily of professional brilliance. The only proof of the argument is in the trying of it.

One could offer as evidence work produced under teachers who, led by their own intuition and sensitivity, have broken through to honest controversy and imaginative creativity in their classrooms. Such evidence might illustrate the standard of quality implied, but it would not underwrite the approach to the curriculum for which I have argued. The direct evidence I can offer is personal and slender, largely because my own professional situation does not easily lead to opportunities for the routine teaching which provides the true test. However, with this reservation, my own experience may be worth reproducing.

In an effort to submit my thesis to some practical test, I was able to make the opportunity to teach in a school nine double periods over the space of nine weeks. The class chosen was a Scottish junior secondary class in a comprehensive school. It was regarded as a difficult one, though not impossibly so, and its attainments were humble, though not abysmal. The boys were 'Newsom pupils'. Discipline was not straightforward. Half the class were studying technical subjects, while the other half were denied this opportunity because of staff shortage and limitations of equipment – and there was some resentment of this. The class also contained two boys who had been expelled from school and readmitted, always a disturbing situation. Finally, the boys were in the final term of their school career, restless and eager to leave.

It is difficult to comment upon the teacher, since I taught them myself, but I think that it is fair to say that, though competent as a schoolmaster, I am more effective with students than with pupils. Perhaps my biggest disadvantage was that the natural dialectal background of the pupils was Glaswegian, whereas my own linguistic origins are English. Experienced secondary-modern and junior-secondary-school teachers will recognize that this divergence of language is a considerable disadvantage, particularly in a short spell of teaching.

I have given these details because it is important to establish that the experiment was not conducted under artificially favourable conditions. The class was selected only in the sense that the headmaster was asked for a difficult third year, the time was the unfavourable summer term of the last year of school, and the teacher was certainly in no position to offer himself as a model and was not tailor-made for the situation.

At our first meeting I asked the boys what subjects they regarded as interesting and important enough to be worth our talking about. 'Women,' came as a snigger from the back row. The suggestion was immediately accepted and written on the board to head the list. In general the subjects were those I mentioned earlier in this chapter, though war was proposed initially as 'The Bomb', and leisure was also suggested. Often a subject had to be extracted in discussion from a groping statement, and the question: 'What's he after?'

In order to test whether one might avoid sex without losing face, a point which seemed important, I explained to the class that their sniggers and disturbance at the introduction of the subject probably meant that we should find it a difficult one to discuss as strangers and might do well to wait until we had got to know one another and gained practice in talking together. They readily agreed to defer it to what turned out to be an all-too-short discussion at our last meeting.

War was selected. Some of the main points were made at the first meeting. At the second meeting several of the boys brought books from home. These included American war comics, novels, pictorial histories of the two wars such as are sold by door-to-door canvassers, and a tattered copy of a war-time Ministry of Information publication about the blitz. We talked about the possibilities and limitations of these materials, and I raised the question of experience: 'What did it feel like?'

Time was short. Rupert Brooke's 'Soldier' had to be made to serve as a bridge. Brooke's attitudes were shaped by a hundred years of peace and the traditions of glory and duty and honour which could not be explored in detail. Briefly we looked at this background. From there we moved on to Sassoon and the disillusionment of the trenches. A passage from an almost forgotten memoir, *A Subaltern on the Somme* by Mark Seven, was extremely effective. Four double periods had now passed. Discipline, though not always automatic, was by no means difficult. Real discussion was beginning to take place and the class was being welded into a group by the common interest in the subject. It seemed time to ask for some writing.

The class was asked to attempt to interpret the experience of going up to the trenches for the first time. They wrote in the second half of a double period, having discussed the topic in the first half. The following pieces illustrate the result.

Composition G

My first impression of the front line as we topped the rise was of a huge muddy plain which reminded me of a huge sea which had the water drained away. As we came closer we noticed the shell holes and the dead bodies lying about which brought home the thought that I could end up lying dead in the mud and everyone just walking over you not really noticing me except when they had to lie duck-boards over me which finaly tramped me into a worthless heap in the muck.

As we eventually squelched through the mud in the Communication trench we met coming out of the trench more men who looked gaunt and unshaven and exhausted but they were all glad to be alive. When we eventually arrived in the trenches which were filled with mud the only thought that came to my head was why the hell die for a few yards of worthless muck untill I realised that you were fighting for your mates and relations that had been killed.

As I settled down in the mud with my groundsheet around me I had at least the comforting thought I was not dead yet although the last shell killed one of my mates. But who knows the man who would kill me might be sleeping a few yards ahead.

Composition H

As I neared the top of the rise I felt sick to the bottom of my stomach because I had a good idea on what I was going to see.

When I reached to top I trembled with fear, then, looking on to the battlefield I witnessed a most bloody scene of destruction. I was paralysed with fear as I watched those poor devils lying there some dead others dying. Then I managed to trudge on to the trenches to greet some of the survivors of whom some were overcome with shrapnel shock.

I was shocked as I looked at the dead and the dying I new war was bad but this massacre was uncalled for. I cried as I thought of the wives children and sweethearts that would be left behind.

All this was stuck in my mind I have a wife and children should I fight on? I felt like throwing my gear away and run, run away from all this killing but my country needed me so as I trudged on my thoughts were on the living, not the dead.

Composition I

When we reached the top of the hill I stopped and stared down onto the battlefield where I would probably spend the last few weeks of my life unless I was damned lucky. It was like a part of hell torn to pieces by continuous battering of shells and men had died in the thousands for this grubby little piece of land. As we crossed the duckboards several soldiers passed by with their clothes caked in mud, their faces miserable and unshaven with the weeks of torture they had been through. We made our way along the trenches as quickly as the mud would let us towards our destination which was the 'front line' the very thought of it made me quiver all over. Suddenly there was a terrifying explosion immediately followed by screaming men in agony. We all stared at each other not knowing what to do when the word was passed along that two men had been killed and another three severely injured. One of the dead men was one of my mates 'Jack Danton'. So Jacks copt it already I said to myself. I wonder how long it will be before I am in the same spot. At that moment I was pushed from behind by a big sergeant who said, 'Hurry up there we cant bloody hang around here all night waiting to get blown to kingdom come.' Shaking and clutching my rifle I sludged on until I reached my quarters for the night. It was 2 feet deep in mud and smelt like a sewage pipe, as I got my blanket out a voice spoke to me out of the darkness. 'Got any fags mate,' it said, 'Sorry chum I dont smoke. There was no reply so I wrapped my blanket round me and cowered into one of the corners. I never felt so alone in all my life, this was one night I wouldnt get any sleep.

It would be quite wrong to make any extravagant claims for this kind of writing, and wrong, too, to expect finished results from a teaching contact of some six hours. Any approach which yielded its results as rapidly as that would be suspect, and what seems to me to show in these compositions is a starting-point. There is an attempt to write more and to write more intensively than is the habit of such boys. The work does not show discipline, but it begins to show signs, I think, of something to be disciplined. Taken with an improvement in attitude, interest and behaviour, it seemed to me to indicate a way ahead. I felt that in a year of continuous and developing teaching something worthwhile might be achieved. The class had begun to develop a culture relevant to issues which moved them, but their personal responses were only just beginning to emerge. Conformity had only just begun to pass over into individual thinking.

In the little time remaining to me I wanted to try to develop improvised drama, and through it to look briefly at the Second World War. An attempt to improvise on the basis of J. B. Priestley's *Desert Highway* was not initially promising. In discussion we decided that the material was too far from the familiar, and that a vehicle for dialect must be found. The form eventually adopted was that of two Glasgow women gossiping as they cleaned their tenement windows. This produced a good deal of vigorous and lively material, which was slanted towards our problem of war by asking the boys to gossip against a background of rationing and air-raids and telegrams announcing casualties. The result was a kind of documentary, broad dialect gossip through which the experience in war of the ordinary working-class housewife was plumbed. In general this approach too seemed reasonably promising.

I cannot base much upon such a fragmentary teaching contact. Indeed, those without experience of adolescents in the non-academic secondary school will probably see little of promise in it. My own feeling was that despite the difficulty of time there was enough to encourage rather than discourage such an approach. There was an honesty peeping through the writing, signs of a willingness to improve it, a growing interest in the work of the class and an improvement in the ability to discuss. Further, the apparent emotional content of the compositions was surprisingly sensitive for so tough a class, though the experience did not seem to disturb them.

The problem of providing a lively experience of education in the secondary-modern school is an exceedingly difficult one, and anyone who claimed to have solved it would be bold indeed. I should go no further than to say that the adoption of a curriculum centred on fundamental adult interests and the resolution to work through experience rather than fact, and to face that experience honestly, seemed to produce a classroom situation which experienced teachers might find it possible to develop profitably. Many of the approaches more often employed lead to an orderly sterility which offers fewer promising educational opportunities.

References

1. Lawrence Stenhouse, *Culture and Education* (London: Nelson, 1967).
2. Dorothy L. Sayers, *Gaudy Night* (London: New English Library, 1963), p. 288 (paperback edition).

Part Two:

The Humanities Curriculum Project

Introduction: Trying it out

The Humanities Curriculum Project bibliography[1] tells me that I have published sixteen papers on the Project, and I have half as many unpublished papers. Selection, therefore, is not easy; nor is it easy to avoid repetition for, although many of the papers are nuanced towards their audiences, most of them rehearse the central points of Project theory.

In order to open the section with an overview of the Project, I have begun with a late paper, written at just about the time the Project ended in 1972, and published in a review of *Educational Research in Britain*.[2] This gives an account of the design and structure of the Project with something of the tidiness of hindsight, and provides a context for the other papers. I have cut from this first paper the argument for neutrality, since that is available from other papers to follow.

The remainder of the papers are printed in date order.

The first of these is dated 13th February, 1968. The Project had a consultative committee, chaired successively by Sir Geoffrey Crowther, Mr Cyril English and Dame Muriel Stewart. This paper is headed: Consultative Committee Working Paper No. 2. At this point I am not sure what the theme of Working Paper No. 1 was, but this second working paper was obviously concerned to establish an agreed basis for the Project as we then saw it.

There were a number of thickets to hack through. First, we wanted to take emphasis off Schools Council Working Paper No. 11,[3] which we did not like because of its pessimistic estimate of the intellectual abilities of our clientele. Fortunately, we were able to do this by transferring our allegiance to the Council's Working Paper No. 2,[4] with whose aspirations we were in sympathy; and this emphasis seemed to accord with the views of the Council so far as we could interpret them.

Second, we had a problem which I had brought upon us. The remit of the Project had been written and agreed between Joslyn Owen, Joint Secretary of the Schools Council, and myself in some haste on a taxi journey from the Council's Belgrave Square offices to Euston Station. Coming from Scotland, I had not realized, since I was not familiar with the English trend towards integrated studies, that the remit might suggest that Humanities would accept a responsibility to teach the subjects whose boundaries it crossed. The paper is therefore concerned to define 'humanities' in our terms, and to juxtapose that definition with the remit in order to establish that interpretation of it.

Another problem which beset us was that we were readily perceived as 'child-centred', 'progressive' and 'informal', since the climate of the time suggested that that was what innovations were likely to be. This paper is staking out a position that is knowledge-centred and looking towards a rather formal style of teaching, such as might form the basis of a contractual understanding between teacher and students. Only formality can contain teacher authoritarianism. If we conceive of authoritarianism as arbitrary use of authority, then informal relations readily favour it. In informality the power of the superior is unbounded.

It is also worth mentioning in connection with this paper that the Humanities Project was breaking new ground both in quoting a large range of sources and in producing non-book print materials in substantial collections. The nearest precedent was the Jackdaw series.[5] Later enterprises such as *Connexions*[6] were reactions to the Project, as were the various resource kits in humanities subjects which later appeared. It is easy after the event to miss the fact that the Project had a substantial influence on educational publishing; and indeed that the publishers, Heinemann Educational Books, were seen at the time as taking a very great risk.

The third paper in this section is the script I read to the teachers from our experimental schools on the first evening of each of the regional residential conferences we held in July 1968 in order to introduce them to the experiment. I seldom read a paper from a script, preferring to improvise, but in this case the terms of the contract between the teachers and the project team (which was, I suppose, the beginning of 'Teacher as researcher'[7]) seemed so important that I must do so. In the event, it did not mean as much as I had hoped. One has to learn that the first paper at a conference of this sort, when people are still looking around to find out who is there and wondering what the conference will be like is no place to forge a contract, even if you do leave the paper in the participants' possession. Still, it seems worth recording here what we were attempting; and it is true that the relationship towards which we looked was achieved with about a fifth of the teachers involved.

So much for the setting up of the experiment.

The next two papers have learned from that experiment as we observed it in schools.

The first is an excerpt from a paper to the Claremont Reading Conference in California in 1969. It is based largely on the tape recordings we received from our teachers in the experimental schools, but it predates the measurement results which showed that, when the teachers had been given training courses, the Project could be associated with rather dramatic improvements in reading scores.

The second paper was given to educationists and educational psychologists at a Conference on Motivation in Ohio State University in June, 1970. Professors Jack Frymier and Paul Klohr of Ohio State had made long-term visits to the Project in London, and on their return to the United States they organized a Project training workshop in Columbus, Ohio, which was funded by the Ford Foundation. On Jack Frymier's initiative, I was invited to address the conference on motivation which was meeting in Columbus at the same time. I chose the paper because it was a representation of the Project at the end of its experimental period to an audience which, like the readers of this collection, could not be expected to be familiar with it.

Although the Humanities Project is not so near the centre of attention as it was, interest in it has been sustained. Some of this interest is practical. For example, the team of Geography for the Young School Leaver commended the Humanities pedagogy for use where the content of the curriculum was controversial. It was also employed in my subsequent project on problems and effects of teaching about race relations[8] while Jean Rudduck and a group of HCP teachers have produced a book on *Learning to Teach through Discussion*.[9] We also keep coming across pockets of teachers working in the HCP style and often meeting as groups. The materials have been used in North Germany to teach English in the Gymnasium and the method in Austria in trades union education.

However, perhaps even more persistent than the practical interest is the interest of academics and their students in Project theory, and particularly in the idea of the neutrality of the teacher. I have had regular skirmishes defending that boundary – and the renunciation of objectives – ever since the Project ended.

Generally, I get annoyed by critics who make empirical assumptions without looking at the Project in practice or by those who read a couple of papers on the Project and assume without casting their net more widely that we could be philosophically or sociologically naïve after five years' work in a strong team with a budget that allowed us consultancies. In such circumstances I am afraid I have been a bit peppery at times.

However, the final paper in this section, dating as it does from 1977, does seem to offer a late defence of neutrality not, I hope, too distorted by the clash of academic battle. Moreover, the references give a good entrance to the debate on neutrality. Most importantly, however, the paper does make the claim that the Humanities Project teaching style in which materials are discussed as evidence under the chairmanship of a teacher working to the criterion of neutrality, constitutes an alternative pedagogy with powerful effects. This is a claim I would stand by.

References

1. CARE, *Bibliography of the Humanities Curriculum Project* (Norwich: Centre for Applied Research in Education, University of East Anglia, 1978).
2. H. J. Butcher and H. B. Pont, *Educational Research in Britain No. 3* (London: Hodder & Stoughton Educational, 1973).
3. Schools Council, *Society and the Young School Leaver* (Working Paper No. 11) (London: Her Majesty's Stationery Office, 1967).
4. Schools Council, *Raising the School Leaving Age* (Working Paper No. 2) (London: Her Majesty's Stationery Office, 1965).
5. A series of envelope files containing reproductions of contemporary documents etc., published by Jackdaw Publications.
6. *Connexions* (Series), published by Penguin.
7. See Lawrence Stenhouse: *Introduction to Curriculum Research and Development* (Heinemann Educational Books, 1975) Chapter 10.
8. Lawrence Stenhouse *et al. Teaching about Race Relations: Problems and Effects* (London: Routledge and Kegan Paul, 1982).
9. Jean Rudduck (Editor), *Learning to Teach through Discussion* (Norwich: Centre for Applied Research in Education, University of East Anglia, 1979).

The Humanities Curriculum Project

Appearing in Educational Research in Britain (*1973*)[1]

Introduction

The Humanities Curriculum Project was set up in June 1967 under the joint sponsorship of the Schools Council and the Nuffield Foundation for a three year term. It was located in Philippa Fawcett College of Education in south London and administration was handled by the ILEA.

From June until September 1967, I worked alone. Project staff were appointed from September and were initially four in number. A schools officer was appointed from Easter 1968. A supplementary budget for film research was granted by the Schools Council to cover the period to August 1970, and a film research officer was appointed from July 1968. During 1968 two other members were added to the project team and for a short time a research librarian was also employed. For the greater part of the two years 1968–70 the main project had a staff of eight and for a time of nine.

This represented a substantial investment on the part of the sponsors and it was clearly important to evaluate the work done. An evaluation unit was set up in 1968 under the direction of Mr Barry MacDonald and was given an additional budget. Although this unit was ultimately my responsibility as director (for purposes of administration), it seemed important also to ensure its academic independence. The evaluation unit built up to a staff of four.

In 1970 the original three year offer of accommodation in Philippa Fawcett ran out. The project and evaluation project were, however, extended for a further two years. The project team now shrank to four. Its task was to complete materials but also more importantly to organize dissemination of the project and training support. The evaluation unit continued at full strength. For the sessions 1970 to 1972 the project was moved to the University of East Anglia.

It will be clear from the above that we are concerned here with a research and development project executed by a fairly large team. My own responsibilities were general administration, overall control of experimental design, relations with outside bodies ('boundary defence') and an editorial responsibility for one theme.

I have written about the administration of the project for two reasons. Both education and educational research are arts of the possible: work must be related to the resources available. Also it is important to make it clear that in writing this article I am writing about other people's work as well as my own – but from the point of view of one accepting overall responsibility for the design of the research.

Basic Premises

The basic premises of the project are at two levels: it embodies a view of curriculum research, and it is founded on substantive premises in a particular curricular field.

The responsibilities of curriculum research are particularly heavy both because it is based upon substantial investment and because it is action research significant for the well-being of pupils. It is research which should be subject to social policy. This involves us in a paradox from the outset. Those who take part in research need to be driven by curiosity about the possible development of ideas in which they believe. Yet these ideas must not be personal and idiosyncratic, but disciplined by a relation to social policy. The personal interest must be legitimized by reference to social needs. Curriculum research exists to make aspirations into practical possibilities and the aspirations should be those of a substantial number of teachers and educationists. Since education is an area of debate, however, these aspirations will inevitably be those of one section or party in this debate. In a decentralized system such as ours, then, the function of curriculum research is to make alternatives practicable.

Any one research, however, can probably only explore one alternative. Ideally, perhaps, curriculum projects should be paired, each of the pair exploring the consequences of contradictory premises advocated in educational debate. This is seldom possible. Failing this, the best safeguard is to attempt to assimilate curriculum research to the generally accepted canons of social science research. This means an attempt to make work in curriculum speculative rather than evangelical and cumulative rather than *ad hoc*. This is a position difficult to hold for two reasons. First, curriculum is so much a branch of policy that it is difficult consistently to avoid moving from the speculative to the evangelical, especially in the face of a public which expects advocacy and sees the renunciation of the evangelical as a flight from responsibility. Second, the field is so underdeveloped that it is difficult to hold to social science canons: because there is no integrated and developed theory of curriculum innovation, hypotheses have to be derived from case study in an effort to build theory rather than being deduced from theory and used to test it. Moreover, action research can never be undividedly oriented towards theory. Such difficulties are not overcome by failing to face them.

The following procedure was adopted:

1. Select a cogent general educational policy statement in the curricular field in question.
2. By relating its logical implications to the realities of the classroom, produce the outline of a teaching strategy consistent with the aim and feasible in practice.
3. Attempt to develop the strategy, testing its logical consistency in discussion and its feasibility in experimental schools.
4. Make case studies of experimental schools to generate hypotheses regarding the problems and effects to be expected in implementing the curriculum in a wider range of schools.
5. Use this case study experience to design dissemination procedures which will attempt to meet the anticipated problems.
6. Monitor the effects in dissemination both by case study and by measurement.

1, 2, 3 and 5 were the concern of the project; 4 and 6 of the evaluation unit.

It goes without saying that a programme of this kind is too ambitious to be fulfilled in a single project. Many approximations will be needed before procedures are refined. The first step, therefore, was to adopt a policy position.

The point of departure of the project was a passage in Schools Council Working Paper No. 2 (1965)[2] referring to work in the Humanities:

The problem is to give every man some access to a complex cultural inheritance, some hold on his personal life and on his relationships with the various communities to which he belongs, some extension of his understanding of, and sensitivity towards, other human beings. The aim is to forward understanding, discrimination and judgement in the human field – it will involve reliable factual knowledge, where this is appropriate, direct experience, imaginative experience, some appreciation of the dilemmas of the human condition, of the rough hewn nature of many of our institutions, and some rational thought about them. (*para. 60*)

It seemed that there would be few teachers who would not assent to this aspiration as a desirable one for the new school leaver, few who would be able to come near to seeing their way to implementing it in practice and therefore few who would not dismiss it as unrealistic. Here then was an aspiration which seemed impracticable. And it is the task of curriculum research to give such aspirations a practicable expression. Two further passages in the working paper hinted at the problems.

All of this may seem to some teachers like a programme for people who have both the mental ability and maturity beyond the reach of most who will leave at the age of sixteen. The Council, however, thinks it is important *not* to assume that this is so, but rather to probe by experiment in the classroom how far ordinary pupils can in fact be taken. The fact is that nothing can prevent the formation of ideas and attitudes about human nature and conduct. (*para. 61*)

and

But adult procedures in the classrooms . . . will not be successful if a different kind of relationship between teacher and pupil obtains in the corridor or in extracurricular activity. If the teacher emphasises, in the classroom, his common humanity with the pupils, and his common uncertainty in the face of many problems, the pupils will not take kindly to being demoted to the status of children in other relationships within the same institution. Indeed, they may write off the classroom relationship as a 'soft-sell'. (*para. 97*)

These statements seemed of great significance. First, they challenged the divisive Newsom assumption that the school-leaver was to be seen as a special case by emphasizing the common humanity of teacher and pupil and challenging us to treat the leaver as simply a young adult. (In doing so it challenged my own thinking since I had written a book (Stenhouse, 1967)[3] which only imperfectly freed itself from divisive assumptions of this sort.) Second, it suggested that the whole pattern of relationships and of authority in schools would have to be rethought to achieve such a programme. If this were so, a curriculum which faced this demand would have a significance far beyond its own place on the timetable. It would provide a laboratory experience in which teachers could work out a new view of their task and their relationships with pupils. In order to translate this prospect into any kind of practical reality it was necessary to analyse the statements quoted in order to redefine them in operational terms.

An extremely difficult problem, probably inadequately solved, was to produce a statement of aim. The aims of the project must first of all be separated from those of the curriculum. The aim of the project was to make it possible for teachers to develop their work in the direction of the aspirations contained in these basic statements. This meant a continuous development of insight on the part of the team about teacher problems and needs. The function of a teaching aim was briefly to describe the direction of classroom work in order to influence the 'set' of the teacher in the classroom. Such an aim is a summary task definition.

In fact the formulation of a statement of teaching aim was an attempt to produce a simplified statement which summarized the insights of the team into the logic of the teaching. The formulation changed and developed. And the central team itself did not have a blanket consensus.

The aim finally adopted for the Project handbook (1970)[4] was as follows: 'to develop an understanding of social situations and human acts and of the controversial value issues which they raise'. It was intended that this should imply an application of the perspectives of social science, history, the arts and religious thinking to the understanding of human issues. Such understanding should take account of the need to attempt objectivity on the one hand and to tap imaginative sympathy on the other. And it was believed that the crucial problem in handling human issues was controversiality.

The Project also stated five major premises:

1. that controversial issues should be handled in the classroom with adolescents;
2. that the teacher should accept the need to submit his teaching in controversial areas to the criterion of neutrality at this stage of education, i.e. that he should regard it as part of his responsibility not to promote his own view;

3. that the mode of enquiry in controversial areas should have discussion, rather than instruction, as its core;
4. that the discussion should protect divergence of view among participants, rather than attempt to achieve consensus;
5. that the teacher as chairman of the discussion should have responsibility for quality and standards in learning.

In following this pattern of defining aim and premises, we were attempting to express the normative aspect inseparable from curriculum design in terms which exposed it as a controlled variable in the experiment. It was hoped that those who did not accept the premises would still be able to profit from the Project's work.

For example, if – as happens – a discussion group becomes concerned with action rather than understanding, then the fourth premise does not hold. Consensus and consequently compromise is required if a group is to agree action. This is true even in simulation: a group planning a new orphanage as part of its study of the family becomes an action group.

The overall task of the Project was to discover a teaching strategy which would implement these premises in the classroom, to report this strategy, and to support teachers who wished to develop it with training and if necessary with materials.

The Experimental Framework

In order to follow the experimental design intended it was necessary to enlist teachers as experimental colleagues. We wished to cast the schools with which we worked in the role of teachers, the central team in the role of learners.

Accordingly we recruited thirty-two experimental schools which were to work with the central team during the sessions 1968–9 and 1969–70. We saw these not as trial schools, but as development schools. Thus, though we wanted a variety of school settings, we were not concerned with sampling in a statistical sense. At this stage our concern was with producing a prototype rather than with generalizing. Some generalization would of course be possible, but there was no real possibility of sound generalization from the thirty-two schools which developed the strategy in close contact with the central team to the experience of the second generation of schools which might adopt the work.

Our plan therefore was as follows. In summer 1968 we would

hold induction conferences for all our experimental schools. By that time we needed to have an outline teaching strategy. We would present to the schools the premises on which we were working, assuming that since they had expressed an interest in joining the Project, they would provisionally accept them. Then we would present our outline of the problems which would be encountered. Finally, by ourselves chairing discussions we would indicate how far we had got in understanding the role demanded of the teacher if he were to develop this kind of work. For us the premises were a constant controlled variable: our diagnoses of problems and suggestions of method were hypotheses to be tested in schools. They can be treated here only in summary.

We visualized an enquiry into human issues conducted in schools in order to increase the understanding of students in accordance with the aim. Such an enquiry would, we assumed, involve research on the part of pupils, written work, visits, improvised drama, art work and so forth. These we took to be the stock in trade of teachers. The novelty came from the fact that the enquiry dealt with controversial issues and the students were young adults in their last two years of school who needed to be hardened off into independence before leaving.

Given the authority position of the teacher, this seemed to imply that the central classroom activity should be discussion rather than instruction. Our premises cast the teacher as chairman of a discussion in a neutral role. This role needed to be worked out in terms of classroom methods.

The fact that the medium of learning was discussion rather than instruction together with the neutral role of the chairman threw into relief the problem of giving a discussion group access to information. It seemed that the best way to do this was to provide them with documentary evidence. Given the pressure on teachers, it seemed advisable for the central team to help them by supplying materials.

The experimental schools were asked to test and develop hypotheses about teaching method and to test and if possible contribute to the materials offered by the central team. Curriculum was seen as a content – method bundle.

Some Difficulties Encountered

Broadly, the strategy adopted did pay dividends, but it was by no means uniformly successful. We got enough data to pursue our work, but much less than we might have hoped. This was largely due to a series of communication problems which affected both our relations with experimental schools and to an even greater extent the way the work was seen outside the experiment. These problems are worth noting.

1. The attempt to conduct curriculum development on social science lines was not expected and therefore not perceived. This took us by surprise and we therefore failed to stress it sufficiently. In retrospect, the situation is clear. Most British curriculum development had been based upon subject specialists with a mission to reform teaching in their fields. Because humanities was not a 'subject' the situation was rather different. Two leading members of the team, myself and the director of evaluation, were 'educationists'. I had a primary interest in curriculum, the director of evaluation in the sociology of schools and in measurement. Our qualifications were in education and psychology. It was natural for us to think in terms of research design. We did not fully appreciate how difficult it would be to induct our experimental schools into experimental assumptions. Thus we found ourselves struggling to maintain the position of experimentalists rather than educational prophets.

2. We underestimated the authority of national projects backed by the Schools Council and the ambivalent attitude they may generate. We saw the project as testing hypotheses: many of the teachers with whom we worked saw either themselves or us as on trial. Often instead of using their judgement to inform us, teachers allowed what were intended by us as tentative hypotheses to overrule their judgement. Some experimental feed-back was distorted by this attitude. It might be designed to reassure us, to challenge us or merely to protect the teacher concerned. In the end, this has partly been overcome, but it has been a formidable problem.

3. Expectations existed concerning what we would be attempting and it was difficult to overcome them. We had taken an anti-Newsom line: but we were assimilated to Newsom thinking. We had stressed knowledge and understanding but we were expected to be non-intellectual. 'Humanities' as a term was often taken to mean integrated studies: we had interpreted it as a 'human issues programme' and though this could be used as a core for integrated studies, in

most of our schools a subject structure was maintained. We saw ourselves as providing support for a particular development whose place in the school should be determined by policy decisions at school level and should vary from school to school: it was often assumed that we should have an answer to questions about the total curriculum – or even that we wished humanities to take over the leavers' curriculum.

4. We were concerned with long-term development and particularly with teacher development: we were often perceived as attempting an instant and easy solution to problems.

5. The problem we were tackling and the way it was tackled did not make a direct contribution to problems of discipline and control. In some ways it made these problems more acute. It opened them up instead of containing them, and this ran counter to the hopes of many teachers.

There were a number of other difficulties of this sort. In short, we found ourselves trying to redefine the role in which we were cast by precedents.

Objectives

Our decision not to use objectives in our work was highly controversial.

When the Project was set up (and even now), a particular model for research design in curriculum was dominant. This was an output model, based on objectives.

The procedure suggested was as follows. A general statement of aim should be analysed into objectives – I prefer intended learning outcomes – which should be behavioural in the sense that they specified changes in student behaviour (in the psychological sense of that term) which it was intended that the curriculum should bring about. A curriculum should then be constructed and tested, so far as possible by measuring instruments, for its success in teaching the objectives.

This design was not adopted in the Project.

I have written elsewhere (Stenhouse, 1964,[5] 1968,[6] 1970–1,[7] 1971[8]) of my reservations concerning the objectives model. A detailed discussion would be inappropriate here, but some reservations are worth listing:

1. Objectives tend to be *ad hoc* substitutes for hypotheses. They

    do not lead to cumulative theory. Hypotheses are therefore generally preferable.

2. The use of objectives assumes a capacity to predict the results of curricula which is not justified by empirical work.

3. Consequently, statements of objectives tend to be over-simplified and self-fulfilling.

4. A centrally designed curriculum development tested by reference to objectives formulated by the central team in detail must imply teacher-proofing. Our curriculum assumed divergent interpretation of a general aim by teachers.

5. The use of objectives tends to make curriculum instrumental and to distort the intrinsic value of content and process. It leads to the concept of an exercise.

6. There are epistemological objections to the idea that all knowledge and understanding can be expressed in terms of specifiable student behaviours.

7. It may be appropriate for the students following a course to have objectives of their own which are to a certain extent divergent.

8. In an exploratory development which enters little charted areas, there is a need to approach the problem of effects speculatively, and in particular to aim at generating hypotheses from case studies.

9. A curriculum may have important effects on teachers and on schools as institutions, not simply on student performance.

For these and other reasons we adopted a process rather than an output model. Given an aim couched in terms of knowledge and understanding (and perhaps also advanced and complex skills), it is possible to devise a teaching process and teaching materials which are consistent with that aim. In this case the aim is analysed into learning process or input, rather than into intended learning outcomes or output.

This procedure allows a gradual exploration of the logic and structure of a subject area, both during a curriculum project and by teachers developing a project's work. Instead of intended learning outcomes the input model deals with effects which are hypothesized from case studies of practical situations. It aims to produce a curricular specification which describes a range of possible learning outcomes and relates them to their causes. The style of its formulation is: 'If you follow these procedures with these materials with this type of pupil, in this school setting, the effects will tend to be X.'

The problem with the input or process model is its complexity. Among its strengths are that it is amenable to the hypothetico-deductive method and hence gives greater promise of a cumulative science of curriculum; it avoids the philosophically dubious position that all knowledge can be expressed as learned behaviours; it allows of students' having divergent objectives within the same curriculum; and it attempts to face the complexity of the classroom.

The Experiment in Schools

Between October 1967 and January 1968 the trial collection on war was prepared so that it could be printed by Easter. Over 4 000 documents were assembled, from which a collection of just over 200 was selected. A punched card system was used for access to the archive collection.

The first collection was produced in a 'Jackdaw' format. That is, each pupil had a folder of materials for each sub-topic. It was printed in the project. On the basis of feed-back from schools the later collections were restructured: each teacher pack contained a single copy of every document in the collection. A class pack contained twenty copies of each document. Audio-tapes were made by the project team. Later collections were sent out to a printer. As experience built up, the archive collection tended to become smaller in relation to the pack.

In summer 1968 three five-day residential conferences were run to induct the teams of teachers from the thirty-two experimental schools. The teachers were introduced to the materials, the nature of the experiment was put to them, groups worked in discussion with team members chairing, and there was a general discussion.

During the session 1968–9 the schools worked on collections on war, education and the family. Feed-back on materials was by questionnaire supported by interviews with the schools officer or other team members when they visited schools. Information was sought on coverage of the collection, accessibility of the material to the students (readability and sophistication of ideas), and the extent to which materials provoked or supported discussion. Most schools used only a small proportion of materials (as was intended) so that feed-back on any one piece was not extensive. It was also frequently contradictory, particularly as to readability. Collections were radically re-edited as a result of experience in schools: often only half the trial pack survived. New materials could not be tested in schools because of publication dates.

The most controversial aspect of the packs as they emerged was the high reading level. Both schools and project team remain divided on this issue.

One view in the team is that since the method and attitudes implied by the project are difficult of achievement, it would have been better not to face teachers with so great a reading problem and hence with motivational difficulties. The other view is that the method and attitude are inseparably linked to an assault on reading levels. Certainly, there is evidence that schools taking a purist line on method find reading problems present much less difficulty. In particular they shift from a view that documents must be understood before they are discussed to a view that discussion is a means to understanding. They also value students' capacity to get the gist of a document.

Throughout the sessions 1968 to 1970 the procedure for testing materials was much the same.

In order to develop methodology, we asked teachers to send us tapes of discussion. These were selected by the teachers. Recording conditions were often bad and many tapes were virtually inaudible. Nevertheless, we had enough to work on, and some of the tapes were quite striking in their novelty.

At our second teachers' conferences at Easter, 1969, we presented our work on the tapes as a series of propositions or injunctions to chairmen, and we asked teachers to test these during the second year. We were also able to play tapes to them.

As a result of experience following this, we concluded that we had made two errors. The expression of the methodology as injunctions was wrong. First, generalizations did not hold. Teacher judgement was at all times necessary. Second, since injunctions were statements, they were treated as instructions to teachers rather than hypotheses. Accordingly, when we published our project handbook we distinguished major variables in discussion and suggested that teachers train themselves by examining tapes of their own teaching in the light of these variables. This analysis required to be related to their own aims.

I believe that this procedure is a profitable one. Basically, we have attempted an operational role definition for the teacher by relating moves on the part of a chairman to the aims of teaching (logic) and to responses on the part of the group (social dynamics). I have no doubt that our work here has a very wide application both in its method and in its substantive findings.

One of the most interesting results of our experiment in schools was our discovery of a very large number of variables in success and failure (as judged by teachers themselves). Organization, choice of team, social structure of the school and so forth were clearly crucial. This remains true in dissemination. In some cases, for example, we have whole local authority areas in which virtually all schools report success and satisfaction; others in which virtually all schools report failure and dissatisfaction.

This is particularly important since it suggests on analysis that the actual curriculum involved is a much less significant variable in curriculum innovation than might have been thought (particularly since our findings are confirmed by other work); and this points to the possibility of a theory of curriculum innovation which could be cumulative.

Evaluation of the Project

The evaluation unit of the Humanities Project differs distinctly in role from those of many other projects. In the first place, the evaluation of teaching materials was in this project taken to be part of the task of the development team. Secondly, the project offered the evaluator no behavioural objectives. It was anticipated that the greater part of the evaluator's work would be in case-studying schools and indeed the title under which MacDonald was appointed was Schools Study Officer. It was expected that he would study the work of the Project, provide feed-back to the central team about the progress of the experiment in schools, and design a suitable evaluation programme for implementation in 1970–2 when the Project went into dissemination.

Writing of the situation in which he was placed, our evaluation officer explained his problems. 'In an approach which is not based on objectives there is no ready-made niche for the evaluator. He must await events, see what happens, trace the different ways in which the work unfolds and try to link patterns of effects to patterns of teaching. *Outcome* and *process* alike demand his attention. A particular problem is *which* effects to study. In an evaluation programme, it's no use providing answers to questions that no-one is asking.'[9] Since it was likely that the crucial effects would depend in part upon the actions and communications of the Project team, it was necessary to study their *input*, and since it was likely that the effects would vary from school to school, it was necessary to study *context*.

The initial aim of the evaluator was so to describe the work of the Project that it was made accessible to public and professional judgement.

During the first year he concentrated on trying to establish what was happening in schools and on gathering data and generating hypotheses which might help to explain the widely differing experiences and effects reported. This was tackled by broad survey work which generated institutional profiles of schools and by intensive case studies of a small sample. The case study work went on into the second year of the experiment. In a brief outline of his work, MacDonald illustrates the type of proposition he was exploring with the following examples:

1. Human behaviour in educational settings is susceptible to a wide range of variable influences. This is a commonplace yet in curriculum evaluation it is sometimes assumed that what is intended to happen is what actually happens, and that what happens varies little from setting to setting.

2. The impact of an innovation is not a set of discrete effects, but an organically related pattern of acts and consequences. To understand fully a single act one must locate it functionally within that pattern. It follows from this proposition that innovations have many more unanticipated consequences than is normally assumed in development and evaluation designs.

3. No two schools are so alike in their circumstances that prescriptions of curricular action can adequately supplant the judgement of the people in them. Historical/evolutionary differences alone make the innovation 'gap' a variable which has significance for decision-making.

4. The goals and purposes of the programme developers are not necessarily shared by its users. We have seen the Project used variously as a political resource in an existing power struggle between staff factions, as a way of increasing the effectiveness of a custodial pattern of pupil control, and as a means of garnishing the image of institutions which covet the wrapping, but not the merchandise of innovation. The latter gives rise to the phenomenon of innovation without change.

Looking back on MacDonald's work and on conversations with him, I see a significant pattern. He was presented with a project lacking a specification of objectives. Objectives constitute a selection of hypotheses according to hopes. Lack of objectives thrusts on the evaluator of a complex action research with vast numbers of variables the task of selecting hypotheses. The first position, that of the 'descriptive' evaluator, was soon discarded. Instead, it was decided to collect questions asked by decision-makers – the Schools Council, LEAS, heads, teachers, Project team, etc. – and to try to answer them. But deeper study of schools showed that decision-makers often asked the wrong questions or – perhaps better – failed to ask questions which were *in the view of the evaluator* highly significant. MacDonald struggled with the problem of justifying his own judgements of significance and in a crucial series of dialogues with the Project team and with American scholars began to develop propositions which reached towards generalization and distinguished significant variables. At this point, the exercise ceases to be one of evaluation in the sense of measuring against criteria and becomes an attempt to understand innovation through the teasing out of variables and their relation to generalizations. This is what the Germans call 'accompanying research'. Its purpose is seen by the evaluator at this stage as 'that of feeding the judgement of decision-makers by promoting understanding of the considerations that bear upon curricular action'.

The evaluation unit has recently defined its task as follows:

1. To ascertain the effects of the Project, document the circumstances in which they occur, and present this information in a form which will help educational decision-makers to evaluate the likely consequences of adopting the programme.
2. To describe the present situation and operations of the schools we study so that decision-makers can understand more fully what it is they are trying to change.
3. To describe the work of the Project team in terms which will help the sponsors and planners of such ventures to weigh the value of this form of investment, and to determine more precisely the frame-work of support, guidance and control which are appropriate.
4. To make a contribution to evaluation theory by articulating our problems clearly, recording our experience, and perhaps most importantly, by publicising our errors.
5. To contribute to the understanding of the problems of curriculum innovation generally.

MacDonald comments:

Not everyone would agree that all of these are defensible objectives for an evaluation unit set up to study one project. I would argue firstly that objectives are in part a function of opportunities, and secondly that, at a time when curriculum development is becoming increasingly the concern of a number of new and relatively inexperienced agencies, there is a need for those involved in the field to contribute what they can towards an understanding of the problems of change.

The sessions 1970–1 and 1971–2 are the crucial ones for the evaluation unit. During these sessions they are able to study the continuing work in the thirty-two experimental schools and also the progress of the 600 or so schools which initially bought materials. Their design for this study contains clinical, psychometric and sociological elements; and they are using two overlapping school samples, one large and one small. The small sample will be studied in detail and the insights gained will be used to interpret results from the large sample.

The programme of tasks is as follows:

1. *In the large sample of schools (c. 100)*

   a) Gathering input, contextual and implementation data by questionnaire.
   b) Gathering judgement data from teachers and pupils.
   c) Objective measurement of pupil change. (We have, at the beginning of this year, carried out pre-tests of pupils on twenty-one objective tests which represent the combined judgement of teachers, pupils, the central team and ourselves, of likely dimensions of pupil change. This is a massive operation, but will be justified if it can help us establish pupil effects and lead to the employment next year of a small but accurate test battery.)
   d) Tracing variations in teaching practice through the use of specially devised multiple-choice feed-back instruments which require minimal effort by the teacher and are monitored by pupils.
   e) Documenting the effect on the school by means of semi-structured teacher diaries.

2. *In a small sample of schools (c. 12)*

   a) Case-studies of patterns of decision-making, communication, training and support in local areas.
   b) Case-studies of individual schools within these areas.
   c) Study of the dynamics of discussion by audiotape, videotape and observation.

References

1. H. J. Butcher and H. B. Pont, *Educational Research in Britain No. 3* (London: Hodder & Stoughton Educational, 1973).
2. Schools Council *Raising the School Leaving Age* (Working Paper No. 2.) (London: Her Majesty's Stationery Office, 1965).
3. Lawrence Stenhouse, *Culture and Education* (London: Nelson, 1967).
4. Humanities Curriculum Project *The Humanities Project: an Introduction* (London: Heinemann Educational Books, 1970).
5. Lawrence Stenhouse, 'Aims or standards?' in *Education for Teaching*, 64, (1964), pp. 15–21.
6. Lawrence Stenhouse, 'The Humanities Curriculum Project' in *Journal of Curriculum Studies*, 1.1. 1968, pp. 26–33.
7. Lawrence Stenhouse, 'Some limitations of the use of objectives in curriculum research and planning' *Paedagogica Europaea*, (1970–1), pp. 73–83.
8. Lawrence Stenhouse, 'The Humanities Curriculum Project: the rationale' in *Theory into Practice*, 10.3. 1971, pp. 154–62.
9. Barry MacDonald, 'The Humanities Curriculum Project' in *Evaluation in Curriculum Development: Twelve Case Studies* Schools Council Research Studies. (London: Macmillan, 1973), p. 82.

The Humanities Curriculum Project: Consultative Committee Working Paper No. 2

To yield to every whim of curiosity and
to allow our passion for inquiry to be restrained
by nothing but the limits of our ability, this
shows an eagerness of mind not unbecoming to
scholarship. But it is wisdom that has the
merit of selecting, from among the innumerable
problems which present themselves, those whose
selection is important to mankind.

(Emmanuel Kant, *Dreams of a Ghost Seer*, part, 2, Chapter 3.)

The Background of the Project

The Schools Council Working Paper No. 2, *Raising the School Leaving Age*,[1] suggested that the task facing the schools in the teaching of the humanities is 'the bringing of the best traditional view of what constitutes a liberal education within the grasp of ordinary people'. It recognized that the problem is to give everyone some access to a complex cultural inheritance, on the basis of which he can come to an understanding of human nature and conduct, and develop concepts of value.

Following on from Working Paper No. 2, a feasibility study was mounted, financed by the Nuffield Foundation, and the results of this study were published as Schools Council Working Paper No. 11, *Society and the Young School Leaver*.[2] This Working Paper surveyed work going on in some schools, made a number of valuable comments on the organization of schools and on the attitudes that are demanded of teachers who handle adolescent students, took a step towards the definition of the roles of the various partners who must cooperate if curriculum innovation is to be successful, and made some suggestions about the content of teaching. It suggested that the curriculum might be organized in areas of inquiry, a phrase which seems to us more positive and helpful than 'themes' or 'projects'.

A feasibility study is intended to reconnoitre the field and expose a range of possibilities. A project following upon such a study is bound to make a selection from among those possibilities, and to define its task more closely. Much of the valuable thinking in Working Paper No. 11 has been embraced by the Humanities Curriculum Project, but there are two major respects in which the emphasis has shifted. We have come to feel that a good many of the areas of inquiry described or suggested are unlikely to be effective bases for the kind of liberal education conceived in Working Paper No. 2, either because they lack sufficient weight and importance or because they raise too few questions in the area of values. Furthermore, practical experience of working with materials seems to indicate a need for more structure and more closely articulated principles if the sense of quality and direction is to be maintained both in the selection of materials and in the strategy of their use in the classroom.

The Remit of the Humanities Curriculum Project

The Humanities Curriculum Project has been given the following remit:

> To offer to schools and to teachers such stimulus, support and materials as may be appropriate to the mounting, as an element in

general education, of enquiry-based courses, which cross the subject boundaries between English, History, Geography, Religious Studies and Social Studies. The Project is expected to concentrate on such support as will in particular meet the needs of adolescent pupils of average and below average academic ability.

Although the word *humanities* does not enter into the remit of the Project, it is obviously implied both in the title of the project and in the work which has led up to it. We understand by the humanities the study of both human behaviour and human experience. The study of human behaviour is broadly the concern of the social scientist: history, human geography, psychology and sociology. In some sense, these studies aspire to examine human behaviour objectively, viewing it as caused, or as dictated by, purposes which can be understood from observation rather than from detailed subjective analysis. The study of human experience is reflected in the arts and in the biographical aspect of history. It is concerned with the subjective or existential aspects of human life, and one important criterion by which judgements of the arts are made is fidelity to human experience. In adopting this definition, we have in mind the assertion of the Newsom Report that 'boys and girls should learn to exercise a commonsense judgement quickened by imaginative insight'.[3] The capacity for objectivity and the capacity for sympathy must both be developed.

The remit of the Project mentions specific subject fields which have been traditionally represented in the school curriculum; but it is not intended that the humanities should merely provide a vehicle for the teaching of these subjects. It is, moreover, clear that some other school subjects, such as visual art, music and drama have a part to play in the humanities. The commonest way to express the situation is to suggest that these subjects should be contributory to the course of study, but this probably underestimates the contribution of a study of the humanities to the understanding – as opposed to the accumulation of systematic knowledge – of the subjects.

Moreover, it should not be thought that the adoption of a humanities curriculum based on areas of inquiry makes subject structures irrelevant. The crossing of subject boundaries may be viewed as an attempt at what A. N. Whitehead called 'generalization'.[4] The very existence of boundaries to be crossed suggests that there are territories, each with its own laws. To cross subject boundaries successfully one must grasp, or at least see the need for and be sensitive to, standards of quality in each of the subject fields involved. What is demanded of the teacher is not extensive knowledge of all the subjects touched upon, but the recognition of the need, as his teaching develops, to extend his understanding of the principles of each subject area. The problem is best illustrated by taking as an example a subject not generally taught in schools. A teacher who is mounting an area of enquiry on law and order needs to be aware of the existence of a field of study, jurisprudence and legal theory, which has its own tradition. Given this awareness, his education should allow him to explore such a field judiciously. To suggest that teachers cannot cross the boundaries of their subjects, even when they are working on the basis of inquiry and discussion rather than of instruction, is to condemn each of us to live within the narrow confines of his specialist academic education. Of course, the task is a challenging one, but it is not so very different from that which has traditionally been faced by teachers of English or classics, who, in the course of interpretation work, have always ranged over a very wide subject area.

It is worth emphasizing that we have attempted to define our curricular area without appealing to the needs and interests of the students. The tendency to conceptualize curricula which cross subject boundaries in 'child-centred' terms does not seem for us a helpful one. The idea of child-centredness is suspect in a discussion of the education of young adults. Too often it is used patronizingly. We seldom hear the phrase applied, for example, when exponents of a specialized sixth-form talk about the young adult's development of specialist interests.

Of course, the curriculum must be interesting and seem relevant to students, but the selection of curriculum cannot be justified in these terms. In a humanities curriculum one selects for adolescents those topics which are of enduring human interest because of their importance in the human situation. If we select as an area of inquiry 'relations between the sexes', for example, we are neither pandering to an interest nor prescribing for a sick society. We are asserting that this is a category of relationships in which people *ought* to be interested and that any development of this interest *ought* to be founded in our cultural tradition. The school can make a contribution in such areas precisely because of their importance in our cultural tradition. No concession is being made: the teachers may be expected to share these interests with their students.

The Task of the Humanities Curriculum Project

The kind of teaching which the Project is asked to study and support is not in itself new. Many of the ideas behind it can be seen in project-teaching and in the social studies movement which was at its height just after the war. Moreover, seminar work in higher education uses a discussion base, while the modern style of thesis is an inquiry. The problem is that in the past project or discussion-based teaching in the schools has often led to a deterioration of quality. Teachers whose judgements were secure while they were working within an academic and instructional framework, have suffered from the lack of a supporting tradition when they moved over to a different style of teaching The pattern of academic teaching is so much taken for granted that it is easy to forget the profound theoretical roots which lie beneath it. One of the main tasks of a humanities curriculum project must be to help to found a tradition which will support teachers working in this curriculum by helping them to select materials, by increasing their confidence in appropriate classroom strategies and by making secure their judgements of the quality of students' work. Unless the need for such a thoughtful and discriminating tradition is widely accepted by teachers, a humanities curriculum cannot be mounted with any confidence that future developments will lead to the sharpening, rather than the deterioration, of standards.

The most immediate and practical task facing the Project is to provide, as examples, materials for use in the classroom which express this tradition and embody its standards. Lack of materials of high quality makes it extraordinarily difficult for teachers to embark on this kind of teaching without some kind of support from the centre, and it is the task of the team to give this support. At the same time, the materials which are offered to the schools by a project with a limited life must not be regarded as defining a curriculum, but rather as providing helpful examples of the kind of work which can be done in this field. As examples, what they are likely to offer is, not so much unusual or surprising materials, as materials which, by their selection and structure, offer the teacher not merely a resource, but also a suggestion of strategy and standards of quality. It is to be hoped that teachers will be provoked to debate and experiment, and that, in particular, if they question the structures suggested by the Project, their questioning will lead them to develop patterns of teaching which are more varied and imaginative, but not less rigorous or thoughtful, than those represented in the work of the Project. It would be tragic if materials provided by the Project lay inert in the schools over the years and led to a kind of teaching which hardened into ritual. The materials can be restructured and added to as teachers rethink their own approaches. Development is not merely to be welcomed; it is essential. Without it, deterioration must be a threat.

Finally, it will be necessary to evaluate the impact of the curriculum materials and suggestions upon the classroom situation. This evaluation can help to build up the secure critique which must be a vital element in a humanities tradition.

What a Central Team Should Not or Cannot Do

It is important that the limitations of a central team should be recognized, both by the team and by those who may call upon it for service or advice.

A central team can provide materials, information and suggestions, but it should not intrude upon policy decisions. Even in an open style of teaching schools will reflect values, and the responsibility here lies with the head. The balance of the curriculum in a school and details of timetabling are also matters in which a central team should not intrude (except in the special case of trials schools). The team's task is to broaden, not to constrict, the range of choice open to policy-makers.

Moreover, a central team cannot in the nature of the case provide materials or suggestions for local and environmental studies or for school visits. These are intimately linked to local settings, and accordingly work at this level requires to be done in local teachers' centres. Work done by a team such as ours must evoke an energetic local response if it is to yield maximum dividends.

Finally, a team with a limited life, directed to undertake its task in a specified number of years, cannot aspire to produce topical material. This is bound to fall to teachers' groups in development centres, whose efforts will, one hopes, be supported and supplemented by the enterprise of educational publishers.

It is highly desirable that a curriculum project should regard itself as conducting an exploratory operation which opens up ground for teachers and for agencies such as publishers, television companies and makers of audio-visual materials of all kinds.

The Work in Hand

Selection of Areas of Inquiry

Whereas the traditional school curriculum is subdivided into subjects, many of which reflect, albeit wanly, the academic disciplines of university study, the curriculum area in which the project is concerned should, it has been suggested, be subdivided into areas of inquiry. There is an inescapable practical need to split a broad area of study into manageable divisions, and we feel that the concept of areas of inquiry is a useful one.

Areas of inquiry may be regarded as fields of study cutting across the disciplines. In this sense, the curriculum with which we are concerned is interdisciplinary. However, it is not always possible in practice to tease out the strands of the disciplines in an area of inquiry. What is important is the recognition of the need for articulated conceptual frameworks and for the touchstone of critical standards.

In selecting areas of inquiry, we have tried to bear in mind a number of criteria.

First, we believe that the choice of areas should not require to be justified in terms of transfer of learning. We have little evidence concerning the possibility of transfer in this kind of curriculum and it would be foolhardy to argue that techniques of inquiry and casts of thought developed in an exploration of a city's drainage system will transfer usefully to a field such as interpersonal relations. If we wish students to be able adequately to deal with important human issues, these issues must themselves be the stuff of the curriculum. Each area should be one which focuses important personal choices, as in the case of relations between the sexes, or important social choices, as in the case of law and order. Each area should involve both a knowledge of facts and an understanding of experience. Each area should raise problems of value and of the interpretation of values in practice. In short, we are concerned with relatively practical questions viewed in depth.

Regarded from this standpoint, topics such as transport or local government taught in a factual way seem difficult to justify in a humanities curriculum: they are derived from a different logic, perhaps that associated with the teaching of conventional school subjects across disciplines on a project or inquiry base. They raise too few issues of value and those they do raise, they raise obliquely. They deal primarily in facts and techniques.

A second criterion for the selection of areas of inquiry is that they should be areas in which the school has something to offer to the pupils. The school may be taken to represent a central cultural tradition in our society. Where that cultural tradition is weak, the school may be of little help to the students, at least on the humanities side. Thus, confronted with the problem of drugs, the teacher in this field may have no weightier intellectual baggage than De Quincey, Coleridge's Kubla Khan, a couple of articles in *New Society*, and a colour supplement. It is therefore extremely doubtful whether such a problem can be effectively dealt with within the framework of the humanities. Perhaps it is more appropriately handled in science or by the school medical service.

A third criterion is that an area of study should have some internal logical coherence, and should not be based on casual association. Thus, the juxtaposition of political power and power as energy in the physical sense is unsatisfactory, as is the association of irrigation, swimming, boiling kettles, and water on the brain in a unit on 'water'. This smacks of the free association of the psychoanalyst's couch. It is difficult to avoid the conclusion that some curriculum designers see thematic teaching as an opportunity for ingenuity. Themes should probably seem inevitable or hackneyed, rather than clever.

The areas of inquiry with which the central team has started should be regarded merely as examples and not as an attempt to define coverage. They are: war; education; the family; relations between the sexes; living in cities; human dereliction and law and order. It is possible that some of these may be abandoned. If time permits, other areas will be developed.

The Central Archive

The basic task of the Project team, without which nothing is possible, is the gathering of materials. This is a slow and laborious process. Our technique has been to start with a general definition of a theme and on this basis to seek materials relevant to the theme.

Since the idea is to support discussion and inquiry we have not been looking for teaching aids but for pieces of evidence. The distinction can best be explained by example. When a teacher is working on an instructional pattern, he may value a piece of material such as a picture because it helps him to put over a point or conveys vividly something he can only describe palely. When one moves to work on an inquiry base, the material comes to be valued sometimes because it poses a question, but most often because it contains information which can be used to document the issue.

It is this which forces the Project team to collect rather than to write material. You can manufacture aids to instruction, but you cannot appropriately manufacture evidence.

Now, since the project can only make a limited amount of material available to schools, there is a problem of selection. One way to handle this would be to select finally as the material is being collected, but this is dangerous both because the selection is not subject to discussion by others and also because it is too easy to have to retrace one's steps as one comes to see the relevance of material previously rejected.

For this reason our technique has been to build up a collection and then to edit a selection from it. The best illustration of this is the work on war. We have selected about 200 pieces of material from about 2000 pieces collected, and before the schools' collection on war reaches its final form, the latter figure will probably have risen to 3000. In short, we are building our own resources centre and then working from this to structured collections for schools, which are drawn from it.

This might be regarded as a purely domestic affair, a mildly interesting insight into Project work habits, were it not that there is a growing recognition of the need for resources collections in teachers' centres, in the larger schools and in colleges of education. It may therefore be that the techniques of storage and indexing adopted by the Project have a far wider interest than was originally anticipated.

It could be argued that the Project archive and similar collections made by other projects could, if they are consistently indexed, form the basis of a national system of documentation for schools, though, before this can be achieved, there are a good many problems to be solved, especially in the area of copyright. Such a national system would be able to offer invaluable support for the development work done in teachers' centres.

Both pressure of work and copyright problems prevent the development of a documentation service based on the Project's archive at present, but it may be possible to explore the potential of such a service at a later date.

Why Structured Materials?

Before describing the general pattern of the structured collections of materials which the Project hopes to offer to schools, it is important to make clear certain important principles which lie behind the idea of imposing some kind of structure on the materials. The object is to give support and guidance to teachers. Once they gather experience of the kind of teaching involved, teachers will no doubt reorganize the materials supplied and reject some of the guidance. Nevertheless, such evidence as we have suggests that the vast majority of teachers will have to be capable of a radical and searching revision of both their attitudes and techniques if an inquiry-based humanities curriculum is to be successfully adopted in the schools. Moreover, we believe that it will be dangerous to embark on such a curricular innovation in schools where there is not a readiness to face the disturbance of reappraisal which is involved. We shall return to these issues later in the working paper. For the moment, we are concerned only with their implication for structuring.

The humanities curriculum as the Project has interpreted it, involves the school in handling highly controversial issues. Official documents such as the Crowther[5] and Newsom[3] Reports have pointed out that this is inevitable if young adults are to be treated in an adult way. At the same time many teachers are rightly concerned about the need for safeguards if they enter such areas. One of the purposes of producing structured collections of materials is to try to provide a body of evidence in which various points of view are balanced, and thereby to help to release the teacher from the limitations of his own perspective.

Teachers will often also feel uneasy about undertaking work outside their own special subject disciplines. An interdisciplinary curriculum is bound to enter areas in which they are not experts. A collection of materials gives them and their students access to the expertise of others.

Both these points are expressed in the aspiration towards discussion and inquiry. The prime justification for inquiry-based rather than instruction-based teaching in the humanities lies not in any generalized claim to the efficacy of such methods or in an assertion that they make pupils absorbed and active, but rather in the nature of the field itself. Interdisciplinary studies in controversial areas cannot appropriately be based on instruction. This would leave the pupil too vulnerable to his teacher's biases and scholarly limitations. Thus inquiry-based strategies must be adopted, using collections of material which balance the value issues and provide information accessible only to the expert.

It is also apparent that areas of enquiry will involve not only controversial points of view and a wide spread of information but also conceptual frameworks. Thus any collection of material should be structured in such a way as to expose some of the major concepts and distinctions which require to be made in informed discussion.

Structured Collections of Material for Schools

In editing we have two main considerations in mind: the practical strategy of teaching in the classroom and the nature of the fields in which we are working.

The latter consideration implies that an editor should build an articulate conceptual map of the area in which he is working. For example, we do not think it possible to edit materials on war without reading one's way into the work which has been done by scholars on the study of war or to handle law and order without acquainting oneself with at least the rudiments of legal theory. This point should scarcely need mentioning but it requires to be emphasized. A good many teachers have either lacked the time or failed to see that it is necessary to undertake this discipline. A field of study cannot be securely based on information: theory is needed here (as in academic subjects) as a basis for order and for judgements.

We see the classroom strategy as flexible and exploratory; but in order to guide our efforts we have to adopt a generalized model. The central activity is that of discussion controlled by the teacher. A question is raised and defined. Evidence bearing on this question is worked over by the class, by small groups or by individual students. This evidence is fed back into further discussion which covers the background issues critically. The process is drawn together and disciplined in students' work.

For convenience the stages might be labelled:

1. Definition through discussion
2. Information through critical examination of evidence
3. Resolution of issues through discussions
4. Outcome in pupils' work

The provision of materials by a central team bears most directly on the first two of these processes. We are at present following the procedure of breaking each of our areas of inquiry into questions which appear significant in the light of our knowledge of the field. We then seek one or two pieces of material which raise a question and challenge closer examination. Around each question-raiser we assemble evidence as a basis for stage 2.

At the moment, therefore, it appears that what the project will offer to schools is a number of packs or collections of material. It is likely that these will contain printed documents, slides, film strips and audio-tapes. There will be verse, fiction, factual prose, song and occasionally instrumental music, documentary material on tape, photographic material, facsimiles and reproductions of paintings. To these will be added a teacher's book, suggestions for supplementary materials and recommendations regarding background reading.

The basic structure of the packs will be cellular rather than sequential. Each pack will be based on some ten to fifteen questions, but in most cases the order in which the questions can be discussed will be quite flexible. In the case of any one question there will be one or two pieces of material intended to serve as a point of departure, but beyond that the organization of materials will again be a matter of logic rather than of teaching sequence.

It is hoped that this arrangement will allow great flexibility in use while at the same time offering firm support whenever a teacher may feel the need of it.

Some Practical Problems

Although the project is as yet hardly under way, a number of considerable difficulties and problems have already emerged, and it seems worthwhile to air these.

The most important concerns the level of difficulty of the material available. Since our concern is with students of average and below average ability (all but the top 25 per cent and the bottom 15 per cent) the range is immense. If the curricular pattern we are exploring commends itself to the teachers of these students it will be because it is more disciplined and more demanding than anything so far generally achieved with these classes. Therefore, we hope to begin our work with fairly difficult materials and thereafter to modify to cover the range. For example it may be possible once the pattern is confirmed in practice to develop an experimental pack which is almost entirely audio-visual.

Accordingly, we should hope that our early packs will contain a little material which is too difficult for general use, but not too much. We must ensure that we do not underestimate the possibilities.

It is, however, not easy to estimate the level of difficulty at which we should aim, and we are finding a wide conflict of view among experienced teachers. It would be of great help if teachers in school or further education settings who are already working with students of our kind on an inquiry base could send us two or three examples of the most difficult prose or verse their students are handling successfully.

Given a clear conception of the level of difficulty which is acceptable, it is still a problem to keep materials as simple as one would wish. Here the crucial factor is time. For example, if one has located a memoir of early Victorian family life, which is admirable as evidence but too difficult in vocabulary and very mannered in style, then it is virtually certain that somewhere there exists a simple memoir or collection of letters which would fulfil the same purpose. But it could take a month to find such a piece of material. Since we frequently face this problem, we should like to appeal to teachers (and others) who come across unusually direct and simple materials of high quality bearing on our fields of inquiry to let us have these. We can copy them and return them.

Two other problems are less within our power.

The first is that of making available to schools teaching the humanities film extracts, film compilations and television material. This is largely a matter of cost. Since extracts from feature films, documentary compilations and television material are too costly to include in packs of material sent to schools, we must ultimately depend on a hire service. The Project has enlisted the help of the education department of the British Film Institute which will attempt to build out its film extract hire service to meet the immediate needs. Future developments, however, depend on the capital investment of a considerable sum in film and television materials so that a hire service can be started. The problem arises partly because educational films made on an instructional base are not generally suited to enquiry-based teaching, and material which can be used as evidence is not readily available at present.

It should be pointed out, however, that full-length feature films are readily available on hire. A school can easily build up a thematic programme in a film society or within the time table. Feature film is important, not simply as evidence, but also because it may well be the one major art form, capable of synthesizing a wide range of issues and impressions, to which the majority of average pupils can respond.

The final problem and the most intractable is that of copyright. Here all we can do is to warn schools that material may be produced more slowly than we should wish, simply because of the immense labour involved in clearing copyright on collections of two hundred items drawn from varied sources. It is this task above all which is likely to slow up results and we can do no more than ask for understanding and forbearance.

Trials in Schools

When the project was first conceived, it was anticipated that materials would go into pre-trial schools in the latter part of session 1967–1968, into about 30–40 first trial schools in session 1968–1969 and into a much larger number of schools in 1969–1970. This was a crash programme aimed at the raising of the school-leaving age, and for various reasons it has been revised.

Since we have not written our materials but collected already existing materials, copyright must be cleared in all material before it goes into schools. As has already been explained this is a lengthy process and has made it impossible to run pre-trials in session 1967–1968.

The schools selected as trial schools in 1968 will thus be handling our first trials. Indeed, the word *trials*, traditional now in curriculum innovation, is probably not appropriate here. A trial suggests the evaluation of materials approaching a finished state, but in fact the teachers in the trial schools will be in a very real sense pioneers who are involved in the process of shaping the material.

Moreover, new teaching skills will have to be developed and a tremendous challenge will face trial schools here. This is not a case for development defined from the centre. A new humanities tradition will be generated, not by a central team, but by teachers working on the raw materials supplied by the team.

As a result of study of the trials, the material will be modified and teaching strategies will be developed. These two processes must be kept closely related to one another and this can only be achieved by close contact between the project team and the trial schools. Under these circumstances it does not seem profitable to mount trials with a large number of schools in 1969–1970.

Accordingly, we shall continue to work with a small number of schools in an intensive way and at the same time hasten the progress of the materials towards general availability in published form as soon as they are in a shape to justify wider diffusion.

While trials are in progress in schools the materials will be offered to a limited number of colleges of education and institutes and departments of education which will be asked to study the implications of the Project for initial and in-service training.

Of Evaluation and Objectives

The general aim of the Project is to stimulate support and furnish with materials teachers who are trying to bring within the experience of the majority of pupils those moral and human issues which in the past have generally been regarded as open to inquiring discussion only by an educated élite.

Our strategy is based on the assumption that this cannot be achieved before adolescence, and that it can only be achieved by developing a core curriculum which concerns itself directly with these fundamental issues.

This is a most ambitious enterprise, nothing less than an attempt to develop a new central tradition of high seriousness and considerable depth on which the non-vocational element in education can be integrated. Environmental studies, consumer education, education for leisure can all fall into place round such a core. They are important, but without a central tradition of moral weight, the whole experience of schooling is depreciated, and the importance of all the work undertaken in school is diminished.

It would be absurd to regard such a development as the responsibility of a small central team. All they can do is to forge the material and theoretical tools with which teachers can begin to set about a task which for any full accomplishment will require a generation.

It is against this background that we must consider the problem of evaluation. It is commonly asserted that an aim of high generality such as that just stated should be thought across into behavioural objectives, that a curriculum development team should design materials to attain those objectives and that it should evaluate its efforts by a process of testing in the classroom. While not denying that there may be some instructional situations where this procedure is appropriate, we would assert that it is of narrowly limited validity and is certainly not appropriate here.

This is not the place to argue this case in full but the issue is important enough to require some systematic comments.

Aims of high generality are useful as expressing the intentionality in education and helping the teacher to criticize his general orientation *philosophically*. Analysing such aims in greater detail is one approach to the critical justification of one's general position. As such, the activity is useful and important, but it is not an examination of one's behaviour in the classroom.

In complex teaching situations an analysis of aims into constituent behavioural objectives is not a good base for examining classroom practice since the criteria involved in practice are so multiple and complex as to make any specification of behavioural objectives an oversimplification which gives a partial view.

Stated behavioural objectives are particularly unsuited to the scientific study of classroom behaviour because they are not based on the observation of that behaviour but on the teachers' verbalization about it and there is strong evidence that verbal witness of this sort is unreliable.

Stated behavioural objectives are not a good basis for the study of teaching in divergent fields because here one expects different (and sometimes unanticipated) worthwhile responses within the same group of pupils.

Stated behavioural objectives are unhelpful as a basis for the study of the teaching process where the values involved in teaching are so fundamental as to suggest that many of the most significant effects may be observable only after a considerable time – perhaps, indeed, quite late in life.

These points seem to apply generally, but there is a further reservation about the evaluation of the work of curriculum development teams in terms of objectives specified by the team. There is a necessary implication that their curriculum offering is 'teacher-proof' since objectives formulated at the centre are used as testing concepts in the classrooms of many teachers as if the teacher were an insignificant variable. In our area of concern we believe that the teacher's contribution is highly significant and that some teachers may be expected to see solutions to problems, and profitable developments beyond the vision of the central team.

It would be irresponsible to sweep aside a strong tradition of evaluation without offering an alternative approach. Our position is as follows:

The subjects of our curriculum are important in themselves. They are approached through discussion and inquiry. Within the subjects some concepts to be used and distinctions to be drawn are more refined and precise than others. Discussion has its rules. Inquiry has its logic. Attainment in the classroom is limited by the ability of the pupils, their experience of this kind of study and the unique personal experiences outside the classroom which they bring to bear in discussion. The good classroom is one in which one can discern at whatever level is appropriate that the teacher is moving in the direction of more disciplined and sensitive work as judged by the accepted standards of the subject field, of discussion and of logical inquiry. The work of a curriculum development team is to be judged by the extent to which it makes this progress possible.

Evaluation must therefore be based upon the close analytic scrutiny of work in the classroom. This is made technically possible by video-tape, but it will take time to make progress with the theoretical work involved in analysis. In the face of this difficulty, no progress will be made by a crude simplification of the situation in terms of objectives.

We hope to evaluate our work and that of our colleagues in trial schools by case studies involving video-tape observation. Within the limits imposed by finance it should be possible to move towards some objective analysis of our video-tape material, but our basic position must be that in so far as our judgements are not objective, they must at least be subject to public scrutiny. We must present our evidence to teachers and frankly admit that there is much they will have to evaluate in the light of their professional experience and that they cannot lean on the authority of the research expertise.

Diffusion

One great advantage of the decision to face the complexity of the classroom situation in attempting evaluation is that the case study materials we shall be using to evaluate our work will also be broadly descriptive of the work in the classrooms of our trial schools. They thus provide an opportunity for those teachers who wish to embark on inquiry-based humanities teaching to understand the problems and opportunities facing them in a far more profound way than would be possible on the basis of a working paper such as this. In short, they serve the purpose off diffusion as well as of evaluation.

This advantage is the more important since we believe that we are working towards a situation asking for a radical reinterpretation of the role of the teacher in the classroom. Four main considerations push us in this direction:

1. adolescent pupils need to be introduced to the responsibility of thinking for themselves by doing so;
2. if controversial material is to be introduced into the classroom, professional ethics demand that the teacher see to it that his pupils are not limited by his own biases;
3. since discussion of controversial material leads across subject boundaries, the teacher is bound to find himself often relying on his status as an intelligent and educated person rather than on his specialist subject knowledge;
4. there is evidence that in many schools the social barrier between the pupil and the teacher is an impediment to committed work on the part of the pupil.

All these considerations lead one to suggest that in inquiry-based humanities teaching the teacher should abandon his instructional role, and develop the skills demanded of a seminar chairman or the chairman of a court of inquiry. Indeed a major reason for our emphasis on the provision of material evidence is our belief that in this style of teaching information should enter the classroom in this form rather than through instruction by the teacher. The teacher's contribution should be his grasp of critical standards, his ability to interpret evidence, and his capacity to stimulate and organize further work.

Verbally stated, this shift of role may seem obvious. The living experience of achieving it in one's own teaching is demanding and momentous. The success of the development we are concerned to support will depend almost entirely on the capacity of teachers to meet that experience.

This is to ask so much of teachers that we are convinced that diffusion should be gradual and controlled. Nothing could be more disastrous than a bandwaggon effect, running beyond the capacity of in-service facilities and teachers' centres so that teachers embarked on a new venture insufficiently supported.

Having charted these problems and difficulties, we feel we can fairly add our conviction that in personal terms the potential rewards of this kind of teaching are most exciting.

The Hypothetical Nature of the Project

The Humanities Curriculum Project is working in a difficult and complex area where relatively high risks are justified by the promise of immense rewards. It will often have to cooperate with teachers in the definition of problems before it can help to solve them. Its attitude must be tentative, sceptical and experimental.

This paper has attempted to define a position as clearly and precisely as possible, but it must be emphasized that this position has at the moment only the status of a hypothesis. The definition is not that of assertion. It is an attempt at the precision which makes it easier rather than more difficult to modify a position in the light of experience.

References

1. Schools Council, *Raising the School Leaving Age* (Working Paper No. 2) (London: Her Majesty's Stationery Office, 1965).
2. Schools Council, *Society and the Young School Leaver* (Working Paper No. 11) (London: Her Majesty's Stationery Office, 1967).
3. *Half Our Future*: A report of the Central Advisory Council for Education (England) (London: Her Majesty's Stationery Office, 1963) (The Newsom Report).
4. A. N. Whitehead, *The Aims of Education* (London: Williams and Norgate, 1932).
5. Central Advisory Council for Education, England, *15 to 18* Vol I: Report (London: Her Majesty's Stationery Office, 1959) (The Crowther Report).

The Humanities Curriculum Project: an introduction for experimental schools (*1968*)

I have asked you to come together this evening, not simply to welcome you, but also to put before you in the plainest possible way what I think must be our working relationship if you join us.

We want colleagues to take part in an experiment with us. It isn't a situation in which we make something and you try it, but one in which we explore something together. We have already tried to explain this in letters, in discussions when we have met some of you and your heads, and in visits. We are quite sure that in some cases we haven't got it across. This weekend we must make the basis of cooperation between us quite plain and, as the picture emerges, you must finally decide whether you can honestly work with us or not. Whatever the outcome, we hope that the actual experience of the weekend will be an interesting one.

What are we up to then? We are part of the preparation for the raising of the school-leaving age. The date has been deferred. There is plenty – it may prove too much – of time to experiment.

We are charged by our sponsors, the Nuffield Foundation and the Schools Council, with the task of mounting, in collaboration with schools, a series of experiments in the teaching of humanities to adolescents on an inquiry base. We mean by the humanities an integration of social studies, arts, and religion.

I think that what we are trying to do is quite new, but at first it doesn't sound it. The kind of teaching we look towards has familiar elements. If you join us you will, of course, feed into your teaching local visits and studies, library work and so forth – familiar enough – and draw from it written work or documentary tapes or improvised drama or whatever kind of work seems to you most worthwhile. But as a centre for this work there will, we hope, be a type of discussion which is quite unfamiliar in schools. We want to develop this kind of discussion and to study it in the setting of the total pattern of teaching.

We could do this initially in ten schools. Both for financial reasons and for experimental reasons we could not do it in a hundred. We have in fact made contact with thirty-two schools which have expressed enough interest in the experiment to attend this series of induction conferences.

I want to introduce you to our detailed thinking by drawing your attention to the plan behind me. This is the ROSLA (Raising of the School Leaving Age) unit at a school in Berkshire. Here, at the bottom left, are spaces for dirty craft, clean craft, and at the top left, a space for kitchen work. But here, at the right, are two rooms marked 'study reference' and 'discussion' and, in the very centre – as we think, appropriately – there is an area marked 'resources'. We want to ask 'What is to go on in the humanities in these spaces?' An advanced ROSLA unit like this of course offers almost ideal conditions. In most of our schools we should have to improvise to get the same opportunities. But an ideal is always useful as something to struggle towards. These plans give a model for an educational unit. We are seeking a model for the teaching inside it.

Those rooms could be filled with bored adolescents or with adolescents entertained but not educated. We want to do something to help make sure that they are filled with disciplined inquiry and discussion work – and with the resources to support such work. We do not know exactly what that discussion work should look like nor exactly what those resources should be. Hence the need for our experiment. We do have hypotheses to test and we need colleagues in school who are interested in testing them thoughtfully.

What do we ask of teacher colleagues?

First. That they accept the desirability of mounting free and open-ended discussion of controversial, social and personal issues with adolescents in their classrooms.

Second. That they have reached this conclusion thoughtfully, recognizing this as difficult work which will tax both them and their pupils and are prepared to try to press towards higher standards than have so far been achieved.

Third. That they accept the need to work towards a relationship with adolescent school leavers which helps them to grow up by stressing their maturity and responsibility, rather than attempting to prolong their childhood and dependence.

Fourth. That they are prepared to create a suitable environment for discussion in their schools. This means in the main a classroom set out for discussion, in which desks or chairs and tables have been rearranged to make a room where discussion is more appropriate than instruction, instead of a room where instruction is more appropriate than discussion. It means also the provision of resources for discussion. That room needs to have an appropriate collection of reference books, a growing collection of photographs, newspaper clippings and similar materials, and wall boards on which to display these.

Fifth. That they become members of the Humanities Curriculum Project team, in the sense that they accept fully the aims and implications of what is being attempted, though not in the sense that they are to be blamed for the failure of our hypotheses to work in the classroom. We want to work with teachers who care and who are tough minded and persistent. We do not expect to work with teachers who are virtuosos in discussion techniques.

Finally, we ask that teachers in the Project shall be prepared to be studied, even filmed, and to study themselves in the class-room.

This is in fact more than any curriculum experiment in this country has asked of teachers before. We recognize this and we hope that our appreciation of your cooperation will express itself both in practical help and in understanding of your problems. What do we ask of ourselves in this experiment?

First. That we provide clear and coherent hypotheses so that experimental teachers are in no doubt as to the kind of thing we are trying to find out.

Second. That we provide – in the words of our remit – stimulus, support and materials for our experimental schools to the limits of our time and ability.

Third. That once teachers have broken through their initial difficulties and begun to feel at home in the style of humanities work we are studying, we should be responsive to the reports they give us and the needs they define for us. We shall want as much thoughtful comment as we can get from you. All our teachers' handbooks and notes will be regarded as drafts, to be shaped by your comment. In the nature of the case we have had to produce a first batch of materials without consulting experimental teachers. Consequently these materials, in sound, vision and print, span a wide range of difficulty and will cover a variety of approaches. Your biggest problem in the early stages will be to find your way round them. A great deal of selection and change will be necessary before we find the best form in which materials can be published and made available to teachers outside the experimental schools. What you are getting is a first attempt, produced in five months.

Given that we are able to reach this basis of cooperation with a group of teachers, what will be the purpose of our common work? I think we must try to break through to a new style of teaching whose strategy we come to understand. We need to develop high standards of quality and we shall hope to get adolescents of around CSE level working in a more adult way and at a higher standard than is commonly the case at the moment. We must try to find the right kind of materials for this sort of teaching which we have developed together and to mould these materials into some publishable shape. We must, once we have succeeded at CSE level, try to push down the ability range.

If we can achieve this together, if we can define our tradition for ourselves, then our problem is quite simply that of communicating our hard-won experience to our colleagues in other schools. We must try to do this through working papers describing our work, through film and tape where this is appropriate, through our handbooks and notes for teachers and through our teaching materials. We hope that by the end of the Project we shall all agree about what we value in humanities teaching and we may be able to suggest tests or styles of examination which will do justice to what we value and which can be adapted for CSE. The measure of our work will in the end be how successfully we can get across to teachers whom we shall never meet the fruits of our experience over the next couple of years. During this weekend we on your central team will face a somewhat similar problem on a smaller scale. As I have already said, there is one respect – style of discussion – in which our hypotheses lead us way from the familiar. The central team have lived together for nine months, reading and arguing about this style of discussion and trying it out in school situations. We have come to call it 'discussion disciplined by evidence'. During this weekend we must put flesh on that phrase for you.

We take it that there is a need for discussion rather than instruction. There are many reasons for this. We must help adolescents to participate in their own education and begin to attain some independence of thinking before they leave school. If we have taught them to lean on our authority, they will too easily transfer their allegiance to any other authority which offers. Discussion seems a better central classroom activity than instruction as a base for the kind of free environmental studies, library work and writing, which so many schools have developed. Perhaps, above all, we feel that in controversial areas, conscientious teachers have to resort to discussion in an attempt to prevent their pupils from being limited by their own biases. Each of us who is a parent will know the extent to which we should hope that our children's teachers bore this ideal in mind. What is at stake is not simply the issue of indoctrination but rather the difficulty of a teacher in representing fairly and cogently a point of view which he respects – or feels he ought to respect – but does not hold.

Our observation of attempts at discussion with adolescents has suggested to us that it is difficult to get them talking and, once they are talking, extremely difficult to achieve a discussion which goes much deeper than a half-baked exchange of prejudice. We hope that a discussion which is an interpretation of evidence will go some way to meet both these problems. It will help pupils to talk because they have something to talk about, and it will help teachers to maintain a satisfactory level in discussion by forcing pupils back on evidence.

This style of discussion is central to our purpose, and it is here that we must ask you first to focus your attention. At the same time you will need to ask about the work which fits round it both in terms of pupils' work which prepares them for discussion and in terms of the work they must draw from it. We are preparing a handbook on discussion, which will be posted on to you shortly – as soon as we can get it ready. It is not a bible. It embodies our own experience, the experience of some pre-pilot experiments in schools, and the experience of those who have thought and written about discussion in the past.

The topics for discussion we have so far begun to develop are war, education, the family, and relations between the sexes. Some work and thought has also been given to the topics: people and work, living in cities, poverty, and law and order. Let us state our aims at this stage quite simply. We want pupils to have a deepened understanding of these topics or problems. The question the teacher needs to keep asking is: are my pupils coming to understand war or education or relations between the sexes more fully, and are they developing in this area what Newsom called 'judgement quickened by insight'?

In order to move in this direction, we ourselves must have a deeper understanding of the issues worth discussing. Few of us have studied these problems systematically. As an aid we are producing topic handbooks, which set out a logical framework for discussion. The one on war is now available. As soon as we can get it into your hands, you will also have a booklet on discussion in the face of evidence. These booklets will be revised in due course in response to your comments and criticism. We might have stopped there. We might have said: 'On that basis will you set about collecting materials for us?'

This did not seem to us satisfactory. A handbook of suggestions for teaching war and a handbook on discussion would be of very limited use to teachers. How could you get time to find the evidence on which to begin your experiments with discussion?

Accordingly, we set about making collections of evidence

which could serve as stores or banks, starting points for resources centres intended for discussion. The first of these collections or banks, that on war, is ready in a special experimental form, and you will meet some parts of it at this conference. Our first attempt will have to be modified in the light of experience, but it *is* experience we need rather than opinion. If you can achieve the style of discussion towards which we are looking, then we believe that opinions based on past experience of other types of teaching will be seen to be unreliable. We must ask you not to judge the materials on a superficial acquaintance, but only after study and use. You must have confidence that in the long run we shall achieve the right balance. We, and the Schools Council and Nuffield Foundation, are here to respond to your needs once you have gone far enough with this kind of teaching to define them clearly. At the moment what we need is agreement in the philosophy of what we are trying to do rather than agreement that we or you have yet succeeded in doing it.

The collection of materials we are offering you is constructed on two principles. It is intended to have a structure which reflects the subject. Thus a collection on the effects of war on society is split into sections such as the effect of war on families, or on education. This structure embodies suggestions for discussion. It prompts the question: what happens to family life in wartime? or what happens to schools and pupils? These questions can give a guide for gathering your own materials. Almost all these questions have been tested in the classroom. The questions to be raised by the education pack are also available. These have all been tested in the classroom.

The collection on war consists of about 240 items – far more than we can ultimately publish. We must lose, I think, at least ninety items. We are asking you to help us in our choice – provided always that you are judging on the basis of experience of their use in discussion teaching. The collection we end up with has to cover a wide ability range. It must stretch the top of CSE. It must contain materials useable as far below CSE level as proves possible. We shall welcome warmly any materials you yourselves find and send to us in an attempt to improve the collection. We shall also welcome suggestions of passages from available published anthologies and text-books which are relevant.

Two experimental principles must be borne in mind. First, as in an intelligence test, at this stage there must be some material too difficult for all our pupils. Only in that way can we make sure that we have got up to the highest difficulty level possible. But in all cases, we want you, having started with simpler material, to push upwards and upwards seeing as you tighten the screws how high your pupils can get up the ladder of difficulty we have built into the pack. Sometimes you may do this by adapting our materials. We believe that you will best help if you are impelled by a determined desire to break down the barriers to your pupils' understanding. There is something of the four-minute mile about this. If your pupils are not at the end working at a more adult level than ever before, we shall not have succeeded.

The second experimental principle is different. We do not regard it as our business, but yours, to decide what is fit to teach in terms of censorship. Here we shall accept your report that material is unsuitable without your having taught it, though we hope to get the agreed opinions of teams of teachers rather than of individuals. Be warned that our materials carry no authority in this respect which is intended to override your own judgement. In marginal cases you may wish to try materials before making a decision in the light of their effect on a class, but you must obviously do so discreetly.

Both for this reason and because the material is in general controversial, schools are advised to take parents into their confidence. We have found that parents in general welcome the attempt of teachers to handle such matters responsibly.

How should you start? And when should you start? Every school will be in a different situation. If you are confident that these innovations in teaching can be gradually built into your present work, and if you have time to study the materials before next term, then you might build the Project into your plans for September. But you might start at half-term or in January. We shall have some materials on education available in September to help your planning. The original urgency of the raising of the leaving-age is mitigated. Prepare before you start and do not start against your better judgement.

We are not supplying you with the whole fabric of a course. At least fifty per cent of the course in your school must come from you. You must also allow for the fact that you may have to improvise if parts of our material are found to be unsuitable. At the same time, bear in mind that we shall give you all the help we can in planning or in improvisation if you want it.

All this has had the knell of caution ringing through it. I have had to make it that way to be quite clear that initially at least we shall be adding to your problems rather than presenting you with easy solutions. Our latest member of staff said that what attracted him to the job was the challenge of worthwhile difficulty.

But let me be quite clear. Once you have decided you can work with us you are not customers but colleagues. We shall be working together on the most absorbing curriculum innovation that could be imagined. No support for you which is in our power will be stinted. I and some of my colleagues are keeping large amounts of free time next session to come and discuss problems with you. It will also be possible to contact us during August.

The Nature and Interpretation of Evidence

From 'An Experiment in the Interpretation of Evidence in Small Groups.' An address to the Claremont Reading Conference, 1969.

When discussion groups meet under a chairman, they tend initially to look to him for authority. They assume, when he is a teacher, that he knows the answers and is setting up discussions with a hidden instructional agenda. Their responses are often attempts to guess what the teacher wants rather than to face the task of understanding through the discussion of evidence. When they do work in terms of evidence rather than in terms of the teacher, they often regard evidence as raw material out of which to make a didactic case, or expect that the more evidence is produced, the more a discussion group will come to agree with them. Often they adopt a sceptical approach and try to make the least of a piece of evidence. Only gradually do they learn to make the most of evidence and to aim at deepening their understanding.

Groups often tend to regard evidence as bearing on fact or event. It takes time to understand that a poem can be evidence of the existence of a possible mood or affective reaction, an ambiguous photograph can be evidence of the general dynamics of a social situation, a piece of didactic prose can be evidence of the existence of a given point of view. The skill and judgement involved in learning to differentiate one's response to different types of symbolic material develops only through experience.

All evidence contains some value element, even if only in the categories chosen for a statistical table. Most evidence is ambiguous, in the arts purposely so. The interpretation of evidence therefore involves judgements which are based on the intersection of the meaning contained in the symbol and the experience of the interpreter. In facing ambiguous evidence the most productive procedure is often to produce a range of likely and unlikely interpretations. The gradient of likeliness implies an interpretation.

Successful discussion work gains its shape and unity from the dynamic flow of discussion. To subject evidence to traditional comprehension exercises kills the discussion. The students must be trained to ask questions about the meanings of words or passages: the chairman must not do so. Misunderstandings can only be dealt with if they make themselves manifest in the discussion. It seems that the teacher as chairman cannot safely ask any question to which he knows the answer.

The process of interpretation of reading in groups is complex and we do not yet have the material to support a detailed analysis. What is already clear is that, at the secondary school level where most worthwhile reading materials are rich and ambiguous, it is only too easy for the teacher to dominate the reading of the text by his own interpretation. Reading through discussion is a device not only for overcoming value dependency but also for breaking through dependency to autonomy in reading.

Groups gradually recognize that in facing a controversial issue they must take the evidence into account and use it to deepen understanding of the issue. They also come to grasp the point that value judgements go beyond the evidence to a decision which cannot be proved to be the only correct one. For this decision the individual must accept full responsibility without the security of dependence on the authority of another. It is this transition from dependency to responsibility which is the main purpose of this kind of teaching. Only in the light of such learning can the nature and status of evidence in controversial issues be grasped.

The Pattern of Discussion

At present, the most successful pattern of discussion emerging from practice in schools is slow in pace, deliberative, reflective. It commonly has long pauses. It would appear that a fair indicator of whether a discussion group is likely to thrive is whether long pauses are terminated by teacher speech or pupil speech. Where the teacher cannot ride out the long pause, the group will unload more and more responsibility on to him, handing back the task he has set them and settling for a comfortable dependency.

Leading questions are always destructive of discussion. They imply that the teacher knows the answer and contribute to the development of the 'guessing game' described in the previous section.

There is a problem of balance in most discussion groups. When this is due to dominant personalities commandeering the discussion it is possible to evolve strategies to redress the balance. For example, the chairman may summarize the argument of the dominant individual or group and then lead the rest of the group to discuss that view while those who have put it forward remain silent now that they have effectively stated it. The most difficult imbalance to deal with is that in which some individuals are silent because they feel that they are not able enough to reach the standard of the others. We have not yet found a solution to this.

We have to case-study individual non-participants to ascertain whether they benefit from being in the group. We are optimistic about this. It would seem that teachers are confident that students can learn by listening to them and if this is true, we should expect that they can also learn from listening to their peers.

A key to success in discussion appears to be that both teacher and group should concentrate on understanding the issues. The work should be intensely task-oriented. For various reasons, too complex to rehearse here, it seems profitable to avoid specifying behavioural objectives in this kind of work. Principles of procedure and hence criteria for controlling the operation can be derived from the general aim of understanding, the principle of controversiality and traditional discussion procedures. In a discussion where the participants face evidence rationally and sensitively divergent student objectives may well be served. One of the characteristics of this kind of work may be to release students from the dominance of teachers' objectives.

The Role of the Chairman

The role of the recessive, non-dominant but inquiring chairman is a difficult one for teachers to fill. Teachers are often accustomed to dominate their classrooms, and their techniques and personality adjustments to their professional role may be maladaptive in the discussion situation. There is intense intellectual interest and reward in following the discussion and also a particular satisfaction in turning oneself into a thoughtful student of one's adolescent pupils' thinking. But it would be wrong to minimize the difficulty of the transition that teachers are required to make if they are to master their role in this style of discussion. They will need all the help they can get.

Convinced that chairing discussion work in controversial issues is a skill which is likely to be learned slowly and thoughtfully, we have set out to offer the teacher the means of self-appraisal and self-development. We have inducted our experimental teachers by means of a four-day course based mainly on simulation, and expect to train agencies already in the field to mount such courses.

In addition to publishing teaching materials and case studies of individual school settings, we shall offer teachers a set of procedural rules for discussion and an array of hypotheses about how they are likely to behave within these rules. Both rules and hypotheses will have been tested in our experimental schools; and they are intended to give to each team of teachers embarking on discussion work in controversial areas a viable experimental framework. They provide a definition of the problems and a starting point, not a hard-and-fast prescription. Rules will require to be reviewed once the teachers have gathered experience.

Typical of rules would be:

'The chairman may summarize to clarify a point of view put forward in the group in order to promote understanding. He should get the agreement of those whose view he is summarizing that his summary is a fair one. He should avoid summarizing two points of view at once since it is difficult to do so without playing one off against the other in such a way as to suggest a preference on his part.'

Typical of hypotheses would be:

'Whenever a student expresses a view with which the chairman disagrees, the chairman's next question to the group will tend to force the critical examination of that view. Whenever a student expresses a view with which the chairman agrees, the chairman's next question will tend to move the argument onwards without subjecting that view to full critical examination.'

The Authority Structure of the School

Insofar as the authority structure of the school is based on teacher dominance and authoritarian and custodial attitudes, the work of the Project has profound implications for change in the school as an institution. It would appear difficult to stimulate a relaxed and free-speaking atmosphere in a discussion group contained within a repressive and authoritarian school. When such an atmosphere is achieved, it leads to tension with other more authoritarian teaching patterns and forms of organization. Most school principals taking part in the project recognize its potential as an agent of change in teacher-student relationships.

If this broad implication is true, it would appear that the attempt to develop autonomy in reading skills and in value judgement strikes at the heart of the problem of authority in staff-student relationships. English observers see this problem of authority as a central issue in the raising of the school-leaving age and the retaining of adolescents in school.

The Humanities Project and the Problem of Motivation

A paper given to a conference on motivation, Ohio State University, June, 1970.

At present, the age of compulsory school attendance in England is five to fifteen. From 1972 all students will be retained in school until they are sixteen by the legal raising of the school-leaving age. The project in which I have been engaged is part of the research and development programme mounted in preparation for this extension of schooling. We have been engaged in exploring the problems of teaching in the area of controversial issues with students aged fourteen to sixteen. We have produced teaching materials and we have experimented with methods. Although the pattern of curriculum and teaching which has emerged is appropriate to a wide range of ages and abilities, we have concentrated our attention on the needs of students who will leave school at the earliest possible opportunity – what you would call 'drop-outs'. We have therefore had to reckon with low motivation and usually low school achievement.

In her book, *Deciding What to Teach*, Dorothy Fraser offered a definition of a controversial issue which we took as a starting point for our thinking.

> A controversial issue involves a problem about which different individuals and groups urge conflicting courses of action. It is an issue for which society has not found a solution that can be universally or almost universally accepted. It is an issue of sufficient significance that each of the proposed ways of dealing with it is objectionable to some section of the citizenry and arouses protest. The protest may result from a feeling that a cherished belief, an economic interest, or a basic principle is threatened. It may come because the welfare of organizations or groups seems at stake. When a course of action is formulated that virtually all sectors of society accept, the issue is no longer controversial.[1]

In short, a controversial issue is one which divides teachers, pupils and parents.

Britishers and Americans do not need to remind one another that in modern pluralist democracies controversial issues abound. Even where there is a widespread consensus of principle, there is disagreement in the interpretation of principles in practice. Most will think war highly undesirable; but disagreement will flare as soon as we discuss particular wars. Ought the British to have gone into Suez? Should America be in Vietnam? What are the rights and wrongs of the Arab-Israeli conflict? And this is the front line of values: where principles meet practice.

(*Four paragraphs on Schools Council Working Paper No. 2 and the basis of the Project are here omitted.*)

Given that one is working in the area of controversial issues, and that one wishes to handle them in groups and not through individual study, there appear to be three possible strategies which can be employed in the school.

One might argue that the school should attempt to transmit an agreed position adopted as a matter of policy. This fails in practice because it is impossible to obtain the agreement of parents or policy makers on the huge range of issues involved. Moreover, even if it were possible to lay down an agreed line at policy level, the teachers would still disagree among themselves and the schools would find themselves involved in an organized and systematic hypocrisy, which would make them extremely vulnerable to the criticism of students. This approach is also unacceptable in terms of our aim, since it cannot possibly further the understanding of a controversial issue to pretend that it is not, in fact, controversial.

A second possibility is that each teacher should be free to give his own sincerely held point of view. But the inescapable authority position of the teacher must in this case leave him open to the charge of using the classroom as a platform to promote his own views. In the face of such criticism, the profession would have committed itself to defending the teacher who advocated pacifism to the children of regular army soldiers or who advocated pre-marital sexual intercourse in the face of parental disapproval. This position seems scarcely tenable in practice, though attractive to many at first view. In theory it might be possible to get around the difficulty by ensuring that teachers whose opinions were relatively heterodox were not given appointments. Questions about a teacher's political, religious and moral beliefs and practices would then become appropriate at interviews for teaching posts. This is unacceptable to the teaching profession.

At first sight it does not look as if this second approach is objectionable from the point of view of enhancing understanding, but in fact our experience in classrooms suggests that the authority position of the teacher is much stronger than most teachers realize, and that it is almost insuperably difficult for him to put forward his own points of view without implying that controversial issues can be settled on the basis of the authority of others.

The third strategy, and the one adopted by the Project, is to attempt to devise a method of teaching which should make it possible for the teacher who will train himself to do all he can to protect pupils from his own bias, while advancing their understanding. This involves the teacher in a procedural neutrality in handling controversial issues which could be the basis of a professional ethic for dealing with controversy in the class-room.

It must be made clear that the position taken at this point by the project is not value-free.

In the first place, the decision to include controversial issues in the school curriculum for adolescents implies a value judgement, and the choice of issues to be tackled is based on the value judgement that they are issues of importance. We have made decisions of value at the most fundamental level at which values impinge on the curriculum, namely, in answering the question, what is worthwhile and therefore worth teaching?

Our decision here was significant for motivation. There are those who argue, at least partly on motivational grounds, first, that the curriculum should grow out of the interest of the student and second that it should be founded in his own experience. We decided to make educational decisions with regard to the content in which we would attempt to interest the student, and we set out in many cases to extend experience in a very direct way, for example, in the area of war.

When a school principal claimed that his fifteen-year-old students were not interested in relations between the sexes, we did not attempt to justify our inclusion of this topic by arguing that they were. Rather we claimed that they ought to be, and that if they weren't, it was his job to try to interest them in any topic as important as that one to adult persons in our society.

We have also made value decisions at another level. We have asserted that teaching procedures and curriculum materials must be justifiable in terms of certain values which are fundamental to education. Education must always involve a preference for rational rather than irrational procedures, for sensitivity rather than insensitivity, for imaginativeness rather than unimaginat-iveness. It will always be concerned to examine and establish criteria and standards. The appropriate attitude of teachers to pupils will always involve respect for persons and consideration of their welfare.

Finally, even in the area of substantive controversial issues in which we ask the teacher to accept the criterion of neutrality, we are asserting the democratic values which call for an open debate and dialogue on those issues 'for which society has not found a solution that can be universally or almost universally accepted.'

We have, then, adopted value positions at three points by trying to answer the questions: what should be taught? what educational values should be realized in the way it is taught? what are the implications of democratic values for the degree of doubt and openness with which controversial issues should be taught?

On the basis of the considerations outlined above, the Project team felt that it must attempt to develop experimentally and evaluate a pattern of teaching with the following characteristics:

1. The fundamental educational values of rationality, imagination, sensitivity, readiness to listen to the views of others, and so forth, must be built into the principles of procedure in the classroom.

2. The pattern of teaching must renounce the authority of the teacher as an 'expert' capable of solving value issues, since this authority cannot be justified either epistemologically or politically. In short, the teacher must aspire to be neutral on controversial issues.

3. The teaching strategy must maintain the procedural authority of the teacher in the classroom, but should contain it within rules which can be justified in terms of the need for discipline and rigour in attaining understanding.

4. The strategy must be such as to satisfy parents and pupils that every possible effort is being made to avoid the use of the teacher's authority position to indoctrinate his own views.

5. The procedure must enable pupils to understand divergence and hence must depend upon a group working together through discussion and shared activities. In such a group, opinions should be respected, and minority opinions should be protected from ridicule or from social pressure.

6. In sensitive issues, thought must be given to preserving privacy, and protecting students, e.g. illegitimate children, children from broken homes, children of prostitutes, should be borne in mind when discussing the family or relations between the sexes.

7. Above all, the aim should be understanding. This implies that one should not force pupils towards opinions or premature commitments which harden into prejudice. Nor should one see particular virtue in a change of view. The object is that the pupil should come to understand the nature and implications of his point of view, and grow to adult responsibility by adopting it in his own person and

assuming accountability for it. Whether or not the pupil changes his point of view is not significant for the attainment of understanding.

It seemed that the basic classroom pattern should be one of discussion. Instruction inevitably implies that the teacher cannot maintain a neutral position. In the discussion the teacher should be neutral on the issues which form the agenda of the group, but he should accept responsibility for the rigour and quality of the work. Accordingly, the teacher was seen as a neutral and relatively recessive chairman, though not a passive one, since it would be his job to develop quality in the students' work by shrewd, though sparing, questioning.

A discussion which aims at understanding cannot be merely an exchange of views. It must be a reflective enquiry fed by information. But it is almost impossible for the teacher to be a source of any but the most rudimentary information in a discussion group without breaching his neutrality and taking a dominant role. Therefore the group's best means of access to information is through the consideration of evidence.

(*Five paragraphs on the nature of evidence are here omitted.*)

In preparing these materials we made two decisions which are highly relevant to the problem of motivation.

We assumed that materials cannot be written or adapted by the Project team if they are to be regarded as evidence. This meant that they were collected or anthologized, and we were immediately faced with an acute problem in reading levels, taking into account the fact that we were dealing with early leavers. On the whole we adopted an ambitious policy, including a lot of material which would be at or even beyond the limits of our students' reading capacities. We hoped that students would be taken farther than they had been before in at least grappling with such materials. We did not court the desire to learn by simplifying reading levels.

Further, we reproduced our materials either in facsimile or in plain and easily read type. We avoided the enticements of decoration or illustration unless these were in the original, partly because of the desire that our materials should be authentic and partly, in the case of illustration, because an illustration is already an interpretation. I do not think that our materials are by any means unattractive, but we have not employed design in an attempt to motivate by making materials particularly attractive or tempting.

The collections have a structure which is intended to ensure that the teacher is likely to have at his disposal at least one piece of material to cover any issue likely to arise within a given topic area. In other words, a main function of the structure is to help to achieve coverage. A subsidiary function is to help the teacher to find his way around the collection in the same way as structure helps a reader to use a library.

The structuring of the materials does not imply that they are intended to be used in a pre-determined sequence. Rather they are to be made available to the group in response to points arising in the discussion. A teacher prepares for this kind of teaching by knowing his way around the collection and not by making up his mind in advance what pieces of evidence he will use in any given discussion session.

(*Three paragraphs on the organization and conduct of the Project's experiment in schools are here omitted.*)

I said at the beginning that we had problems in motivation. You will not be surprised to know that in the classrooms of teachers working with us students are sometimes undermotivated. It is true that some students say:

Humanities is different. You just don't go in and sit down like the rest of them and write a lot of rubbish in your books and that, you know.

and

I think you take more interest in it because the questions we are asked are just the sort of questions we would ask for ourselves.

and

If the other teachers worked in this way, they would learn that we're not just boys who, you know, they tell us to do a thing, they put something on the board and you just write it down and take it for granted what they've written there you know is true. I think they could realize that we have opinions of our own and we have quite a good standard of opinions and we think for ourselves.

But others say:

I'm opposite – I'd rather be sat in the classroom writing down the work and listening to what the teacher says.

But these are not the problems I should expect to interest you.

You don't need someone to stand up and tell you that not all children in school are as highly motivated as a sports team in a cup final game.

What I think may be of interest is the way that problems of motivation interweave an innovatory pattern of teaching; and perhaps particularly a pattern of teaching which results from taking a hard-line on motivation at certain decision points, for example in not following the interests of students or seeking to make the materials they use particularly attractive. What will emerge, I think, is a complex of problems and issues so inextricably interwoven in the classroom situation that it is still difficult to subsume them under a single theoretical approach.

Let us start by looking at the role of the teacher as discussion chairman, and relating this to problems of motivation.

Our setting up of a model of neutral chairmanship has attracted a good deal of critical comment. Some of the reserve expressed has been on grounds of social, ethical or educational responsibility, but some has, I think, been related to motivation. People have argued that we are taking away from the classroom the teacher's personality and enthusiasm. It does seem that, in spite of much talk of pupils' interests and child-centredness, most of our teachers see their own charisma and enthusiasm as a major, perhaps even as the prime, element in motivation in the classroom.

Now, of course, it can be. But few teachers have this charismatic quality. And I think we have a model of teaching which calls for a different teacher role. If a teacher explains carefully to a group the task they are expected to take on, explains that he will support them within limits, and defines his neutral position and the grounds of his neutrality, then the effect can be to induce the group to accept independent responsibility for the learning task. It is not inevitable – too many other variables are involved – and it takes time, and often a struggle with the students, before they will accept the redefinition of the situation; but this is a viable model from the point of view of motivation.

Of course, the teacher must live up to his definition of the situation, and this is not easy, for his role cuts across the habits that come from instructional teaching. Few teachers appreciate the extreme subtlety and strength of their authority position in the classroom. It is often transmitted by barely perceptible cues. For example, the chairman of a discussion group who persistently asks the group questions to which he himself thinks he knows the answer implicitly asserts his position of superiority and authority and indeed often makes the group feel that the discussion is merely an oblique teaching method which cloaks the teacher's instructional position.

Again, because of his general authority position in the school, the teacher is a potential source of rewards. If one is, as we are, attempting to get the group of students to accept full responsibility for their own learning, then they must find rewards in the task itself and in their own progress as a working group and as individuals. A teacher as chairman cannot afford to say 'yes' or 'an interesting point'. This sort of reward clearly tends to set up a guessing game in which the students are more concerned with interpreting the teacher's behaviour in order to understand what he has in mind than with interpreting the issues before them in the light of evidence. The teacher needs to see that the students are rewarded by being carefully listened to and fed with questions which help them to articulate and express their own points of view.

The teacher himself needs to learn to listen. Many teachers, even in running discussion, interrupt as many as 80 per cent of all student statements. It often appears that they are trying to be helpful – to re-express more effectively what they think the student is trying to say, to make for pace and movement in the discussion. But this runs across the organic motivation of the discussion situation, and appears dysfunctional in the long run, because it is so frustrating.

Many teachers have been trained to ask eliciting questions, to lead pupils towards the answer which is desired. In the discussion situation this is undesirable. Again, students focus on the teacher. They are readily aware that his questions are intended to lead them to some answer. It is all rather like the game of hide the thimble where the audience sings louder as the searcher gets nearer and more softly as he moves away again. The motivation is that of a puzzle, not that of a task.

Eliciting questions are particularly destructive when they are used to guide the interpretation of evidence, and it is in this context that the teacher finds them most difficult to avoid. He has read the piece or seen the picture before, and he has decided what they ought to see. The students know this, and come to lean on him as an interpreter who will intervene and mediate between the evidence and themselves.

Of course, one might say that the teacher does know better, ought to point to the conclusions to be drawn, ought to direct students to the 'correct' interpretation of a poem or short story or photograph. But it seems that this is not strictly so in practice, for when one plays tapes of teachers using eliciting questions in this way, one finds that their own colleagues seldom agree in the interpretation they are trying to evoke from the students.

Moreover, neutrality is motivationally important. When we first explored a neutral role for the chairman, we embarked on this course on political grounds, but neutrality appears to be pedagogically functional in at least two ways.

Whenever a group is given a task to handle in discussion and it accepts that task and works on it, then the intrusion of the teacher on one side of the discussion short circuits and devalues the process. Students say: 'You can only have a proper discussion if the teacher doesn't take sides.' Only in that way can one make it genuinely their discussion. If they are working on a problem, keep out. This even applies to giving one's opinion when the discussion is over. Teachers have found that when at the end of a discussion session they have yielded to the temptation to give their point of view, the students have often come to regard the previous discussion as a competitive situation. Those who had argued the point of view endorsed by the teacher are triumphant, the others are crestfallen.

The second point about teacher neutrality is a negative one, though none the less important for that. There are indications that the teacher's assumption of a neutral and non-authoritarian role damps out his capacity to transmit to his students his low expectation of their performance. Recent researches have suggested quite strongly that teacher expectation is a major element in holding down the achievement of pupils of average ability, and there are some indications of a strengthening of the capacity of pupil groups to face difficult reading materials as a result of working in the Project. Teachers have found students coping with materials which they considered to be beyond them. One might formulate the hypothesis that when the teacher is neutral and recessive enough to wean a group of students from dependence on him and induce them to accept responsibility for achieving understanding, then the reading level of that group is higher than that of any individual member in it.

To sum up, and to generalize beyond our context of controversial issues: if any topic is suitable for teaching through discussion, then that implies that the taught group should take on a task. The teacher as chairman of such a discussion group, should not intervene in the discussion to advance a view or influence a conclusion, though he should offer open questions which ask for reflection and self-critical thinking on the part of the group, and he should help them towards information they require. This means that he requires to interpret motivation, not to organize it. He needs to be aware of the currents of the desire to learn in the group and to feed them; and this demands that he be responsive, rather than directive.

In many teaching situations the teacher pre-structures for motivation. In discussion situations he must also contribute to structure, but his task is to sharpen and form what is already immanent in the work of the group.

Now, of course, this involves some understanding of group dynamics, or at least some sensitivity towards them. One must, for example, understand how voting splits a group, and learn to work instead towards negotiated consensus. One must be immediately aware when one's own responses grate across the grain of the group. And certainly, teachers' work often does suffer from such difficulties. But often the problems are more narrowly educational. They are connected with lack of clarity of aim or lack of mastery of subject matter.

I want now to consider some factors in the promotion of the desire to learn in discussion situations of the kind we have been exploring, dealing first with factors more in the field of group dynamics and then with factors which seem to me more clearly educational.

A prominent problem in the minds of most teachers is participation. Ought one to try to get every student to speak in discussion and if so, how? Since our professed aim is understanding, there is no *prima facie* reason why we should value participation. The problem seems to be that most non-participant students wish to participate and are under-motivated if they do not, but that some students do not want to participate, but simply want to listen, and these are likely to become hostile if they are pressed to participate. It is easy to say that the teacher should encourage, but not press; but students have said that when the teacher encourages and is obviously pleased when non-participants come into discussion, he makes them self-conscious and puts them off.

The important point seems to be to prevent the discussion

being commandeered by a sub-group. To ask distributive questions – questions which, like 'What do other people think?', invite comments spread round the group – seems to be a helpful technique. But it looks as though the most important factor may be to slow down the pace of discussion in the group, aiming at a reflective discussion with pauses for thought and the examination of evidence. This allows slow reactors whose style is naturally reflective to get into the discussion. It may be that the type of slow discussion which is least superficially entertaining to the lay observer is most highly motivated within the group. There is also some evidence that the pace of discussion can gradually quicken, once a reflective style has been established, without cutting people out.

It appears that the chairman can within limits control the pace of discussion by the pace, hesitation and thoughtfulness of his own contributions. Also, he may ask people to think for a period before anyone comes in.

Closely related to this point, because again it is fundamental to the style I have called reflective discussion, is the need to teach a group to accept discussion as a way of cooperating rather than competing. It is important that discussion aimed at understanding should not become debate, a forum in which each person struggles to enlist support for his particular view. Competition motivates, but not towards the thoughtful understanding of other people's points of view.

Given the background of normal classroom instruction, of educational competition, of habits of debating and of the assumption initially adopted by any group that it is trying to achieve consensus, there is a danger of a group climate in which all the motivational dynamic runs counter to the aim of reflective understanding. The teacher needs to be clear about this aim and its implications for the pattern of work in the group if he is to teach them another way of working. This is particularly difficult for him if, as is common in our experience, the assumptions of the work are so unfamiliar that he cannot create a model in his mind, but must work out the problems as he goes in the classroom.

Two other problems of motivation are rooted in the content of discussion: the nature of controversiality and the nature of relevance.

Notionally, controversiality motivates. Dorothy Fraser speaks of a controversial issue as one which arouses the citizenry. However, some of the teachers working in the experiment claim that the issues lack controversiality for the students. So far as we can gather from observation and tapes, this is most often due to the teacher's failure to see controversial issues, perhaps because he has a preconception as to what is the issue at stake. For example, if a teacher is discussing an anti-Vietnam demonstration and his students all side with the police rather than the demonstrators, he feels he is left without a controversial issue, whereas the issue clearly is: 'What limitations do you wish to see on the power of the police? Could you lay down a code of conduct for police dealing with civil demonstrations? How would you react to breaches of that code?' In other words, there is presented the major problem of how we control the power we create to ensure law enforcement and keep the peace; but often the teacher fails to see this because it is eclipsed by the issue foremost in his mind.

There is a need for the teacher to be familiar with a wide range of issues discussed in the literature of the subject topic he is exploring with the students, and to be sensitive to issues of some importance which lie beneath superficial nodes of consensus in the group.

Relevance is a like problem. It occurs in two forms. Since the teacher is the curator of a large collection of evidence, he makes a judgement of relevance every time he introduces a piece of material; and since he has a responsibility to ask questions, he must ask relevant questions. Now often, in practice, the teacher fails in his judgement of relevance in the eyes of most observers. This appears to be due to lack of knowledge of subject matter, and perhaps sometimes to lack of grasp of the principles of logical thinking.

There is an interesting tie up here between our observations and those of Richard Jones in his *Fantasy and Feeling in Education.*[2] In reflecting on the observation of the use of Bruner materials in the classroom he writes: 'Relevance, then, is the key to availing the instructional process of emotional and imaginal issues' (p. 208). And he notes that 'it has often been the disappointing case in this writer's experience that the more adept a teacher becomes at providing children with opportunities to express their inner lives, the more glaring may be her failures to establish relevant points of correspondence in the subject matter if her own knowledge of the subject matter is shallow' (p. 208).

The loose ends begin to come together. American work in social studies with fifth-graders throws up patterns discernible in an English controversial issues programme for adolescents.

I think the underlying pattern is roughly this. The older academic tradition asked students to work without seeing the logic of their studies. Motivation was achieved through a system of extrinsic rewards and punishments embellished with the cosmetics of the teacher's personality and enthusiasm. The revolt of the progressives – saving Dewey, who was grossly misinterpreted – tended to child-centredness and intrinsic motivation, but neglected the systematic development of subject logic. Now authentic instructional materials produced by new curricular developments are challenging teachers to make a synthesis of the progressive tradition and the academic tradition.

In the developing situation it becomes clear that the difficulty teachers face is in having enough understanding of motivation and enough grasp of the subject of instruction to recognize in flexible classroom situations those moves, bids and strategies on the part of the students which promise relevant motivation.

Now, of course, the experimental psychology of motivation is relevant to this problem as is research in the subject areas of the curriculum. But the most urgent need is for workers interested in motivation to face the problem of application by the close study and interpretation of the classroom. This means a good deal of pioneer exploratory work based on tapes, videotapes or direct observation. We need to look at the educational process in close up.

References

1. Dorothy M. Fraser, *Deciding What to Teach*. Project on the Instructional Program of the Public Schools. (Washington, D.C.: National Education Association, 1963).
2. Richard Jones, *Fantasy and Feeling in Education*. (New York: Harper and Row, 1968. Paperback edition, 1970).

An Appeal for Evidence of the Effectiveness of an Alternative Role to that of Neutral Chairman in Promoting Rational Inquiry into Moral Issues

From the Journal of Further and Higher Education *1.2.1977, pp. 50–54.*

This late defence of the Project's position is drawn from an academic interchange with John Hyland, then of the University of Lancaster. He has very kindly given me permission to reprint the introduction to his paper which provoked my reply.

Teaching and Legitimate Influence in Moral Education by John T. Hyland

Introduction

This article is concerned with one of the central questions of moral education: is it legitimate for teachers to influence the moral beliefs and opinions of their pupils? Legitimate teacher influence will be taken to cover all the teaching which is consistent with the development of rationality and autonomy in pupils.[1]

The most common arguments in the contemporary debate on this topic stress the importance of 'teacher neutrality' in moral education. Indeed, this notion of 'neutrality' has preoccupied (not to say bewitched) educators in the last few years and, as Alan Montefiore[2] remarked in a recent symposium on the neutral teacher, much of the interest in the topic stems directly from the work of the influential Humanities Curriculum Project. Just recently one of our leading moral philosophers. R. M. Hare,[3] has turned his attention to the subject and has expressed qualified approval of the approach to value issues outlined by the Project team.

I wish to examine the implications which this stress on neutrality has for moral education. In particular, I will contend that the neutral teaching strategy advocated by the Humanities Project is incompatible with the objectives of the moral educator, and that attempts to change the emphasis by referring to this strategy as 'impartial' rather than 'neutral' or by drawing distinctions between 'substantial' and 'methodological' (or 'procedural') neutrality only serve to confuse matters and do not help us to understand the nature of the moral educator's task. Finally, I will argue that, though a teacher must be committed to fundamental moral values if he is to be a moral educator, this does not preclude the possibility of the employment of rational procedures in the enterprise.

The Humanities Project did not address itself to moral education as such, nor did it question whether it is legitimate for teachers to influence the moral beliefs and opinions of their pupils.* However, it is relevant to the development of rationality and autonomy in students, since it explored experimentally the conditions constraining an appeal to reason in schools.

It is important to grasp that the Humanities Project from the outset described itself as a research project.[4] It attempted to suggest how teachers might, by a course of educational action, present to themselves and study some of the problems in the interaction of the authority of schools and the nature of knowledge which have subsequently come to be discussed under the rubric, 'knowledge and control'.[5] An initial and tentative statement of these problems by the director of the Project[6] led into, but was superseded by, the work of the Project. The problem was also stated in Schools Council Working Paper No. 2, where the aim of forwarding understanding, discrimination and judgement in the human field was suggested and the hypothesis that such an aim would be frustrated by the authority of the school and teacher was adumbrated.

Crucial to an understanding of the Project is its criticism of the objectives model. Since the effects of a curriculum cannot be reliably anticipated (it is argued) principles of procedure must be justified in terms of premises at the outset. Subsequent experience will enable an evaluative judgement to be made in terms of effects.

---

* The Humanities Project was concerned only with such moral issues as were judged to be controversial in terms of its adopted definition of controversiality. It was also concerned with controversial issues of other kinds. It did not question that the school inevitably influences its students and pupils, for example, through assembly and the teaching of academic subjects with moral content. In particular, it was concerned with adolescents, not with young children. Since these were logical points, I rather naughtily left it to the philosophers to think them out.

                                                                            L.S.

Now, the context of the Project provided an unusual opportunity to explore the modulation of authority in teaching because the humanities could be construed as involving controversial issues and this provided a justification for teacher neutrality. This justification was a political one, based on the empirical definition of controversiality proposed by Dorothy Fraser,[7] the principal point of which is that a controversial issue divides the citizenry, taken with the suggestion that some teachers would see themselves as accountable to the citizenry. Such teachers would, it was felt, be interested in the possibility of teaching to a criterion of neutrality in order that they could reassure parents that they were doing everything in their power to absolve themselves of the charge that they might be using their authority to promote views which conflicted with those of the home.

The Project has worked with such teachers in pursuit of a teaching aim: to develop an understanding of social situations and human acts and of the controversial value issues which they raise. The inclusion of 'social situations' in the aim was intended to hint at the social sciences, and of 'human acts' to hint at history and the arts. The value issues might be aesthetic as well as moral. A helpful way to think of the Project is in terms of a study of 'contemporary history' and like history it is largely concerned with the judgement of the particular and substantive. Its focus is not on the formulation and justification of ethical principles. But like literature or sociology or history it involves a discourse into which moral sensitivity and moral judgement are inevitably woven.

In this context Hare is right in characterizing the position of the Project: 'In discussing substantive questions the teacher ought not to set himself up as an authority on the right answers, but . . . he may try, nevertheless, to ensure that pupils examine issues in the light of appropriate evidence and with due respect for critical standards.'[8] For example, the teacher should help students to gather evidence and conduct discussion on whether it is better to live in city or country, or what might be the motives of the officers involved in the Hitler bomb plot, or what are the arguments for getting married or whether to tackle the cycle of deprivation by removing children from their parents, but he should not (within the Project strategy) argue for living in the country, or that the bomb plot officers were all patriots or that marriage is for mugs or that slum children should be institutionalized. All these examples are drawn from real instances of work in classrooms.

Now, of course, the distinction between substantive and procedural values is not clear-cut; but Hyland[9] is quite simply in error if he argues that only clear-cut distinctions are significant for practice. The distinctions drawn here can be used as criteria in teaching and, when these are interpreted within the HCP tradition, the result is a teaching style so radically different from that normally observed as to constitute an alternative pedagogy.

So far I have argued that the specification adopted by the Humanities Project can be defended in terms of certain premises as an intelligent experimental response to a dilemma in the accountability of schools and that, effectively operationalized, it provides the framework of an alternative pedagogy.

Moreover, although it is extremely difficult to meet the criteria of the neutral chairman role, the evidence strongly suggests that the main barriers are not logical, but are associated with teacher skills, pupil expectations and the authority of the school. In the face of these difficulties the question naturally arises whether it is worth tackling them merely for the sake of accountability to the citizenry. On the whole, I think not: if I am right, then the ultimate justification for the Project must be found in its effects.

I assert that the observational evidence suggests that in the development of oracy, literacy and the capacity for reflective inquiry the procedure of the discussion of evidence under a neutral chairman is quite unusually effective as compared with orthodox teaching procedures. The test might be to compare tapes of good HCP work with tapes of alternative procedures, and it is, of course, comparative judgement of the sort this would allow which has convinced the body of teachers who value the strategy.

Such a comparison will, I believe, show among other features a development within HCP of moral discourse and moral judgement. At this point the Humanities Project touches Hyland's concerns for moral education, and the point is surely so heavily empirical that it cannot be considered adequately without the careful comparative analysis of classroom transactions. It is the philosopher's conviction that he can do the work from his armchair that is the problem! This is what allows Mary Warnock[10] to conclude that the teacher who tries to be neutral will fail as a teacher – without observing the activity itself.

I am claiming that the Project procedure does markedly better than any other teaching strategy I have been able to observe in emancipating students from dependence on authority to acceptance of the need to justify judgement by reasons. In this sense it is *adult* education.

The most contentious value position built into the Project is the belief in the use of speculative reason operating upon doubt as the medium of advance towards truth. Men who do not know what is true of things take care to hold fast to what is certain, so that, if they cannot satisfy their intellects by knowledge (*scienza*), their wills at least may rest on consciousness (*coscienza*).[11] This position associates the Project with those in religion who believe in the primacy of conscience, with Charlotte Mason's doctrine of neutrality as a form of respect for the pupil as a person,[12] and with MAN: a Course of Study's injunction to the teacher to 'validate the search'.[13] With Freire,[14] the Project shows concern for education as an instrument of freedom through the development of students' powers. With Gramsci it shares the idea that 'the last phase of the common school must be conceived and structured as the decisive phase, whose aim is to create the fundamental values of "humanism", the intellectual self-discipline and the moral independence'.[15] Across a whole range of religious and political views we can find the dispute between knowers and seekers. The humanities Project strategy validates the student's right to be a seeker by containing the teacher's need to declare himself a knower.

The aspiration is necessarily unsuccessful to some degree, but complete success is inevitably so rare in education (as in all human endeavour) that we must be sure that we have committed ourselves to something worth failing in – both in terms of worth of aspiration and in terms of the effects of flawed performance.

It is within such a context that I turn to some of Hyland's problems.

First, respect for persons expressed procedurally is a matter of respect for persons in the working group. There is a dilemma in the face of the expression of, say, a racist view which shows a lack of respect for persons in a broader sense. The choice is to oppose the view and place one's position as chairman at risk or to settle down to a long process of discussion within the group in the face of evidence (including evidence expressing the view the teacher would represent in his own person). It is an agonizing choice. A group with whom one had a good understanding might tolerate a procedural failure in a chairman under such stress. But in our project on teaching about race relations we have actually found that in direct confrontations of the kind we are now envisaging even the non-neutral, non-HCP teachers tend towards the HCP response. 'We ought to send all the wogs home' evokes 'What makes you say that?' or 'How would that look in practice then?' rather than 'I won't have that kind of talk' or even 'Let me argue against you.' A majority of teachers *in practice* appear to incline to a more neutral role in precisely those circumstances which Hyland and others visualize as most invalidating it: to be argued down by the teacher in such circumstances is not, they believe, to be convinced, but to be defeated.

Bailey's[16] position that the Project seems to imply that value judgements cannot in the last resort be rationally defended seems odd in the face of the fact that the Project appears to be attempting to implement rational discussion as a means towards value judgements. If a licence to discuss value judgements implies relativism, then surely all those who discuss ethics are implicated!

But the plot thickens when Wall asserts 'that thinking for oneself about moral issues must satisfy certain criteria and be subject to certain restrictions'.[17] Is he arguing that autonomous morality is dependent upon the special expertise of the moral philosopher? If not, the development of a grasp of the appropriate criteria is surely likely to depend upon progressive attempts at moral reasoning. The application of HCP to moral education would on this argument rest upon the effectiveness of the strategy in evoking moral inquiry among the pupils: it stands up well to this criterion I think. For it appears that the ordinary procedures and climate of the school are not favourable to the development of moral inquiry, or indeed of reflective discussion, at any rate among adolescents of average attainment. I think this is because of the use of authority to warrant knowledge. But I'd be glad to learn from audiotapes of classrooms of roles other than that of neutral chairman which seem to Hyland – or to other readers – to offer alternative approaches to the problem of developing autonomy based on reason. How does a teacher (as Hyland suggests) 'ask if honesty is more important than kindness in a particular situation' while declaring his own answer, and at the same time encourage inquiry? As to the problem whether honesty and kindness are virtues which make up the framework within which moral thinking can take place, those who can raise such a problem need to seek an answer; but it is not an issue that we have found raised so far, for the normal assumption seems to be that they do.

References

1. K. Strike, 'Autonomy and Control: Toward a Theory of Legitimate Influence' in *The Philosophy of Open Education* ed. D. Nyberg, (London: Routledge and Kegan Paul, 1975), p. 177ff.

2. In *Philosophers Discuss Education* ed. S. C. Brown (London: Macmillan, 1975), p. 196.

3. R. M. Hare, 'Value Education in Pluralist Society' in *Proceedings of the Philosophy of Education Society of Great Britain*, 10, (1976), pp. 7–23.

4. Lawrence Stenhouse, 'The Humanities Curriculum Project' in *Journal of Curriculum Studies*, 1.1.1968, pp. 26–33.

5. Michael F. D. Young, *Knowledge and Control* (London: Collier Macmillan, 1971).

6. Lawrence Stenhouse, *Culture and Education* (London: Nelson, 1967).

7. Dorothy M. Fraser, *Deciding What to Teach*. Project on the Instructional Program of the Public Schools. (Washington, D.C.: National Education Association, 1963).

8. R. M. Hare, 'Value education in a pluralist society' in *Proceedings of the Philosophy of Education Society of Great Britain*, 10, (1976), pp. 7–23.

9. John T. Hyland, 'Teaching and legitimate influence in moral education' in *Journal of Further and Higher Education*, 1.2.1977, pp. 41–9.

10. Mary Warnock, 'The neutral teacher' in *Progress and Problems in Moral Education* edited by Monica Taylor. (Slough, Bucks: NFER Publishing Company, 1975).

11. Vico, Giambattista (1720–21) *Scienza Nuova* para 137, translated by Bergin and Fisch. (Ithaca, N.Y.: Cornell, 1968).

12. Charlotte Mason, An Essay towards a Philosophy of Education (London: Kegan Paul & Co, 1925).

13. *MAN: a Course of Study* was developed by the Educational Development Center, Cambridge, Mass. and is published and disseminated by Curriculum Development Associates of Washington, D.C. The British dissemination agency is the Centre for Applied Research in Education, University of East Anglia.

14. Paulo Freire, *Pedagogy of the Oppressed* (London: Penguin Books, 1972); *Cultural Action for Freedom* (London: Penguin Books, 1972); *Education: The Practice of Freedom* (London: Writers and Readers Cooperative, 1974).

15. Antonio Gramsci, *Selections from the Prison Notebooks of Antonio Gramsci* edited and translated by Quintin Hoare and Geoffrey Nowell Smith. (London: Lawrence and Wishart, 1971), p. 32.

16. Charles Bailey, 'Neutrality and rationality in teaching' in *Values and Authority in Schools* edited by David Bridges and Peter Scrimshaw. (London: Hodder and Stoughton, 1975).

17. G. Wall, 'Moral autonomy and the liberal theory of moral education' in *Proceedings of the Philosophy of Education Society of Great Britain*, 8.2.1974, pp. 231–3.

Part Three: 1972–82

Introduction: Following it up

Since the Humanities Project ended in 1972, its theme has been continued in a number of ways. In a programme of research on the problems and effects of teaching about race relations funded by the Social Science Research Council and undertaken with Gajendra Verma, Bob Wild and other colleagues, I was able to look at the problems of authority in teaching in an area where certain attitudes were valued. (Stenhouse and Verma 1981,[1] Stenhouse *et al.* 1982[2]). The attempts to disseminate the work of that project pushed farther the principles and practice of sharing research and dissemination responsibilities with teachers (Sheard and Sikes 1978;[3] Sikes 1979;[4] Rudduck and Stenhouse 1979[5]). Then, from 1980 a project on library access and sixth-form studies, supported by the British Library Research and Development Division, provided an opportunity to study the process of emancipation into independent study in the sixth form. In these and other projects there continued an interest in case-study methods as a means of democratizing and demythologizing educational research.

Alongside these major projects there were other themes and other occasions through which the experience of the Humanities Project could be developed and expressed. The papers in this section are the products of such occasions. None of them is constrained by the need for consensus within a working research team.

The first paper in this section was a contribution to an issue of the *Cambridge Journal of Education* that was devoted to teaching in higher education. It is an attempt to apply some of the lessons learned in the Humanities Project to small-group discussion in other contexts. The focus is on the importance of formality, rules and contract in containing the authority of the teacher in participatory small-group work; and the point is made perhaps more clearly than it had been in the immediate context of HCP where it was expressed in the definition of the roles and responsibilities of the chairman.

In passing, I ought to note that the work of HCP has been consolidated, generalized and built out by Jean Rudduck, who directed projects in small-group teaching in higher education,[6] and later worked with a group of experienced HCP teachers to produce a book on *Learning to Teach through Discussion*.[7] The self-monitoring style of teaching developed in HCP was driven forward yet more rigorously by another colleague, John Elliott, in his Ford Teaching Project.[8]

Contract is also at stake in the following paper, this time in the planning and conduct of the secondary school curriculum. As a member of the Schools Council Working Party on the Whole Curriculum 13 to 16, I contributed this draft towards Chapter III of the report:[9] Aims and the Educational Covenant. Inevitably perhaps in such a committee, the sharp lines of the draft were softened by compromise. I was disappointed enough by this weakening of the force to take the trouble to obtain the agreement of the committee and the Schools Council representatives to my retaining copyright in my draft with a view to publishing it; but it has not previously appeared in print. Rereading it I find I still believe it to be a good basis for the background principles of a curriculum review in the broadest sense. Most schools would be pretty radically changed if they took it seriously.

The next paper is concerned with the improvement of schooling in rather a different way. 'Curriculum Research and the Art of the Teacher' was a keynote address to the 1978 conference of the Association for the Study of the Curriculum. It takes the development of the art of teaching to be the crucial factor in the improvement of schooling; and it sees curriculum as the medium in which individuals develop that art, deriving its power by virtue of its expressing ideas as classroom practice.

This concept of curriculum as a medium embodying epistemology and pedagogy and making them subject to classroom experiment is sufficiently unfamiliar to be difficult to grasp; and yet I believe that it is the experience of examining crucial issues in the nature of knowledge and the nature of teaching as they are expressed in classroom practice that is most important for our development as teachers. This view is, of course, potentially threatening to the academic establishment in education. By analogy, we might see curricula as equivalent to musical scores, and relegate talk or print about education to the status of words about music. Such a conceptualization clearly increases the power of the teacher relative to that of the academic student of education.

The last two papers attempt a synthesis.

'Towards a Vernacular Humanism' is concerned with the redistribution of access to knowledge, and thus of the means of autonomy and judgement. Its aspiration is towards a humanism that is popular rather than élite. Taking a discussion transcript from a Humanities Project classroom as evidence, it argues that an important element in the development and enrichment of discussion of human affairs and human issues is the accessibility of evidence. On this basis, an argument is mounted for a more humanistic and more vernacular social science which would be more accessible to the layman, a form of social science closer to contemporary history than to the abstraction of positivism. By the same token the findings of educational research ought to be as accessible to teachers as is possible.

The collection ends with my inaugural lecture in the University of East Anglia, 'Research as a Basis for Teaching'. Taking up again the problem of the relationship of the authority of the teacher to the representation of knowledge in teaching, I try to link this across a broad front to the idea of research-based teaching. Inquiry and instruction are put into relationship: inquiry serves to question instruction and define its status. It is inquiry or research as a means of learning that provides the learner with the insight that accepted knowledge is questionable knowledge which for present purposes does not need to be questioned. The psychological threats of this approach to knowledge are explored and application is made to both university teaching and school teaching. The paper concludes with an argument that research is applicable directly not only to the humanities and sciences whose prime purpose is the extension of knowledge, but also to the professional disciplines, where what is at stake is intelligent action.

References

1. Lawrence Stenhouse and Gajendra K. Verma, 'Educational procedures and attitudinal objectives: a paradox' in *Journal of Curriculum Studies*, 13, 4, Oct. 1981, pp. 329–37.
2. Lawrence Stenhouse *et al. Teaching about Race Relations: Problems and Effects* (London: Routledge and Kegan Paul, 1982).
3. David Sheard and Patricia Sikes, 'Teaching for better race relations?' in *Cambridge Journal of Education* 8.2/3. 1978, pp. 165–72.
4. Patricia J. Sikes (editor), *Teaching about Race Relations* (Norwich: CARE for NARTAR, University of East Anglia, 1979).

5. Jean Rudduck and Lawrence Stenhouse, *A Study in the Dissemination of Action Research* Final Report on Social Science Research Council Project, 1979, HR 3483/1.
6. Jean Rudduck, *Learning through Small Group Discussion*. (London: Society for Research in Higher Education, 1978).
7. Jean Rudduck (Editor), *Learning to Teach through Discussion* (Norwich: Centre for Applied Research in Education, University of East Anglia, 1979).
8. Ford T (no date) Ford Teaching Project. Unit 1: Patterns of Teaching (5 booklets); Unit 2: Research Methods (8 booklets); Unit 3: Hypotheses (2 booklets); Unit 4: Teacher Case Studies (4 booklets). (1st edition, Norwich: Centre for Applied Research in Education. Now available from Ford T/CARN, Cambridge Institute of Education).
9. Schools Council *The Whole Curriculum 13 to 16* (Working Paper No. 53) (London: Evans Methuen Educational, 1975).

Teaching Through Small-Group Discussion: formality, rules and authority

A paper appearing in the Cambridge Journal of Education, *2.1.1972, pp. 18–24.*

This paper is concerned with participatory small-group teaching in situations where the tutor talks, let us say, less than 25 per cent of the time, where he is concerned to throw a great deal of responsibility on to the students and to develop their autonomy, and where he accepts that the work of the group should take account of the needs of all its members. There is no suggestion that all small-group work should be of this sort, merely that this is one useful kind of work.

Small-group discussion, with its related activities, including role play, simulations and educational games and problems, is essentially cooperative and essentially participatory. The basic principle is to place all the resources available within the group at the disposal of all the individuals within it. The group must feel that everyone's needs count.

This is not easy to achieve within the competitive assumptions of our educational system. Nor is cooperative working typical of most spontaneous groups, at least in our society. Accordingly, tutors generally have to teach students to work in groups, to value different styles and types of participation and to resist the temptation to commandeer the group to serve one's own needs. The problem of developing satisfactory small group work depends as much on student training as on teacher training.

I wish to argue here that successful participant small groups in education are likely to be formal rather than informal. They call for rules and conventions. Many seminars fail because tutors see them as informal occasions.

A spontaneous example of the development of conventions is reported by Bjerstedt.[1] 'It was demonstrated by Beck[2] (1956, 116 *et seq.*) that groups solving problems often showed initial phases where dominant individuals played an important role followed by phases where this dominance was replaced by some kind of regulated "division of labour": each individual was expected to try in turn (*Reihum-Phänomen*). As ability to do the task in question developed, the dominance rank order (in certain respects comparable to the pecking order of hens) was thus replaced by rules of procedure; to express it more picturesquely, but also more loosely: "right of strength" was followed by "right of law".'

Small groups develop as part of their sub-cultures principles of procedure which have the status of conventions or rules. Successful teaching in participatory small groups depends on the establishment of procedures appropriate to educational aims, and this can best be done if conventions and rules are made explicit by the tutor. Usually he will be able to propose a number of rules and conventions at the outset, but others will have to be evolved in the group. In the latter case they should still be made explicit and clearly related to the group's task.

The intrusion of the tutor into the small group now needs to be considered. When he enters the group, he is immediately located in a position of authority and leadership, and he carries two types of authority. R. S. Peters[3] has distinguished these as being 'in authority' and being 'an authority'. The teacher is 'in authority' in so far as he is the representative of 'an impersonal normative order or value system which regulates behaviour basically because of acceptance of it on the part of those who comply'. He is 'an authority' by virtue of 'his special competence, training or insight'.

The teacher in higher education is in authority as a representative of his institution, and in this respect his authority is heavily reinforced by his position as internal examiner. This authority is consciously present to his students: he is seen as defining the task and the situation in which it will be tackled.

The teacher is *an* authority by virtue of his knowledge of the subject. Most students regard most teachers as experts, and the teacher is seen as a man of knowledge. There is also a sense in which the teacher is in authority within his role as an authority. He can be seen as adding to his own knowledge of the subject a grasp of 'the impersonal normative order or value system' which represents the subject as a discipline. He is familiar and at home with both academic institutions – conferences, journals, personnel – and the criteria and norms accepted in his academic field.

The consequence of this authority position of the teacher is that students brought up in our system expect him to play the role of instructor in the sense that they expect him to take responsibility for their learning. They assume an attitude of dependence. Now there are occasions – even in small groups – when instruction is appropriate. But there are also many occasions when students have to accept responsibility for their own learning, to develop autonomy as scholars, and hence to learn to use the tutor as a consultant and guide rather than as an instructor. It is in this context that participatory small groups are appropriate.

Yet the tutor cannot simply and easily renounce the authority which leads students to believe that the initiative and effort should come primarily from him. He enters the small group trailing with him the authority of his own knowledge of the university or college of which he is a delegate and of the academic field of which he is a representative. This authority may be reinforced by personal charisma and by the authority of age. All in all the teacher cannot escape the responsibilities of a leadership position and the problems in the area of authority-dependency which this sets up.

If a teacher handles his authority unselfconsciously as a matter of personal habit, he usually induces a relatively passive dependency relationship.

Students are reluctant to participate and anxious to interpret the rules of the situation. If he does not make the conventions explicit, his students can interpret them only by observing the tutor. Their task is to study his behaviour in order to understand the situation in which they are placed. He is for them an experimental subject. Unless they can develop from observation consistent theories about what he is up to, his authority will appear arbitrary. The need of the students to develop such theories will reinforce the teacher's position as centre of interest in the group. The students will be teacher-oriented rather than task-oriented.

Sometimes when a teacher is attempting to convey to the group procedures of thinking, he can find no way of defining them except through his authority. Such is the method of Socrates in the Platonic dialogues; and it accounts for their one-sidedness. I would argue that in small group situations he should avoid this if he can; and this suggests that he should explicitly confine his authority in the group by rules and conventions.

I have argued that participatory small group situations, which are often seen by tutors as spontaneous and informal, are likely to be most effective as educational enterprises when they are relatively structured and formal. The group needs to adopt explicitly rules and conventions governing procedures and the role of the tutor in the group also requires some formal definition accessible to the students. If I am right, this is an encouraging position for teachers since it suggests that competence in small-group teaching is to a large extent capable of being learnt. It is not some personal or intuitive possession in the absence of which the teacher cannot be effective.

The next step is to examine what rules, conventions and roles are 'appropriate'.

Here there are two areas of consideration: the logic of the task and the psychology of groups. Crudely, we might regard the first as the message and the second as the medium; and we should immediately blur the distinction and say that medium and message are inextricably entangled. For example, a group dependent on the authority of persons is not likely to learn effectively the authority of research procedures.

Educational tasks are concerned with the promotion of learning. The task is often defined in terms of an aim; and aims are often analysed as cognitive, affective or psycho-motor. This seems to me a laboratory distinction rather than a teaching distinction, and I prefer to distinguish knowledge, application, understanding and skills.

By knowledge I mean sheer information. The distinction cannot be rigidly maintained, but most teachers will be able to give the concept meaning in their subjects. In teaching the need for knowledge expresses itself as concern for 'coverage'. Every teacher is familiar with a feeling of concern about covering the ground, and students feel this too. I do not believe that participatory small-group teaching is an effective way of providing coverage. What is required is individual study, individualized learning programmes and/or lectures. (These do also have other functions.) Nothing is more destructive of participatory small-group teaching than concern for coverage in this sense; and any such teaching must take place in a context of coverage supplied by other experiences.

By application, I mean the application of principles to particular cases. The principles may have been learnt as knowledge or may be taught through application. They are at a higher level of generalization than cases, but gather their strength from their effectiveness in application to cases. The task of application is a suitable one for small-group teaching.

Understanding is essentially relational. It consists in establishing significant relationships of knowledge or of knowledge and skills. Application is one such relationship. The essential point about understanding is that it is both personal and public. An understanding implies a grasp of a relationship on the part of an individual. It is an experience leading the individual to claim 'I understand'. Understanding in this sense is opposed to not understanding. But it is characteristic of education that it is concerned with public criteria by which understanding can be assessed. A personal understanding must be tried out against such criteria. In this sense, understanding is opposed to misunderstanding. The promotion of understanding is a suitable task for small-group teaching.

Skills are performances which are generalizable to some degree. That is to say they can be practised. One problem in this is that they may be practised as exercises in situations which are relatively meaningless. The application of skills, like the application of principles, is a suitable task for small-group teaching.

Participatory small-group teaching is thus effective as a critical exchange in which significant relationships are suggested and explored in order to promote an understanding of the structure and logic of knowledge or a grasp of the problems of applying knowledge or skills in various situations.

Tasks which would be suitable for small groups might be, for example, applying engineering principles to the design of a particular bridge, promoting an understanding of the wave/particle duality of electrons or of *Hamlet*, or applying skills in the design of electronic apparatus to an experimental problem in psychology.

Now, given any such educational tasks as these, it is possible, though challenging, to work out the logic of the task in terms of rules for the group and roles for the teacher. But it is also possible so to push the logic that we fail to take account of the psychology of the group. This is an important failing in an educational setting since the group is there to learn, that is, the task is there for the sake of the group, not the group for the sake of the task. In a real-life situation, the test is whether the bridge stays up. In an educational situation the test is whether *all* members of the group learned in designing it. Moreover, lack of attention to the psychology of the group can lead to crises and even problems of control.

Now, of course, sensitivity to groups is important, even vital. But it is also helpful to recognize that there are certain patterns of small-group work which have stood the test of experience and obviously help us in finding a ground-base of rules and roles which harmonize the logic of the task and the psychology of groups. Many such patterns have been reported in the literature, for example, by Abercrombie,[4] Collier,[5] Nisbet,[6] Richardson[7] and Rudduck[8] in this country. My concern here is to argue that a pattern appropriate to the logic of the task needs to be adopted, rules and roles need to be defined as explicitly as possible within that pattern and the proceedings need to be handled with faithful adherence to those rules and with sensitivity.

In summary, the position I am advancing is as follows:

1. Effective group work depends upon the establishment of rules and conventions – it is formal.
2. The teacher will be most effective if he defines his role and thereby makes his use of authority also rule-governed, and his areas of initiative clear. Small-group work is not forwarded by the renunciation of authority, but by its definition. Effective leadership is relatively formal.

3. Both group rules and teaching roles need to be logically consonant with the demands of an explicit task.
4. Group rules and teaching roles need to take account of the psychology of groups.
5. A variety of reports of patterns of small-group teaching exist and provide a range of choices which have some claim to meet the demands of 3 and 4 above.
6. Given that effective small-group teaching is relatively formal and that reported patterns offer precedents, it is possible to increase one's effectiveness in working with groups by learning, i.e., effectiveness is not merely a function of personality supported by mystique.

References

1. Åke Bjerstedt, '"Interaction competence" among children: the rotation phenomenon in small groups' in *Journal of Psychology*, 61, (1965), pp. 145–52.
2. R. Beck, *Grundformen sozialen Verhaltens* (Stuttgart: Enke, 1954). (Cited by Bjerstedt).
3. Richard S. Peters, *Ethics and Education* (London: George Allen and Unwin, 1966).
4. M. L. J. Abercrombie, *Aims and Techniques of Group Teaching* (London: Society for Research in Higher Education, 1971).
   M. L. J. Abercrombie, P. M. Terry *et al.* 'Whatever happened to group dynamics?' in *Proceedings of the Conference on Small-Group Teaching*, University of London Institute of Education, 4–5 January, 1971.
5. K. G. Collier, 'Syndicate methods: further evidence and comments' in *Universities Quarterly*, Autumn, (1969), pp. 431–6.
6. Stanley Nisbet, 'A method for advanced seminars' in *Universities Quarterly*, June, (1966), pp. 349–55.
7. Elizabeth Richardson, *Group Study for Teachers* (London: Routledge and Kegan Paul, 1967).
8. Jean Rudduck, *Learning through Small Group Discussion* (London: Society for Research in Higher Education, 1978); *Learning to Teach through Discussion* (Editor) (Norwich: Centre for Applied Research in Education, 1979).

The Aims of the Secondary School

A draft towards a Schools Council working paper on the whole curriculum.[1]

1. The curriculum can be seen as an expression of a covenant between the schools and society. Aims must be seen in the context of claims.
2. The first claim on the school is that of the pupils, for whose welfare the school exists.
3. There are some difficulties in thinking in terms of the needs of pupils, for who is to define them? Perhaps it is better to think in terms of the *demands* pupils can reasonably make of the school.
4. The pupils have a right to demand that the school shall treat them impartially and with respect as persons.
5. The pupils have a right to demand that the school's aims and purposes shall be communicated to them openly, and discussed with them as the need arises.
6. The pupils have a right to demand that the procedures and organizational arrangements of the school should be capable of rational justification and that the grounds of them should be available to them.
7. The pupils have a right to expect that the school will offer them impartial counsel on academic matters, and if they desire it, with respect to personal problems.
8. Pupils who live in home or environmental circumstances which make it difficult for them to meet the demands which the school from time to time places on them have a right to expect special consideration and compassion from the school.
9. Pupils have a right to expect that the school will make unabated efforts to provide them with the basic skills necessary for living an autonomous life in our society.
10. Pupils have a right to expect that the school will provide them with a general education which will equip them to enter upon a job and which will provide an adequate basis for further specialized education and training. Where unemployment is high, the school cannot meet the first of these demands, and morale suffers without the school having it in

its power to remedy the situation. The second of these demands implies that the school should pay as much attention to the demands of such courses as ONC as to the demands of its own sixth form.

11. Pupils have a right to expect that the school will do its best to make available to them the major public traditions in knowledge, arts, crafts and sports, which form the basis of a rich life in an advanced society.

12. Pupils have a right to expect that the school will enable them to achieve some understanding of our society as it stands and that it will equip them to criticize social policy and contribute to the improvement of society.

13. Parents also have claims upon the school.

14. Parents have a right to demand that the school show a degree of respect and understanding for parental policy with respect to the upbringing of the child and for parental values. The schools, however, are not expected merely to endorse parental values.

15. Parents have a right to demand of the school some understanding of their problems with respect to the upbringing and particularly the education of their children. For example, parents often face the problem of a child growing away from them as a result of extended education and there is a real conflict of values between family solidarity and individual achievement in such cases. The school does not operate in a vacuum and nor do its aims and values have any unquestionable validity.

16. Parents have a right to expect that the school will attempt to meet the legitimate claims of pupils impartially.

17. Society has claims upon the school.

18. Education and the quality of living depend upon the productivity of industry. Society has a right to demand of the school that it equip its pupils to contribute to the economic commonweal. If pupils are seen as making a contribution which does not cast them in the role of instruments, but develops their initiative, there is no conflict between this demand and the interests of the pupil (see 10 above).

19. Society has a right to expect that the schools ensure that pupils have a general knowledge of law and democratic process and a respect for public property including, however, an understanding of how to use political process to change the law and how to defend oneself from injustice.

20. Society has a right to expect that the schools will foster talent of whatever sort which can make a contribution to the richness of life.
21. Society has a right to expect the school to foster, so far as it is within its power, the ability to realize as an individual the paradoxical combination of conviction and tolerance of others which is fundamental to democracy.
22. There is, in addition to these claims, an obligation on the school to attempt to realize in its teaching the standards of quality, integrity or truth inherent in the content it teaches.
23. It is clear that the claims and obligations laid on the school are too onerous to be met. They are the criteria to which it should work, recognizing that (like all worthwhile aspirations) they are not perfectly achievable.
24. Given such criteria, the task of embodying them in the curriculum is in part at least a technical one. It is also a matter of establishing a degree of precision as these very broad values are translated into the practice of the school.

Reference

1. Schools Council, *The Whole Curriculum 13 to 16* (Working Paper No. 53) (London: Evans Methuen Educational, 1975).

Curriculum Research and the Art of the Teacher

From Curriculum, *1.1.1980, pp. 40–4. (First delivered as an address to the 1978 conference of the Association for the Study of the Curriculum.)*

What is a curriculum as we now understand the word? It has changed its meaning as a result of the curriculum movement. It is not a syllabus – a mere list of content to be covered – nor is it even what German speakers would call a *Lehrplan* – a prescription of aims and methods and content. Nor is it in our understanding a list of objectives.

Let me claim that it is a symbolic or meaningful object, like

Shakespeare's first folio, not like a lawnmower; like the pieces and board of chess, not like an apple tree. It has a physical existence but also a meaning incarnate in words or pictures or sound or games or whatever.

In our imagination let us bring it into this room. The doors open and it enters on a porter's barrow, since it is too heavy to carry. Two large boxes are full of books for pupils to use in the classroom. A third contains educational games and simulations and a fourth, posters, slides, film strips and overhead projector transparencies. The big box over there is the film set – or is this the videotape version – and the smaller one beside it contains audiotape and gramophone records. The seventh, and in this case the last, box holds the teachers' books and materials.

Who made it? Well, perhaps a curriculum research and development group funded by Nuffield or the Schools Council or the American National Science Foundation or Stiftung Volkswagenwerk. Or perhaps a group of teachers from various parts of the country working under an editor for a publisher. Or perhaps a teachers' centre group. Or a school – Abraham Moss or Stantonbury or some less fabled place.

So there it stands, a palpable educational artefact. But what use is it to a student or a teacher? Often apparently, not much. Like some wedding presents it is in a month or two more likely to be found in the attic than in the living room. But that analogy is not quite right. A better one is the affluent outhouse containing the unused golf-clubs, canoe, sailing dinghy, skis, ice skates and glider. All the possessions which implied not simply ownership but learning, the development of new skills, on the part of the owner. Mr Toad's curriculum of derelict skiffs and canary-coloured caravan. Material objects cast aside because the teacher was not prepared to face the role of learner they forced upon him.

'No curriculum development without teacher development', reads one of the poker-work mottoes we hung on our wall during the Humanities Project and haven't taken down. But that does not mean, as it often seems to be interpreted to mean, that we must train teachers in order to produce a world fit for curricula to live in. It means that by virtue of their meaningfulness curricula are not simply instructional means to improve teaching but are expressions of ideas to improve teachers. Of course, they have a day-to-day instructional utility: cathedrals must keep the rain out. But the students benefit from curricula not so much because they change day-to-day instruction as because they improve teachers.

The most satisfying aspects of the Humanities Project, MAN: a Course of Study, and the Race Project, from my point of view, is the fact that they have each produced virtuoso and highly intelligent teaching. This in turn has transformed teachers' images of themselves. They have become powerful people because of their confidence in their art.

In our present educational situation there is no prospect of benefit to pupils more significant than the improvement of the art of the teacher.

A curriculum, if it is worthwhile, expresses in the form of teaching materials and criteria for teaching a view of knowledge and a conception of the process of education. It provides a framework in which the teacher can develop new skills and relate them as he does so to conceptions of knowledge and of learning. We are concerned with the exercise of skills in the service of meaning; and I believe that to be an acceptable definition of the practice of an art.

The teacher is an artist whose medium is interpersonal transactions of knowledge. Knowledge here means information and meaning so structured as to expose the problems of the warrant for truth and to provide the organization of ideas – Barzun called it 'intellect' – which supports active thinking and reflective assimilation of new experience.

Now the really important thing about curriculum research is that, in contrast to books about education, it invites the teacher to improve his art by the exercise of his art. Teacher education has too often assumed that reading books is the way a teacher gets access to ideas which can be expressed in his practice. Whether they are philosophical works or accounts of experience – such as A. S. Neill's books on Summerhill for example – books tend to put the teacher in the power of the expert. Who can carry a full teaching load and still keep up with the university education lecturer who specializes in Plato or Dewey or Piaget or the expert prominent enough to be allowed to – and even financed to – visit Summerhill – and Countesthorpe and Stantonbury and Gordonstown.

On the other hand, traditional educational theory – book learning about education – is something you can be very good at without actually getting to know any teachers. In America your status as a university professor of education is actually higher if you have never taught in schools, even when your fame is based on telling schoolteachers how you think they should teach. In a Scottish College of Education the lecturers in education are traditionally exempted from – and thus barred from – supervising teaching practice in order to ensure that they have sufficient time for study to prevent their standards from falling to those of the English.

I am, however, not arguing that all educational thinkers and doers should be teachers, but that all should pay teachers the respect of translating their ideas into curriculum. And that means enough contact with classroom reality or enough consultancy with teachers to discipline all ideas by the problems of practice.

Only in curricular form can ideas be tested by teachers. Curricula are hypothetical procedures testable only in class-rooms. All educational ideas must find expression in curricula before we can tell whether they are day dreams or contributions to practice. Many educational ideas are not found wanting, because they cannot be found at all.

If someone comes along asking you to adopt an idea or strive after an objective, political maturity or basic literacy, ask him to go away and come back with a curriculum. Or give you a sabbatical to do so for him. What does 'back to basics' mean? What books? What procedures? What time allocations? What investments? MAN: a Course of Study in every school? It is the only graded scientific reading scheme I know!

Some people shout their plans for the reform of their football team from the terraces, Cloughie provides a curriculum instead. There are as many education rowdies as football rowdies about today. And one or two are ex-players!

But I am not simply being practical about ideas, or saying that all ideas ought to be subject to testing by teachers and expressed in forms that make that testing possible. I am claiming that the expression of educational ideas in curricular form provides a medium for the development – and if necessary the autonomous self-development – of the teacher as artist.

To say that teaching is an art does not imply that teachers are born, not made. On the contrary artists learn and work extraordinarily hard at it. But they learn through the critical practice of their art.

Idea and action are fused in practice. Self-improvement comes in escaping from the idea that the way to virtuosity is the imitation of others – pastiche – to the realization that it is the fusion of idea and action in one's own performance to the point where each can be 'justified' in the sense that it is fully expressive of the other. So the idea is tuned to the form of the art and the form used to express the idea.

Thus in art ideas are tested in form by practice. Exploration and interpretation lead to revision and adjustment of idea and of practice. If my words are inadequate, look at the sketchbook of a good artist, a play in rehearsal, a jazz quartet working together. That, I am arguing, is what good teaching is like. It is not like routine engineering or routine management.

Note, however, that the process of developing the art of the artist is always associated with *change* in ideas and practice. An artist becomes stereotyped or derelict when he ceases to develop. There is no mastery, always aspiration. And the aspiration is about ideas – content – as well as about performance – execution of ideas.

Thus the process of developing one's art as a teacher – or the art of teaching, which develops through individual artists – is a dialectic of idea and practice not to be separated from change. May I quote Mao Tse Tung without your generalizing my views about life from my choice of source?

> 'Whoever wants to know a thing has no way of doing so except by coming into contact with it, that is, by living (practising) in its environment.'

and

> 'If you want to know a certain thing or a certain class of things directly, you must personally participate in the practical struggle to change reality, to change that thing or class of things, for only thus can you come into contact with them as phenomena; only through personal participation in the practical struggle to change reality can you uncover the essence of that thing or class of things and comprehend them.'

Certainly, this seems true of art, including the practical art of teaching. Perhaps Mao's deviationism was to transpose 'praxis' as a cornerstone of an epistemology with Germanic roots and render it as an expression of the experience of one to whom politics was in practice an art.

In advancing the view that curriculum constitutes both the medium of education of the pupil and the medium for the teacher's learning of the art of teaching, I am making a claim sufficiently novel for me to feel that an analogy may be helpful, but the analogy must not be taken to be too close. It is a crutch to understanding to be thrown away as soon as possible.

I compare a school to a good repertory theatre. With a manager – the head; a company of actors – the staff; a technical support staff – the librarians, lab technicians, audio-visual experts; and an audience – the pupils or students. Both theatre and school embody the interaction of different groups of people: artists on the one hand, their public on the other. It is as intelligible for a repertory company to claim to have educated its audience as it is for a school to claim to have educated its pupils.

But note that a good repertory company is also concerned with the development of its actors as artists and of the skills and arts of its technicians too. And the medium of this development is the very same medium as that which entertains – motivates – and educates its audience. It is the curriculum of the theatre: the plays.

The good company chooses plays on several grounds. They must overall appeal to an audience. An empty theatre is not really a theatre at all. They ought to be justifiable as worthwhile. So they will say, 'We are sorry we did *Confessions of a Windowcleaner* in May: we know it's rubbish, but it allowed us to do *Antony and Cleopatra* to a smaller audience in February'. Importantly, however, they should also develop the actors. 'We chose *Antony and Cleopatra* rather than *Othello* because Larry and Viv were just at the point where those parts would most contribute to their development. And, you know, the audience profits immensely from the development of our art. It is not done at their expense.'

There is yet a deeper level at which the artist learns: he not only learns his art, he also learns through his art. Thus the actor learns about life and people and moral dilemmas through participation in plays. And similarly, I learned through *teaching* literature and history something of what literature and history have to teach.

Curriculum is the medium through which the teacher can learn his art. Curriculum is the medium through which the teacher can learn knowledge. Curriculum is the medium through which the teacher can learn about the nature of education. Curriculum is the medium through which the teacher can learn about the nature of knowledge. And curriculum is the best medium through which the teacher *qua* teacher can learn about these because it enables him to test ideas by practice and hence to rely on his judgement rather than on the judgement of others.

This learning of the teachers need not and should not conflict with the welfare of the pupils. This is not just because pupils benefit from the development of the teacher's art in the long run. It is that the teacher's art is to benefit the pupils and is not being adequately practised unless that benefit is there. Of course, there are failures, but at some point failure has to be abandoned.

To summarize and concretize what I have been claiming. MAN: a Course of Study makes the ideas of Bruner testable and is in turn testable by them. The Humanities Project makes the ideas of Schools Council Working Paper No. 2[1] testable, and is testable by them. And so for all those curriculum projects which are not teacher-proof but open to teacher judgement.

This means that the improvement of schooling through curriculum research and development is about the improvement of the art of the teacher. It is not about the improvement of students' intended learning outcomes *without* improving the art of teaching.

The curriculum movement of the 1960s and 1970s has pursued the hypothesis that the improvement of the knowledge content of education can be achieved only by developing the art of the teacher to make possible inquiry, discovery and discussion-based modes of learning. The shift is like the shift from apron stage to proscenium or from realism to the theatre of the absurd. The argument is that pupils need to know earlier what mature experts understand about the speculative function of knowledge.

The barriers to that development, apart from the contextual lack of understanding provided by some local authorities, teacher educators, HMI and the like, are that for the most part neither teachers nor pupils recognize teaching as an art. Hence teachers do not see their own development as key to the situation, in the same way as actors or sculptors or musicians do. And pupils do not understand – nor do teachers generally share the understanding with them – the significance of experiment in the classroom and their role in it.

No change can be introduced without being explained and justified to pupils. No experiment can be mounted without its purposes, duration and criteria being presented to pupils and without their being invited to monitor its effects on them, both in process and in outcome.

We must be dedicated to the improvement of schooling. The improvement of schooling is bound to be experimental: it cannot be dogmatic. The experiment depends on the exercise of the art of teaching and improves that art. It depends too on the art of learning and improves that art. The substantive content of the arts of teaching and learning is curriculum.

I am claiming, therefore, that the most important substance of in-service education or autonomous self-development can best be curriculum. Curriculum presents educational ideas interpreted in the art of the classroom. You will never improve the art of teaching by mere reading lists any more than you will improve the art of acting by mere reading of Stanislavsky. Reading has its place: its place is to support reflection about action. And the medium of classroom action is curriculum.

A great deal of work put into curriculum in the last decade or so appears to have yielded less than in fact it has. This is because there is a tendency to regard the implementation of curriculum as dependent upon in-service education. Where curriculum has really changed classrooms there has been in-service education in support. So it might seem that curriculum research and development cannot work without in-service education.

But put the proposition the other way round. To what extent has in-service education improved schooling? To the extent, I would answer, that it has worked through research in curriculum or teaching. We might do better to consider that curriculum study is the condition of successful in-service education, rather than in-service education the condition of successful curriculum research. It is an important message as we enter a period of potential heavy investment in in-service work.

If we are not careful we shall be back on reading lists and contributory disciplines. Only the pursuit of research directly applied to curriculum and teaching puts the teacher educator in the position of giving intellectual hostages to the teacher. Only research in curriculum and teaching puts the teacher in the power position; for he is in possession of the only valid laboratory, the classroom.

A decade of in-service education which neglects the curriculum research of the last fifteen years will not only be wasting the greatest potential of an immense investment; it will also be leading us to an unnecessary disillusion about the potential of in-service teacher development.

Reference

1. Schools Council, *Raising the School Leaving Age* (Working Paper No. 2) (London: Her Majesty's Stationery Office, 1965).

Towards a Vernacular Humanism

A paper given to the Dartington Conference, 1978.

My theme is an old-fashioned one; emancipation. In its roots, the Oxford English Dictionary tells us, it is, in Roman law, the action or process of setting children free from the *patria potestas*, the parental jurisdiction. But this is a mere nominal freeing unless it be supported by another definition the dictionary offers: delivering from intellectual, moral, or spiritual fetters. The essence of emancipation, as I conceive it, is the intellectual, moral and spiritual autonomy which we recognize when we eschew paternalism and the rule of authority and hold ourselves obliged to appeal to judgement. Emancipation rests not merely on the assertion of a right of the person to exercise intellectual, moral and spiritual judgement, but upon the passionate belief that the virtue of humanity is diminished in man when judgement is overruled by authority. That it is necessary in practice that personal judgement be so overruled by authority is testified by the universal existence of legal codes; but every overruling of judgement diminishes civilization; and the most civilized state is that in which the citizens are successfully trusted with the responsibility of judgement.

It is in this context that I want to recall the conception of humanism. And I am appealing to a rather widely recognized definition of that term. The eleventh edition of *Encyclopaedia Britannica* in 1910 described humanism in these terms:

> Any system of thought or action which assigns a predominent interest to the affairs of men as compared with the supernatural or the abstract. The term is specially applied to that movement of thought which in western Europe in the fifteenth century broke through the mediaeval traditions of scholastic theology and philosophy and devoted itself to the rediscovery and direct study of the classics. This movement was essentially a revolt against intellectual, and especially ecclesiastical, authority and is the parent of all modern developments whether intellectual, scientific or social.

And the 1973 edition of the same encyclopaedia adds 'As ecclesiastical influence waned, the protest of humanism was turned against secular orthodoxies that subordinated man to the abstract concepts of political or biological theory.'

In its origins humanism was supported by a reinterpretation of the classical literatures of Greece and Rome.

Mediaeval Christianity, following mediaeval scholastic theology, asserted that man's life on earth had value and significance only in relation to the fate of his soul in a life after death. The law that governed the affairs of the living stemmed from a supernatural god and the question was whether this law was better interpreted by mystical intuition codified in the authority of the Church or by the use of human reason, which, if it were functional, must have been created by God to lead man towards Him. Rationalists there were: Abelard, for instance, but the overwhelming authority was the law of the Church and rationalism itself was a logical analysis based on a theological metaphysics. A crucial problem was the nature of a trinitarian god. Issues of space and matter were expressed, not as four-dimensional theories, or as curved space, but as the problem of how many angels could stand on the point of a pin. In short there was little empirical study of any kind, and particularly of human affairs.

If Keats, who was supported by three hundred years of humanism, could encounter Homer in translation 'Like some watcher of the skies when a new planet swims into his ken', we see how the classical world might impact upon those imprisoned in the assumptions of scholasticism. Take as simple an example as the first book of Plato's Republic: the enjoyment of the celebrations, the reflections on the satisfactions of prosperity in old age which is seen as the fulfilment of human experience, the – literal – sophistication of debate, and the whole held together by the personal influence of Socrates, surely the archetypal television don. I suppose that each of us here can recall in the past the excitement of some period of intellectual emancipation from the *patria potestas* which marks in our personal biographies a dawn in which it was 'bliss to be alive'. That must have been how it felt to be a member of the humanist discussion whose essence lay in the fact that it opened human affairs to the play of judgement rather than to the authoritative interpretation of an overriding divine law; and with the exercise of judgement the way was open for notions of responsibility or irresponsibility seen as criteria of the process, rather than of salvation or damnation as objective assessments of performance.

But the age was a religious one, as certainly as ours is secular. Salvation and damnation remained important, but for the Protestant there was no reassurance in the authority of the Church which could underwrite the responsible conscience of the individual, and it became possible to conceive it a social duty to attempt to strengthen the powers of every man and to balance them so that his capacity to doubt, to fear and to question might be satiated by his power to reason and to judge. Such was the conviction which underlay the development of popular education in those countries, generally Calvinist or Lutheran, in which the individual conscience was seen as the source of spiritual, and by an inevitable extension civil, judgement. It was the need to equip the citizenry to face this inescapable responsibility which animated John Knox's proposal for an educational system in Scotland, for example. In the Lutheran tradition in particular the religious and the secular elements in this movement were intertwined. Thus the leaving examination for the *almueskole*, the Norwegian vulgar school, was the confirmation examination in the Lutheran Church.

Of course, we are talking of aspirations, rather than perfect achievements. In education, and particularly in schooling rather than higher education, the problems of establishing a relationship across the generations between an adult, generally prone to the assertiveness which is tamed in most of us only by the exercise of self-discipline, and a cohesive group of recalcitrant young people, unwilling to postpone ribald satisfactions in the present for the doubtful prospect of future wisdom, have led teachers to subordinate pupils by taking upon themselves the authority of knowledge, in defiance of the epistemology of the speculative humanism which I have been admiring. Yet it is arguable that the sharp authoritarian questioning which 'kept them on their toes' gave at least some pupils in the Scottish schools the weapon to assert an autonomy, albeit a belligerent one.

There was however, another strand of humanism less democratic than Protestantism which found expression in the English rather than the Scottish educational system. This humanism rejoiced in man in society by emphasizing style rather than reason as a vehicle of self-expression. The differing traditions of debate in the golden ages of the unions of the University of Glasgow and the University of Oxford catch the distinction rather well. It is, I think, this emphasis on style which has been, between the age of Disraeli, who himself embodied it, and the

Second World War, the main means and the main barrier to emancipation through education.

We are still two nations, because we produce through education a majority who are ruled by knowledge, not served by it, an intellectual, moral and spiritual proletariat, characterized by instrumental competencies rather than autonomous powers. I believe that no-one in the business of education should accept that situation as it is. If it is not to betray all that is most worthwhile in the European tradition, education must be centrally concerned with becoming the instrument of a redistribution of the means of autonomy and judgement. Yet the schools have become scholastic, conceiving knowledge as a matter of law rather than speculation, of assertion rather than enquiry, and of style.

It might be profitable to revisit humanism. The kind of humanism which 'was essentially a revolt against intellectual, and especially ecclesiastical, authority and is the parent of all modern developments whether intellectual, scientific or social'. But that humanism was essentially the humanism of an élite, because it fed upon the classics which were locked in the languages of ancient Greece and Rome. If we are to reinterpret humanism, then we must look towards a vernacular humanism, which, through the uses of languages domestically familiar to him, opens to the student a ready access to knowledge and that experience of its fruitfulness which Keats had from Homer through Chapman's intervention. An educational programme which would make realistic this aspiration is difficult to mount even under the most favourable conditions. It involves the formidable problem of expressing knowledge in those forms and activities which both invite and strengthen the judgement of the learner. Also it asks us to find an appropriate way to support, without constricting, people who are being weaned from the comforts of the authority of the *patria potestas* which asks only a cloistered virtue, to assume a more adventurous 'personal responsibility frequently involving commitment in the face of uncertainty'.

That phrase is taken from the Schools Council Working Paper No. 2 on the raising of the school-leaving age which was written by the late Derek Morrell and an H.M.I., John Witherington.[1] I think it is fair to claim that both authors were steeped in the humanist tradition to which I have referred; and although there are in the working paper clear signs of the difficulty of breaking down the barriers of a humanism of the élite, it is nonetheless a remarkably imaginative and perceptive document.

Writing of the humanities in school, the authors have this to say:

> But despite some slight awkwardness it is convenient to use the term 'humanities' to refer to that group of subjects which is predominantly concerned with men and women in relation to their environment, their communities and their own self knowledge. Within this area of the curriculum the teacher has a great deal of room for manoeuvre. It is also quite evident that the modern world cannot be understood without impinging on the field of economics, and that sociology, psychology and anthropology have a contribution to make to a teacher's armoury, even though these descriptions are unlikely to appear on the pupils' timetable.

> But the main issues are, not so much what ground to cover in the sense of what subjects to teach, but what information ideas and experiences to grapple with, through what media, and by what means. The problem is to give every man some access to a complex cultural inheritance, some hold on his personal life and his relationships with the various communities to which he belongs, some extension of his understanding of, and sensitivity towards, other human beings. The aim is to forward understanding, discrimination and judgement in the human field – it will involve reliable factual knowledge, where this is appropriate, direct experience, imaginative experience, some appreciation of the dilemmas of the human condition, of the rough hewn nature of many of our institutions, and some rational thought about them.[2]

I still find this a moving statement of an aspiration towards a humanistic education for all. And it is the text from which the Humanities Curriculum Project, of which I was formerly director, set out. In retrospect, I feel that the Project might best have been called: 'The problems and effects of teaching the humanities to adolescents'. Of the problems Working Paper No. 2 had something to say. After its statement of aspiration the authors make this comment: 'All of this may seem to some teachers like a programme for people who have both mental ability and maturity beyond the reach of most who will leave at the age of sixteen'. And they comment that the Schools Council think it is important not to assume that this is so and urge that we should 'probe by experiment in the classroom how far ordinary pupils can in fact be taken'. The problem of making effective contact with the pupils as persons is noted, and it is suggested that 'if both teachers and pupils are to move towards more adult relationships, breaks in a previously settled routine will help'. The report faces the whole range of the curriculum in this spirit and goes on to review problems of school organization and the pupil-teacher relationship where it notes that:

> Adult procedures in the classroom . . . will not be successful if a different kind of relationship between teacher and pupil obtains in the corridor or in extra-curricular activity. If the teacher emphasises, in the classroom, his common humanity with the pupils, and his common uncertainty in the face of many problems, the pupils will not take kindly to being demoted to the status of children in other relationships within the same institution.[3]

In short the authors of the report saw the barrier to emancipation through education as lying in the relationship of the adolescent pupil to the authority of his teachers and of the institution of the school.

In our project we interpreted humanities as 'human issues of universal concern' and our claim was that such issues were empirically controversial in the sense that parents, pupils and teachers would disagree about them. Thus we were able to argue, by way of the school's responsibility to the parents and the pupils, that this was an area in which the teacher could not be an arbiter of truth or warranter of knowledge. Facing the problem of knowledge and control in this form, we argued that the relaxation in authority which was necessary for the emancipation of the pupils was in the teacher's claim to be *an* authority by virtue of his knowledge, and not in the teacher's claim to be *in* authority by virtue of the legitimation of his role. Perhaps I may remark in passing that in my view most teachers meet the adolescent challenge to authority by adapting the texture of the transmission of knowledge to make it a control mechanism at the expense of speculation and by using a claim to be an authority to escape the need for rational justification of their policies in authority. I sympathize with their problem and I believe it is difficult to escape from their position without making advances in the art of teaching.

It was to this task that the Humanities Project addressed itself when it evolved a pedagogy in which pupils were asked to consider evidence bearing on human issues under the chairmanship of a teacher who would exercise a procedural authority over the discussion without taking sides. The neutral chairman role is one in which the teacher attempts to embody into the procedures of learning fundamental educational values, while not obtruding his own substantive social, political or ethical values. The position is a complex one and the form of teaching is difficult to realize successfully against the background of the institutional pressure of a school whose overall climate is designed to support the comparative authoritarianism of instructional teaching.

I cannot profitably spend much time on an exposition of this project here and so I prefer to give the transcript of a videotape in which I see the budding of the vernacular humanism to which I am aspiring. The tape is an unusually successful one. It was made in a South Wales secondary modern school in an area where grammar schools took more than half the pupil population. In short, the pupils are just ordinary people. No claim is made that the tape is evaluative of the work in the Humanities Curriculum Project. This is an unusually successful example. *I* use it not to make promises but to define an aspiration.

This group is from an all boys junior comprehensive school, set in a surburban area of South Wales. Both the chairman and the students have one-and-a-half years' experience. There are fourteen boys in this mixed ability group of fifth years. They are discussing the nature and causes of poverty. This excerpt was recorded in a television studio.

Boy: No . . .
Teacher: Does poverty equal filthy conditions?
Boy: No sir, because that artist, he wasn't living in filthy conditions . . .
Boy: Only because he didn't have a house at all.
Boy: Well if he had a house, I don't think he'd be living in filthy conditions.
Boy: You can't tell, can you?
Boy: No, 'cos he was happy, wasn't he?
Boy: We were talking a short while ago about um . . . a duke might consider himself . . . if he was short of cash, couldn't buy something, he'd consider himself in a state of poverty, if he couldn't buy a castle or something.
Teacher: If he couldn't buy a Rolls-Royce.
Boy: Yeah, if he couldn't buy something really expensive, which to his own mind, as compared to his standard of living would be a state of poverty, whereas compared to anyone else would just be a luxury. So there's probably differences of, you know, poverty, for different people at any rate . . .

Boy: In the lower class . . . well lower class, it's a . . . how shall I put it?

Boy: Poverty stricken people?

Boy: I can't say lower classes really, 'cos that'd be . . .

Teacher: Go on, we understand what you mean.

Boy: . . . lower classes, big families usually meet with poverty, I've noticed that.

Boy: Perhaps it's not that big families lead to poverty, but they get poverty stricken because they've got so many children . . .

Boys: It's the same thing . . .

Boy: You could mean poverty leads to big families, they're in a state of poverty, the family, and then they have more kids so they get more money.

(Boys all speak together for 5 secs — indistinct)

Boy: . . . They're not very intelligent you know . . . I want to press this point more I think, because surely a person who's poverty stricken who keeps having more children all the time, like this woman, she had six children, well, it's just ridiculous, isn't it?

Boy: It's more money . . . it's more money.

Teacher: Keith is suggesting that the poverty-stricken indulge in producing children as a source of income . . . *(laughter)* . . . that's what you said, isn't it? Is it true?

Boy: But they get the money to feed the children don't they?

(Boys all speak together for 10 secs — indistinct)

Boy: . . . it's stupid saying they have children just to get more income.

Boy: I didn't say it as a fact, I just said it as perhaps a means by which . . . *(inaudible)*

Boy: The main scale is that the families with more than two children . . . and one child's under seven, they don't get so much for a child under seven. He's got to be seven before they get anything and that's still not enough for him.

Boy: You don't get anything for the second child I don't think . . .

Boy: The first child . . .

Teacher: The first child.

Boy: Well there was a chap along here with eleven children and he was out of work and they were managing pretty comfortably.

Boy: . . . *(indistinct)*

Boy: Have you any knowledge of their financial conditions?

Boy: I've seen the children and I know they're not exactly running round in rags and at Christmas they get these toys, the same as any other children.

Boy: They might have a lot in the bank or something, you don't know.

Teacher: Is this an indication of the fact that poverty does not necessarily equate with squalor, that here's a family who was hard up, that could turn out very, very tidy children?

Boy: Yes, . . . (*indistinct*) . . . and because Will said that.

Boy: If you have a look at any family that lives in poverty, I would think that they would have over three children.

Boy: Why do you . . . why do you associate children with poverty?

Boy: Well, I don't know, that's just the common factor I see in all, you know, poverty stricken things . . . in any country.

Boy: What happens if they're ill, they don't have children . . . that's another one isn't it?

Boy: It's not as great as children, I don't think,

Boy: I think it is, just as great.

Boy: I think I see what Peter means because we discussed this in America, Texas or something, wasn't it? With that woman and she had children and she couldn't afford to send them to the doctor's and things like that. Wasn't it a piece of evidence we read . . . about that . . . we had a piece . . . a sheet of paper with a picture of . . .

Boy: About that town, where they all moved out . . .

Boy: Yes, where they all moved out and left . . .

Teacher: . . . the fact the mine closed down.

Boy: Yeah, yeah, that's it.

Boy: That was in America, wasn't it?

Teacher: It was.

Boy: Yeah, that's right.

Boy: If we're going to solve this problem we've got to educate these people in contraceptives. This is about the only thing that I see we can do. And once you've cut down the children, you haven't got so many dependants upon the family, upon the working man himself. This is going to lighten his burden.

Boy: I would have thought they would have known about contraceptives.

Boy: Do you?

Boy: No, but I'm not a man am I?
(*4 secs laughter*) . . . I mean I'm not thinking of having children, am I?

Boy: Well I don't think you could have children yourself. Well come on then, look you're sixteen years old now, aren't you, you could get married tomorrow.

Boy: Yeah, but I'm not thinking of having children.

Boy: Well what are you going to do . . . (*indistinct*)

Teacher: What is the point Keith?

Boy: I don't know. I've forgotten now.
(*4 secs laughter*)

Teacher: It is a matter of education on contraceptives. Someone has suggested education generally, but is it just a matter of education, can education in anything solve this problem?

Boy: Well they are educated, aren't they?

Boy: In what way?

Boy: They are given education, but they don't take any notice of it.

Boy: They don't want to know.

Boy: No.

Boy: Well they haven't been educated have they?

Boy: Well they've had the opportunity.

Boy: Yes, but they haven't been educated.

Boy: It's not our problem.

Boy: If they won't accept it. This is the point. How do they get people to accept education at all? I mean if they have been to school, you know, they've had a laugh right through school like, ok, they are a bit older now but what's to say they are going to pay any notice if you push them back in school or try to teach them anything at all.

Boy: Yes, but most of them regret it afterwards, Keith.

Boy: No, I don't think they will. It's the standards of living. I don't think they think about these things, you know, they go to Bingo for the night or something like this. They would not want to go back to school.

Boy: You're talking now about women – we are talking about children.

Boy: I am talking about anybody – they maybe go to the pubs or whatever they want to do but I don't think they want to learn.

Boy: No, they don't.

Boy: We don't want to start pushing anybody back into school, anyway. They're not going to like it anyway.

Boy: Not into school. If you could have some sort of Centre or something . . .

Boy: Yes, but if you are going to say, 'Oh you are not educated, get in there.'

Boy: I don't think I would do it as crude as that.

Boy: No, but the meaning would get over to them.

Boy: It is not get in there – if you want help come to us.

Teacher: If a Centre were established just to what extent do you think it would be successful? A Centre, now, of a kind of intermediate Centre for the rehabilitation of slum dwellers.

Let me compare the education offered by the Humanities Curriculum Project to that offered by the classics. There is, of course, an argument for the teaching of classics which rests upon the notion that intellectual problems are more easily soluble by a mind exercised in conjugations, declensions and syntactical constructions, but this is not the humanist argument. The humanist argument is that the ancient languages unlock an incomparable store of literature, history and philosophy, particularly suited, both by its freshness and by its position as a foundation of later western thinking, to provide the content of an education for the young. In the kind of discussion we have just seen I believe that we have a parallel yield to that expected of the classics and one accessible to the many rather than only to an élite. The vernacular form helps to overcome the linguistic barriers: the substitution of a reflective and cooperative discussion for one of dialectical conflict does much to overcome the barriers of style. There is enough in the work we have done in schools, I am claiming, to promise that a vernacular humanism could under the right conditions be made accessible to a very wide range of people. But when I make this claim I am doing no more than lay the foundations of a bridge on one side of the river. A vernacular tradition in popular education has implications for the frontiers of knowledge.

And so I want to argue the importance of a humanistic social science and a strong humanist tradition in the media of the arts today. For only these can provide adequate support for a humanist education.

There is a sense in which the eighteenth-century age of enlightenment and reason was the final flowering of the classical humanist stock. There was a substantial minority public sufficiently familiar with the classics to support an elegantly allusive literature and this was a public at the same time responsive to many of the developments in philosophy, in history and in science. We were just at the beginning of that fruitful interaction between science and technical problems which enriched both the pure and the applied fields and made science a technical and specialized area of human activity. Fundamental to this progress was the capacity of science to deal in law-like generalizations which did not in principle allow of exceptions. Apparent exceptions must be explained in terms of the interactive effect of theoretical laws.

It is crucial that social science in its origins accepted the model of the physical sciences as the basis for a study of human affairs. The foundations of modern psychology lie in such an approach; and there are implicit elements of it in sociology and even in anthropology. The issue of whether physical events are inherently lawful is, of course, a matter of philosophical dispute. But it is clear that, whatever may be the case in principle, the assumption of lawfulness applied to human affairs leaves a substantial residual problem of explanation. This is signalled for example in the restrictions of behaviourism, which limits the range of data to be considered, and those of inferential statistics, which seeks to build probabilistic laws which by the device of probability admit of unexplained exceptions.

On such foundations rest approaches to social sciences which are non-humanistic in two senses. First, because they deal in probabilistic laws in which the irregularity and exceptions are not explained, they do not appeal to lay human judgement but incline to override it by quoting odds; and second the social sciences have produced a technical language whose referents do not coincide with lay observation and which does not therefore provide a medium for reflection about the experience of human affairs.

This tradition of social science has, I believe, run into considerable difficulties when it has been applied to fields of complex human action such as education, which is the area in which I myself am best informed. In an important and well-known address at the meeting of the American Psychological Association in 1974 Lee J. Cronbach, one of the leading figures in American psychology, discussed the limitations of a nomothetic, or law-seeking, approach to psychological research and observed:

> Originally, the psychologist saw his role as the scientific observation of human behaviour. When hypothesis testing became paramount, observation was neglected, and even actively discouraged by editorial policies of journals.

And he concluded his speech:

> Social scientists are rightly proud of the discipline we draw from the natural-science side of our ancestry. Scientific discipline is what we uniquely add to the time-honoured ways of studying man. Too narrow an identification with science, however, has fixed our eyes upon an inappropriate goal. The goal of our work, I have argued here, is not to amass generalizations atop which a theoretical tower can some day be erected. The special task of the social scientist in each generation is to pin down the contemporary facts. Beyond that, he shares with the humanistic scholar and the artist in the effort to gain insight into contemporary relationships, and to realign the culture's view of man with present realities. To know man as he is is no mean aspiration.

In this formulation I feel that there is still the implication that there is an objective facticity about man as he is which is to be pinned down in the sense of reduced to terms different from those sullied by the experience of living. In effect, the truth about man is conceived as an abstracted truth.

In terms of methodology this abstraction begins in the ideas of comparability and sampling. The idea of comparability implies that the data about man must be organized in comparable and, if possible, quantifiable units. The categories used must be carefully defined so that they are unambiguous in denotation. The observations of different observers must yield the same results. They must be amenable at least to being tallied, at best to being scaled.

This demand that data should be gathered in a way that makes them comparable without the need for fine judgement immediately implies an abstraction so radical as to remove the data from the world of, and hence from the judgement of, experience. Operations performed on these data are not accessible to criticism in the light of experience. They elude capture by wisdom, though they are rationally manipulable. They must be processed within an inviolable logic of their own and the results then related once more to the business of living from which the data were originally abstracted.

Moreover, such data are treated as attributes of populations in the sense that relatively small samples of living reality can be drawn which are to be judged representative of a population of comparable living realities. On this argument an experimental and a control group can be compared as if they were the same; and the results of that comparison can be generalized according to a calculated probability to a target population, related to the samples by virtue of definition and not by virtue of judgement.

The humanistic alternative, or, to be modest, complement, to such a positivist approach to the study of human affairs, is a social science which is a contemporary history. History is concerned not with data which is comparable but with evidence it will undertake critically to compare. And it accepts evidence not only about behaviour, but also about experience. The historian works with sources as diverse as records of parliamentary debates, legislative statutes, newspapers, diaries, letters, photographs, pictures, even music and now cinema and recordings. He compares and relates them by an exercise of critical appraisal and he presents his conclusions to us, not as results which we are to accept on the grounds of an impeccable research technique, but as accounts of life which we are to judge in the light of our own experience, tutored by the broader experience to which we have had access through the arts – including history.

Such a social discipline studies cases, not samples, and studies them with proper attention to their richness and ambiguity. Its basis is a comparative procedure which takes comparability as problematic, and which accepts that the relevance of any study of man in society depends not on the formulation of abstracted laws, but rather upon the situational judgement of the living men to whom the study is addressed. It emphasizes application rather than generalization, and hence it must aspire to strengthen, and never to override, the judgement of those it addresses.

I see the buds of such a contemporary historical study in social science, and I believe that it is important not only that it should be developed by students but more especially that its logic should be so disseminated to the public that there is a rejection of the formulation 'scientists tell us that . . . '; and an acceptance of the right and the responsibility to judge.

This necessary underpinning of a vernacular humanism needs to be supplemented by an accessible tradition of thought in the arts. By the device of fiction – an absolution from the demands of authentication – the arts acquire a licence to explore truth inaccessible to even a humanistic social science or social history. They can address and ask confirmation from the secret experience of life which, they reassure us, can be breached by a felicitous and penetrating communication.

I spoke earlier of a vernacular humanism as one which addresses people in 'languages which are domestically familiar'. I had in mind a comparison of the family circles of Thomas More or John Stuart Mill which domesticated the intellectual tradition of an élite, and those of ordinary people today.

It is apparent, therefore, that I would respond positively to the importance claimed for television by such a representative of that medium as Denis Potter. But all the arts stand at television's shoulder with a capacity to be popular arts. What is demanded of popular art – in television, pop music, novels, paintings and happenings of every kind – if it is to support a vernacular humanism, is that it have a sufficiently strong central strand of integrity and engagement. The enemy of this is not the complementary art of escapism, which must certainly have its place, but an art which creates an unreal world authoritatively related to the real world. This is an art which disseminates generalization through stereotypes, which invites us to accept rather than to question the surface of experience. What is needed is an art created by artists who claim to be like us in their humanity, who insistently disclaim the authority of glamourization and the reification of the looking-glass world of being flown-in from a more compelling reality which is where it all happens.

What chance there is of developing within education a vernacular humanism such as I have described and of feeding it upon a humanistic social study and a humanistic art I leave to this conference to speculate. No doubt it all sounds an idealistic aspiration. But I shall offer one dogmatic proposition by which I am prepared to stand: the contemporary human condition is never the product of success but always, by contrast, the outcome of those aspirations men have thought it worth falling short of.

References

1. Schools Council, *Raising the School Leaving Age* (Working Paper No. 2) (London: Her Majesty's Stationery Office, 1965).
2. Ibid., p. 14.
3. Ibid., p. 22.

Research as a Basis for Teaching

An inaugural lecture in the University of East Anglia, February, 1979.

Fortuitously, this year is the nine hundredth anniversary of the birth of a man commonly regarded as the forefather of the tradition of rational speculation in western universities: Peter Abelard. His world was, of course, very different from ours, and it is one which I am not competent to recreate. But it is part of my thesis that all human knowledge has about it an element of error, and I may perhaps adopt Abelard as a source for my learning even though I am not true to his teaching.

He was, of course, a great dialectician, and by virtue of this a great teacher. We should say today that his research field was dialectics and that it fed directly into his teaching.

'It is,' he wrote, 'one thing to inquire into truth by deliberation, but quite another to make ostentation the end of all disputation for while the first is devoted study which strives to edify, the second is but the mere impulse of pride which seeks only for self glory. By the one we set out to learn the wisdom which we do not possess; by the other we parade the learning which we trust is ours.'[1] To call for research-based teaching is, I suggest, to ask us as teachers to share with our pupils or students the process of our learning the wisdom which we do not possess so that they can get into critical perspective the learning which we trust is ours.

Research-based teaching is more demanding than teaching which offers instruction through a rhetoric of conclusions. Abelard tells us that he slipped from one to the other under the distraction of his love for Heloïse.

> In measure as this passionate rapture absorbed me more and more, I devoted ever less time to philosophy and to the work of the school. Indeed it became loathsome to me to go to the school or to linger there; the labour, moreover, was very burdensome, since my nights were vigils of love and my days of study. My lecturing became utterly careless and lukewarm; I did nothing because of inspiration, but everything merely as a matter of habit. I had become nothing more than a reciter of my former discoveries, and though I still wrote poems, they dealt with love, not with the secrets of philosophy.[2]

My colleague, Professor Malcolm Bradbury, has hinted fictionally that some modern dons may have like problems, though their diaries in the *Times Higher Education Supplement* appear to claim that travel and administration outweigh even family and television as contemporary distractors.

The idea that research is a necessary basis for good teaching is not universally admitted – much less practised – even in universities. Joseph Ben-David, reviewing *Centres of Learning* for the Carnegie Commission on Higher Education, provides an excellent statement of a contrary position. Addressing the difficulty of reconciling research and teaching, he regards the competing demands on time and effort as only a superficial impediment, and reaches out after a more fundamental conflict. He suggests that 'knowledge that can be taught no longer requires investigation, while knowledge that still needs to be investigated cannot yet be taught,' and he claims that 'teaching requires a body of established authoritative knowledge.'[3]

Now, Abelard worked in the context of a 'body of established authoritative knowledge' far more secure than most of us could recognize today: the Scriptures, the writings of the Fathers of the Church, and the authority of the Church itself; and this was not an authority he questioned. Yet his position was almost the opposite of that taken by Ben-David. Established authoritative knowledge hardly required teaching; it was embodied in the Church or was a matter of mere instruction. Teaching was required where doubt or bewilderment caused by obscurity or apparent contradiction in the authorities required clarification by dialectic. His aim was understanding as a fortification, but not the ground, of faith, for he conceded that the final mysteries were inscrutable. Christian doctrine, the knowledge of God and his ways attainable by human beings, was for Abelard 'essentially rational and logical, and . . . it lay within the province of human thought.'[4] Whenever appeal to the authority of the Church and its tradition left space for interpretation and hence for error – called 'heresy' – there was space for research and hence for non-authoritative teaching. The teacher could not, of course, claim to be an authority without offence to the power of the Church.

Only in the presence of doubt is teaching called for, one might gather from Abelard. Only that which has the warrant of certainty can be taught, Ben-David answers. And he can relate his view to the one I have represented by Abelard.

> In . . . relatively closed traditions of higher learning, combining research with teaching presented no difficulty since the difference between elementary and advanced knowledge was not one of substance or certainty, but one of mastery. Original research consisted of novel interpretation or systematization of the tradition and could be done as part of the organization of the material for teaching. For academic teachers in the humanities the ideal of their being original investigators was not a nineteenth-century innovation. The university had been a seat of creative scholarship in philosophy throughout the Middle Ages, and many universities continued to employ original scholars throughout the seventeenth and eighteenth centuries.[5]

This is to attribute the difficulty in reconciling research and teaching to the nineteenth-century development in research in which the German universities were leaders and of which we are all heirs. In this development the pioneer field was history with its attendant technical studies such as philology, palaeography, diplomacy and archaeology. Behind history came the natural sciences and later the social sciences.

Now the environment of research in this new tradition was not the lecture hall where the speculative disputation might be conducted, but the archive, the library, the laboratory or the field site. Research became collaborative by virtue of the network of journals and the talk in coffee-break, but the actual activity was conducted in private. It had become industrialized. The steel-rolling mill is not open to inspection as the local blacksmith is. In place of the speculative disputation open to the student as participant observer, inquiry was expressed in the archive search or the series of laboratory experiments, mute occupations whose meaning was not self-explanatory to the observer.

Ben-David contributes an interesting analysis of the problems of keeping research and teaching in mutual and fortifying interaction, and concludes that by the end of the nineteenth century 'the implementation of the ideal posed serious problems'. To these the American graduate school was one response, associating research-based teaching with the training of professional researchers. Ben-David's diagnosis of the post-war situation is not encouraging.

> There have been no serious efforts at constructive restructuring of the relationship between research and teaching. . . . The resulting frustrations have reinforced the long-standing trend towards the transfer of the seat of advanced research from the universities to non-teaching research institutions.[3]

The Centre for Applied Research in Education was founded by this university in 1970, initially as a non-teaching research institution within a university setting. The fact that we have developed a graduate teaching programme on the basis of the resultant research activity, has prompted me to address the problems explored in this lecture.

The knowledge we teach in universities is won through research; and I have come to believe that such knowledge cannot be taught correctly except through some form of research-based teaching. The grounds for this belief are epistemological. Knowledge of the kind we have to offer is falsified when it is presented as the results of research detached from an understanding of the research process which is the warrant for those results.

Abelard has a lot to teach us here, for he is correct in his understanding that what is represented as authoritative, and established independently of scholarly warrant, cannot be knowledge. It is faith. What is unquestionable is unverifiable and unfalsifiable. It may be true belief, but it is not knowledge in the sense in which we in universities deal with it or are equipped to deal with it. Our knowledge is questionable, verifiable and differentially secure. Unless our students understand that, what they take from us is error: the error that research yields established authoritative knowledge. That this error is widespread must be apparent to anyone who has listened to the questions asked of academics by laymen on television. And if we educate teachers who will transmit this error to their pupils, the error will continue to be widespread. We shall support by our teaching the idea that faith in authority is an acceptable substitute for grasp of the grounds of knowledge, even perhaps a substitute for faith in God. Once the Lord spoke to man: now scientists tell us that. . . .

This epistemological falsification in teaching research-based knowledge authoritatively is compounded by a simple error. We in the course of our research have made and witnessed a large number of audio and video-recordings of teaching, and we find it virtually impossible to locate passages of authoritative exposition by lecture which are not criticized by observers, who are as well-qualified as the lecturer, on the grounds that they contain errors of fact or indefensible judgements. And these shortcomings are perceptible to only a small proportion of students. This intrusion of error into exposition and instruction is not surprising, nor is it a serious criticism of teachers as scholars. The archetypal effort to compress and present knowledge in accessible form, the encyclopaedia, encounters the same problem, for all the resources at the disposal of its editors.[7]

No teacher of normal endowments can teach authoritatively without lending his authority to errors of fact or of judgement. But my case goes deeper than that. Were the teacher able to avoid this, he would, in teaching knowledge as authoritative, be teaching an unacceptable proposition about the nature of knowledge: that its warrant is to be found in the appeal to the expertise of persons rather than in the appeal to rational justification in the light of evidence. I believe that most teaching in schools and a good deal in universities promotes that error. The schooled reveal themselves as uneducated when they look towards knowledge for the reassurance of authoritative certainty rather than for the adventure of speculative understanding.

How to teach a different lesson is an educational problem of considerable technical difficulty. Even though education be voluntary – and it is largely not so – the act of will by which a person devotes himself to a sustained and arduous course is not easy to maintain. The teacher is not concerned simply with the justification of knowledge. He needs to motivate and to set up social situations conducive to work. Leadership is necessary, authority is inescapable. The problem is how to design a practicable pattern of teaching which maintains authority, leadership and the responsibility of the teacher, but does not carry the message that such authority is the warrant of knowledge.

This problem is not unlike that of explaining to a naïve person with no experience of our world that a television set does not make pictures but transmits images of things taking place outside itself. The view of knowledge one can get in a classroom or lecture theatre is most often comparable to that offered by the television set: Plato's simile of the cave holds even if we do not locate reality in ideal forms. Taught knowledge is a shadow or picture of knowledge rather than knowledge as it is apprehended by the researcher who creates or discovers it.

This problem of the relationship of the authority of the teacher to the representation of knowledge in teaching has been a central theme of my own work and that of some of my colleagues in the Centre for Applied Research in Education. In the jargon of our field it is the problem of inquiry- or discovery-based teaching or of teaching through discussion. To my mind the essence of the problem is expressed by declaring the aim of teaching in its fullest ambition to be: to develop an understanding of the problem of the nature of knowledge through an exploration of the provenance and warrant of the particular knowledge we encounter in our field of study. Any education which does not achieve this leaves its recipients disadvantaged as compared with those who have followed courses where it is achieved; for we are talking about the insight which raises mere competence and possession of information to intellectual power of a kind which can emancipate.

On this occasion I do not want to get trapped in the details of educational research. Rather I shall confine myself to three specific problems encountered by those attempting research-based teaching in the sense I have given it. They are: the need to cover ground in a subject; the psychological barriers to this kind of teaching; and the interpretation of the idea of research-based teaching into the practice of primary and secondary schools.

The problem of coverage is generally formulated by asserting that discovery and discussion are such slow procedures for learning that the need for a quantity of information precludes their use. If we are to cover the curriculum we set ourselves, we must needs resort to instruction.

Of course we need instruction. And text-books too. The key is that the aim of discovery and discussion is to promote under-standing of the nature of the concessions to error that are being made in that part of our teaching where we rely upon instruction or text-books. The crucial difference is between an educated and an uneducated use of instruction. The educated use of instruction is sceptical, provisional, speculative in temper. The uneducated use mistakes information for knowledge. Information is not knowledge until the factor of error, limitation or crudity in it is appropriately estimated, and it is assimilated to structures of thinking – disciplines,[8] realms of meaning,[9] modes of ex-perience[10] – which give us the means of understanding.

Two parallel activities need to be pursued: instruction, which gives us access to conclusions which represent in simplified, and hence, distorted, form our best grasp of a realm of knowledge and meaning; and learning by inquiry or discovery, which enables us to understand how to utilize such a representation of knowledge, to assess its limitations and to develop the means of pushing outwards beyond these limitations.

The interaction between inquiry and instruction is perhaps best understood through a concrete instance. A person of my acquaintance is practising as a non-graduate research worker in biochemistry in a government research agency and at the same time taking an undergraduate degree in the Open University. At once, therefore, a professional researcher and an undergraduate, this student is advantaged as compared with those not engaged in research by the clearer perception of the status and use of text-book knowledge made possible by research experience. The justification of research as a basis for learning or for teaching is the perspective to be gained from the hill of inquiry over the plain of knowledge.

But more than this, the seeker, the questioner, the researcher, is always at an advantage *vis à vis* the person who claims to be a knower; hence, the dramatic structure of Plato's dialogues. One can combine inquiry-learning and instruction appropriately only by using the inquiry to teach the student to question the instruction.

Herein lies the psychological barrier to research-based teaching. It may leave me *in* authority, but it asks me to depreciate my claim to be *an* authority.[11] The article on research in the eleventh edition of the *Encyclopaedia Britannica*, the memorial summary of the British perception of knowledge on the threshold of the First World War, observes that 'Investigations of every kind which have been based on original sources of knowledge may be styled "research", and it may be said that without "research" no authoritative works have been written. . . .'[12] The implication is that research, by allowing us to produce authoritative work, makes us authoritative. Such authority is prestigious and highly satisfying personally; but it is vulnerable to the next questioner, and even more so to changes in the paradigm of knowledge.[13] Sir Walter Scott remarked of the persistence of astrology:

> Grave and studious men were loth to relinquish the calculations which had early become the principal objects of their studies, and felt reluctant to descend from the predominating height to which a supposed insight . . . had exalted them over the rest of mankind.[14]

The psychological reluctance to abandon the claim to be an authority is reinforced by fear of the implications for the social order, where such authority holds hierarchy in place, as my colleague, Professor Robert Ashton, perceives: 'Like the schoolmaster, the university don, the householder, the civil magistrate and the King himself, the master (of apprentices) wields an authority which is in essence paternalistic and contributes to the maintenance of order in society as a whole.'[15]

Our deep psychological and social needs for that conception of knowledge which makes the elders curators of truth are yet further reinforced by our need as teachers for institutional authority in the schools and universities in which we work. As Derek Morrell and John Witherington wrote in their Schools Council Working Paper on the *Raising of the School Leaving Age* – from which our Humanities Curriculum Project sought its validation:

> If the teacher emphasizes in the classroom, his common humanity with the pupils, and his common uncertainty in the face of many

problems, the pupils will not take kindly to being demoted to the status of children in other relationships within the same institution.[16]

In authority-based teaching the teacher is Promethean: in research-based teaching the teacher evokes a Promethean response from the student, who casts his master in the role of Hephaestus. In teaching there is always a retaining of power as well as a conferring of power. Research-based teaching, conceived as inquiry-based teaching, shifts the balance of power towards the student. It is his own research or inquiring which gives the teacher the strength to do this. Yet it happens that, fathering an Oedipus, the teacher is tempted to expose him to destroy him.

These are difficult matters, and most of us go for compromises; but they are compromises charged nonetheless with the emotions aroused by the extremes. I claim no more than that a research base offers the teacher a security for his authority in a mastery of seeking rather than of knowing, and hence provides him with a necessary protection in the enterprise of educating those who will, he wants to hope, exceed his grasp.

The view of knowledge and teaching which I have outlined seems at first sight to apply to universities, but not to schools. This is not a limitation I accept.

Research may be broadly defined as systematic inquiry made public. The inquiry should, I think, be rooted in acutely felt curiosity, and research suffers when it is not. Such inquiry becomes systematic when it is structured over time by continuities lodged in the intellectual biography of the researcher and co-ordinated with the work of others through the cumulative capacity of the organization of the discipline or the subject.

Systematic inquiry of this sort – or approximation to it – is a pattern of learning by a thoughtful study of problems. Such study becomes research when it is made public by being published, at which point the student makes a claim intended to evoke a critical response: that the reported inquiry has resulted in a contribution to knowledge, being soundly based and in some sense new.

Saving only this final stage of publication such inquiry is possible as a basis for learning at quite early stages of education. When it takes place the teacher is not an instructor but instead takes the critical role assigned in fully blown research to the scholars in the subject who react to publication. And there is no better experience than to work on this pattern with a teacher who has the imagination to initiate inquiry and the judgement to discipline it. The pupils make trials or essays within the inquiry, and the teacher offers an experienced critical reaction.

Thus, when a teacher of six-year-olds separates two children who are fighting and, using them as independent witnesses, invites the class to question them and attempt to reach a judgement concerning the causes of the conflict, that teacher is already equipping those children to understand that the averred causes of the First World War, which they may some day consent to rehearse for 'O' level history, are not unproblematic. Only such teaching can tend to provide the learner with an acceptable view of accepted knowledge: that is, as questionable knowledge which for present purposes does not need to be questioned.

One of the teachers with whom our Centre is working is known to her pupils in a Dorset middle school as 'the hypothesis teacher', a tribute to her capacity to stimulate hypothetical thinking within the American social studies curriculum, MAN: a Course of Study, which, under the inspiration of Jerome Bruner, reached after a framework to support children in an inquiry into the nature of humanness as it can be understood through the study of animal behaviour, anthropology and comparative sociology, set in a context of values.[17] Bruner spoke of a 'courteous translation' of knowledge into the grasp of children.[18] I think that the courtesy lies in conceding the importance of the right of the learner to speculate, to learn autonomously to criticize and correct intelligent errors which reach after understanding.

Inquiry-based teaching of this sort necessarily aims at higher levels of attainment than are commonly settled for in schools and it naturally needs the support of instruction. Such instruction is best provided, not through the lecture given by the teacher, but rather through books and audio-visual materials, since this enables the teacher to maintain his critical stance towards the instruction. But the teacher will feel secure in such a role only if he is research-minded to the extent of having an inquiring habit of thought. It will be his task to interpret his claim as a man of knowledge to support his capacity to manage an inquiry towards understanding, 'to legitimise the search'.[19] He must not diminish the importance of that search by suggesting that it can be avoided by appeal to him as an authority who can warrant knowledge.

The teacher's qualification is in that knowledge of which the universities are curators, knowledge based upon inquiry organized as research. Such knowledge celebrates the capacity of the human mind to deal with problems or doubts in at least some area of human concern, not by a leap of faith, but by a calculated and secure uncertainty. Confronted by the fact that if there is knowledge which is absolute it is, like Abelard's God, finally inscrutable, we settle for serviceable approximations which can be progressively sharpened by sceptical, but systematic, questioning. Only by keeping teaching in touch with inquiry can we do justice to this element in the knowledge we represent.

The university stands – or should stand – behind inquiry in schools as the curator of that uncertainty without which the transmission of knowledge becomes a virtuoso performance in gentling the masses. We do not live up to our principles, of course, but it is of the first importance that we do not rest from trying to do so, routinely from day to day. Whenever we assert and bully with our authority instead of reasoning on an equal base with those we teach and helping them to liberate themselves from our authority as the source of truth, we invite them to faith rather than to knowledge. And our credentials to teach do not support our claiming faith from our students. The university holds no secrets of life and experience except through what Oakeshott has called 'arrests of experience',[20] the partial perspectives which alone give us a purchase on the limitless universe of experience and hence the possibility of understanding, which we call 'knowledge'.

We are within reach of Abelard, whose 'statement that our beliefs must be understood does not mean that in his view a complete comprehension of divine matters was possible to men'.[21] But while Abelard's element of uncertainty, constituting as it did a limitation of understanding of the divine, was associated with a sense of deficit, for some of us at least the uncertainty of research-based knowledge is a valued asset. The alternative presents itself, not as the mystical apprehension which supports faith founded in God, but as the threat that certainty will be idealogically based and that truth will be dictated by political authority. It is the thesis of Thrasymachus we oppose.

And since Thrasymachus spoke with the confidence of the practical man, let me at this point, warned by experience, combat what I believe to be a misapprehension about the relation of speculation to action. (I am forewarned of this by criticism of our Humanities Curriculum Project, which sought to offer a speculative style of education through dialectic to those who would leave

school at sixteen.)[22] The uncertainty or provisionality of knowledge which I have associated with research is not to be equated
with uncertainty of commitment or failure of the will to act. It
does not preclude faith or commitment as 'that which we held
firmly in our minds', but rather builds upon it and elucidates it.
Commitment needs to be interpreted before it can inform action,
and the man of action is more typically he who can act without
the reassurance that his interpretation is certain than he who can
act only when unafflicted by doubt. Security in uncertainty is
the armour which a speculative education can offer. It is a
valuable equipment for the practical man.

Not everyone will agree with my analysis of the nature of
knowledge and its relation to research and to action. There are
those who, agreeing, will judge knowledge dangerous because it
gives power to the dispossessed and those who, wishing it were
more dangerous, will believe that it lacks the power to break the
domination of the hegemony.[23] But the achievement of secondary
education for all signals, if it does not realize, the aspiration
towards a knowledge-based education at every stage of schooling
and for everyone – not merely for scholars – and commits the
teaching profession to a struggle with the consequences of that
ambition.

Historically the great majority of the children of this country
have been offered in the state educational system, whether
through the elementary school or the secondary modern school,
no more than a rudimentary education in the basic skills and such
an acquaintance with knowledge as might be expected to
inculcate a respect for those who are knowledgeable. Their lot has
been to accept that truths are defined by the authority of others.
This tradition has lain alongside a tradition among the gentry of
knowledge as a mere accomplishment or appurtenance of style.
The juxtaposition of these traditions has not merely impaired our
capability in the industrial arts,[24] it has also defined scholarship
in the liberal disciplines as merely technical, and the results of this
are to be observed in the discontent with higher education of
many intelligent students, who resist the idea that technical
prowess is the precondition of curiosity rather than its servant.

In the familiar tradition the uses of knowledge are reserved for
an élite, while the burdens of knowledge are imposed on the
generality by an imperious pedagogy. Schools provide students
with competences without enhancing their powers. There are
gross inequalities in the distribution of the means of thinking and

hence of the power thinking confers and, consequently, the creation of a proletariat of the intellect.

To provide an alternative tradition of access to knowledge is a formidable problem for teachers, and it is not a problem to be solved by a change of heart. Important as it may be to declare worthwhile aims for education, good intentions do not pave the way to their fulfilment. What is needed is progress in the art of teaching as a public tradition and a personal achievement.

The character of the art of teaching is to represent to learners through social interaction with them meanings about knowledge. The succession of experiences we provide for them, and within the framework of those experiences the nuances of our questions, our judgements of their work, our tutorial advice, even the very gestures and postures of our bodies, are expressive of those meanings, sometimes explicitly, sometimes as elements in what has come to be called a 'hidden curriculum.'[25] Teaching represents knowledge to people rather as theatre represents life.

Some of those who have called teaching an art appear to think that this suggests it is all flair and no learning. As if actors or dancers or musicians have nothing to learn. Others, on the contrary, imply that it is all skill and can be learned by the imitation of models on the pattern of apprenticeship.

Under the régime of the elementary school, which emphasized a training in skills for pupils, teaching itself could be reduced at the level of minimum competency to a set of skills for pupil teachers. Under such assumptions the training of teachers might be conducted through some sort of apprenticeship, for the masters could do in masterly fashion what the apprentices would be called upon to do. This is not true today. It is not only that the past masters would find themselves inadequate in present class-rooms, though I believe this to be true. It is because the act of teaching as a representation of knowledge is inherently problematic.

Teaching which accepts fidelity to knowledge as a criterion can never be judged adequate and rest content. Teachers must be educated to develop their art, not to master it, for the claim to mastery merely signals the abandoning of aspiration. Teaching is not to be regarded as a static accomplishment like riding a bicycle or keeping a lodger; it is, like all acts of high ambition, a strategy in the face of an impossible task.

It is the existence of such vocations with open frontiers for development which provides a basis within the modern university for the second traditional strand in the universities which intertwines with that of liberal education, the professional schools, and among them schools of education. Changes in society, changes in knowledge, related changes in professional role all contribute to professional doubt and uncertainty, which is confirmed by the experience that old recipes no longer work. And I have argued that the controlled and organized exploitation of such uncertainty in the disciplines of knowledge – the research tradition – is central to the modern university tradition. Research as a strategy is applicable not only to the humanistic and scientific but also to the professional disciplines.

Most of you will have noticed the ambiguity in my title. Just as research in history or literature or chemistry can provide a basis for teaching those subjects, so educational research can provide a basis for teaching and learning about teaching. Professional skill and understanding can be the subject of doubt, that is, of knowledge, and hence of research.

In education what might such research look like?

In this country, since the 1950s, the received doctrine has been that the core of education for teaching lies not in research in education, but in the application to education of the conclusions of research in the 'contributory disciplines' of philosophy, psychology and sociology. Most of those teaching these disciplines to teachers have not been able to share a research base with their students, who are clearly quite unlikely to become philosophers, psychologists, or sociologists, since they are on professional courses for teachers. All too easily philosophers, psychologists and sociologists, whose researches are problematic in their own fields, become – only sometimes against their wishes – authorities in courses for teachers.

An alternative to the constituent disciplines approach is to treat education itself – teaching, learning, running schools and educational systems – as the subject of research. This alternative is not characterized by a neglect of disciplines, upon which it draws eclectically, but rather by the fact that what is drawn from the disciplines and applied to education is not results or even the theories which give shape to each discipline, but methods of inquiry and analysis together with such concepts as have utility for a theory of education. The problems selected for inquiry are selected because of their importance as educational problems; that is, for their significance in the context of professional practice. Research and development guided by such problems will contribute primarily to the understanding of educational action through the construction of theory of education or a tradition of understanding. Only secondarily will research in this mode contribute to philosophy, psychology or sociology. And this principle of applied research is, I think, appropriate *mutatis mutandis* in all the professional schools of our universities.

How can I best make clear the implications of such a position? Let me take as a point of departure an example of research and training which I take to be sub-professional.

In Ohio State University I visited the Disaster Center, a research and development unit concerned with making more effective the response of the emergency services to disasters. There I saw in a laboratory an exact replica of the Columbus, Ohio, police nerve centre. Police staff were released to man their familiar positions while simulations of disasters were fed through their information channels and their responses were studied. While I was watching, a simulated airplane crash on a Columbus suburb was enacted. It was cleverly contrived. News that the wife of one of the men on the switchboard had just given birth to a son was fed through as a distractor. Information that the deputy superintendent's family had been badly injured when the plane hit his residence invited the team to override public priorities with private ones. Research and training were well integrated. The task was to find the best procedure, to test it against interference and then to enable the emergency team to react smoothly and automatically without needing to pause for thought or run aground on difficult judgements. The laboratory situation was a godsend. You cannot keep crashing planes on Columbus as a research strategy.

If we were to take this as a model for educational research, then we should provide laboratories which simulate classrooms. Desks carefully carved with graffiti might be assembled, walls might be hung with the Fall of Icarus and centre-spreads from the *Teacher's World*, fans could pump in the scent of sweat and damp clothes mixed with chalk dust. But what of the pupils?

We deal in education – as in medicine or law or social work – with human action which cannot be channelled through headphones. We need real pupils, and we cannot properly engage them in doubtful experiments or even in placebo treatments.

In short, real classrooms have to be our laboratories, and they are in the command of teachers, not of researchers. This is the characteristic of professional schools; the research act must conform to the obligations of the professional context. This is what we mean by action research. It is a pattern of research in which experimental or research acts cannot be exempted from the demand for justification by professional, as well as by research, criteria. The teacher cannot learn by inquiry without undertaking that the pupils learn too; the physician cannot experiment without attempting to heal. As the Tavistock Institute put it: 'No therapy without research, no research without therapy'.[26]

Such a view of educational research declares that the theory or insights created in collaboration by professional researchers and professional teachers is always provisional, always to be taught in a spirit of inquiry, and always to be tested and modified by professional practice. The teacher who founds his practice of teaching upon research must adopt a research stance to his own practice: it must be provisional and exploratory.

It is this that marks him out as a professional, as compared to the Ohio police emergency team; for while the object of the disaster simulations is to allow them to respond effectively without pausing for thought, the object of educational research is to develop thoughtful reflection in order to strengthen the professional judgement of teachers.

This implies that the educational researcher and the teacher must have a shared language. No doubt there is a need for increasing the research literacy of teachers, but there is also a lot of room for research couched in the vernacular. Here the language of history is a good model: George I instituted professorships of history in 1724 for the purpose of training public servants, and historians still speak of politics in language politicians can understand.[27] If we want to influence action, we must have very strong excuses when we abandon the vernacular of action.

It also implies that the teacher be committed to inquiry in the process of his teaching on the grounds that nothing he is offered by teachers of teachers should be accepted on faith. Anyone who doubts this scepticism would do well to study the case of Cyril Burt.[28]

In teaching about teaching as in teaching about the disciplines of knowledge we can offer some tips and rules of thumb, but these should not don the mantle of expertise. Moreover, such lore is sub-professional. Professionalism is based upon understanding as a framework of action and understanding is always provisional.

The infusion of teaching by the spirit of inquiry is difficult enough in the context of teaching the disciplines of knowledge. It is even more difficult in professional schools where the natural cry from the fields of professional action is for the reassurance of certainty to ameliorate the agony of responsibility. It is still more difficult in initial training situations, where some are in more need of instruction in clinging to an overturned dinghy than in navigation. But even here the short cut of accepting a 'rhetoric of conclusions' is one we must struggle to avoid. As the McNair Report said: 'The training of teachers must always be the subject of experiment. It is a growing point of education.'[29] Growing points are uncertainties because uncertainties are potentials. It is the task of universities to keep those potentials open.

The ambition of the programme I have proposed might be understood to remove it from reality. Inaugural lectures in education can too comfortably address the problems of the school in the sky. Not so in this case. I am talking of my everyday practice as an educational researcher and teacher of teachers. But my practice is not successful. Success can be achieved only by lowering our sights. The future is more powerfully formed by our commitment to those enterprises we think it worth pursuing even though we fall short of our aspirations. Abelard's setting out 'to learn the wisdom which we do not possess' commits him and we who follow him to the pursuit of an elusive, ever-receding goal. In such an enterprise research is by definition relevant for its gains accrue, not from a leap towards finality, but from the gradual cumulation of knowledge through the patient definition of error. Its achievement is always provisional, the base camp for the next advance. We shall only teach better if we learn intelligently from the experience of shortfall; both in our grasp of the knowledge we offer and of our knowledge of how to offer it. That is the case for research as the basis for teaching.

References

1. J. G. Sikes, *Peter Abailard* (New York: Russell & Russell, 1961, 1st edition 1932), p. 55.
2. Peter Abelard, *The Story of My Misfortunes (Historia Calamitatum)* translated H. A. Bellows (New York: Macmillan, 1972, 1st edition 1922), pp. 18–19.
3. Joseph Ben-David, *Centers of Learning: Britain, France, Germany, United States* (New York: McGraw Hill for the Carnegie Commission on Higher Education, 1977), pp. 93–4.

4. J. G. Sikes, *Peter Abailard* (New York: Russell & Russell, 1961, 1st edition 1932), p. 50.

5. Joseph Ben David, *Centers of Learning: Britain, France, Germany, United States* (New York: McGraw Hill for the Carnegie Commission on Higher Education, 1977), pp. 94-95.

6. Ibid., p. 124.

7. See Harvey Einbinder, *The Myth of the Britannica* (London: MacGibbon and Kee, 1964).

8. See Paul H. Hirst, 'Liberal education and the nature of knowledge' pp. 113-138 in *Philosophical Analysis and Education* edited by Reginald D. Archambault (London: Routledge & Kegan Paul, 1965).

9. Philip H. Phenix, *Realms of Meaning* (New York: McGraw-Hill, 1964).

10. Michael Oakeshott, *Experience and its Modes* (Cambridge: Cambridge University Press, 1933).

11. The distinction is taken from R. S. Peters, *Ethics and Education* (London: Allen & Unwin, 1966). See also the same author's *Authority, Responsibility and Education* (London: Allen & Unwin, 1959).

12. *Encyclopaedia Britannica* Eleventh edition, 1910.

13. See Thomas S. Kuhn, *The Structure of Scientific Revolutions* (Chicago University of Chicago Press, 2nd edition, 1970).

14. Sir Walter Scott, *Guy Mannering*, Chapter IV.

15. Robert Ashton, *The English Civil War* (London: Weidenfeld & Nicholson 1978), p. 9.

16. The Schools Council Working Paper No. 2 *Raising the School Leaving Age* (London: HMSO 1965), p. 22.

17. *MAN: a course of study* was developed by the Educational Development Center, Cambridge, Mass. and is published and disseminated by Curriculum Development Associates of Washington, D.C. The British dissemination agency is the Centre for Applied Research in Education, University of East Anglia.

18. Jerome S. Bruner, *The Process of Education* (Cambridge. Mass: Harvard University Press, 1966), p. 52.

19. See Janet P. Hanley, Dean K. Whitla, Eunice M. Moo and Arlene S. Walter, *Curiosity, Competence, Community: Man: A Course of Study: an Evaluation* (Summary of original two-volume edition) (Washington, D.C. Curriculum Development Associates, 1970), p. 5.

20. Michael Oakeshott, *Experience and its Modes* (Cambridge: Cambridge University Press, 1933).

21. J. G. Sikes, *Peter Abailard* (New York: Russell & Russell, 1961, 1st edition 1932), p. 36.

22. *The Humanities Project: an Introduction* (London: Heinemann

Educational Books, 1970). A bibliography of this project is available from: The Secretary, Humanities Curriculum Project, Centre for Applied Research in Education, University of East Anglia, Norwich NR4 7TJ.

23. See Antonio Gramsci *Selections from the Prison Notebooks*, edited and translated by Q. Hoare and G. Nowell Smith (London: Lawrence & Wishart, 1971).

24. As has been argued by Correlli Barnett in 'Technology, education and industrial and economic strength', the first of three Royal Society of Arts Cantor Lectures on Education for Capability. *The Royal Society of Arts Journal*, 127, 5271, 117–30.

25. See Philip W. Jackson, *Life in Classrooms*. (New York: Holt, Rinehart & Winston, 1968). The concept is now widely adopted.

26. Quoted by Duncan Smith, 'Action Research and the Ford Teaching Project: a strategy for evaluating classroom practice'. (Unpublished M.Ed. dissertation, University of Liverpool, 1979.)

27. Excellent treatments of the common language and common sense virtues of history are: Jacques Barzun and Henry F. Graff, *The Modern Researcher* (New York: Harcourt Brace Jovanovich, revised edition, 1977) and J. H. Hexter *The History Primer* (London: Allen Lane The Penguin Press, 1972). These are of course a personal selection.

28. See Oliver Gillie, 'Sir Cyril Burt and the great I.Q. fraud', *New Statesman*, 24 November 1978, pp. 688–94.

29. *Teachers and Youth Leaders* (London: HMSO 1944) (Board of Education non-parliamentary paper).

Index

Abelard, Peter 177–9, 181, 187, 193
Abercrombie, M. L. J. 151
ability levels 128
  HCP materials 100–101, 110–11,
    113–14, 167
academic disciplines 42–3, 46
academic education 9–10, 16–17,
  29–30
academic tradition (intellect) 42,
  157
access
  to knowledge 145, 166, 181,
    188–9
  library, sixth formers and 143
accountability 135, 136
action research 34, 35, 58, 74–5,
  191–2
adolescents
  adult interests, curriculum and
    55–65, 122
  education of see Crowther Report
  independence 111–12, 116, 128,
    136–7
  see also emancipation; Humanities
    Curriculum Project
aims (of education)
  concept limitations 47–9, 52–3
  high generality 103–4
  intended learning outcomes 5,
    81–2
  secondary school 144, 153–5
  see also objectives
anthropology 4, 5, 37
application, task of 150
arts 173, 188
  in curriculum 26–7, 33–4
  mode of creativity 26, 42
  and sciences 10, 28
  vernacular humanism and 176–7
Ashton, Professor Robert 184
aspirations, curriculum research 74,
  76, 167–9, 177

Association for the Study of the Curriculum 144
audio visual material, HCP 100,
  101–2
authority, teacher 119
  controversial issues 121, 123,
    126–7, 135, 138
  emancipation and 163, 164–5,
    166, 168
  formality/informality and 70,
    143, 147, 149, 151–2
  in Humanities Project 70, 77, 79
  knowledge and 134, 138, 145,
    178–89 passim
  pupil dependence on 111, 116,
    128, 136–7
  in research-based teaching 178–9,
    181–2, 184–5
  in small-group discussion 143,
    147–9, 151–2
autonomy, pupil 119, 133, 134, 138,
  146–52, 184–5
  see also emancipation; independence

Bailey, Charles 138
Bales, Robert 50
Barber, Bernard 50
Barzun, Jacques 42, 50, 157
Beck, R. 147
behaviour 5, 91
  classroom 24–5, 49–50, 52–3, 104
  influenced by language 38–9
  models (symbolic systems) 43–4
behavioural objectives 5, 81–2
  stated (limitations) 103–4
behaviourism 5, 174
Ben-David, Joseph 179–80
Bjerstedt, Ake 147
books (about education) 159, 162
Borgotta, Edgar 50
Bradbury, Professor Malcolm 178

British Film Institute 101
British Library Research and Development Division 143
Bruner, Jerome 131, 161, 186
Burt, Sir Cyril 192

Cambridge Journal of Education 143
Carnegie Commission on Higher Education 178
Cartwright, Dorwin 50
case studies, use of (HCP) 75, 82, 86, 88, 117, 143
diffusion of materials 103, 105–6
censorship, HCP materials 114
Centers of Learning (Ben-David) 178
Central Advisory Council for Education 7, 9–11, 13, 16
central team, HCP 94, 96, 99, 111
Centre for Applied Research in Education 180, 182
change
art of teaching and 159
social, culture patterns and 12–13
Christianity 21–2, 164–5, 179
class *see* social class
classics 164, 166, 172–3
classroom
action research 34, 35, 58, 74–5, 191–2
behaviour 24–5, 49–50, 52–3, 104
competitive element 130, 147
group work *see* group
morale 50
sociology of 35–6
standards *see* standards
sub-culture 4, 6, 26–7, 147
see also teacher; teaching
Collier, K. G. 151
common culture 9, 14–16, 18
communication
common culture by 9, 14–16, 18
culture as medium 20–21, 23
language of 36–41
mass, adolescent interests and 55–6
see also interaction
comparability, judgement and 175–6
competition 13
in education 8, 14, 130, 147
comprehensive education 3–4, 8, 14

concept formation 38–9
conceptual frameworks 5, 20–34, 99, 157
conformity concept 35, 36, 38, 44–5, 64
Connexions (teaching material) 70
conscience 137, 165
consensus 21–2, 24, 129
consumer education 103
contract (covenant), curriculum as expression of 143, 144, 153–5
control
critical, aims concept and 47–8
social, education as form of 36, 38
see also authority, teacher
controversial issues
chairman's role 118–19, 126–30, 168–9
definitions 120, 130–31, 134–5
discussion 77–9, 98, 99, 106, 111, 116
value positions 120–23, 168–9
see also moral issues; neutrality, teacher
conventions, group 147, 149, 151
Cooley, Charles H. 38
copyright laws 97, 102
core curriculum 103
county colleges 11
coverage, subject 150, 183
creative innovation 25–6, 27
creativity
conceptual framework 36–45
culture and 35, 45–6
role of education 45–6
critic, role of (traditional) 26, 51
critical
control, aims concept and 47–8
principles 52–3, 54
Cronbach, Lee J. 174
Crowther, Geoffrey 3, 69
Crowther Report (1959) 3–4, 28, 98
General Education in the Light of 7–20
CSE-level materials (HCP) 110–11, 113
cues, teacher authority and 126–7
cultural education 18–19
cultural sociology (framework) 36–45
cultural tradition, school's role 96

culture
  academic education and   17
  characteristics of   22–3
  class, social education and   12–13,
    15–16
  classroom sub-   4, 6, 26–7, 147
  common   9, 14–16, 18
  communication and   36–7, 40–41
  creative innovation and   25–6
  face-to-face (classroom)   34, 35, 58
  functional definition   20–21
  patterns, social change and   12–13
  transmission of   23–4, 34–5, 36
Culture and Education (Stenhouse)   5–6
curriculum
  arts and sciences in   26–7, 33–4
  content   20, 32–3, 79
  core   103
  differentiation   3, 8, 10
  'hidden'   189
  humanities in   6, 55–65
  interdisciplinary   95–6, 98
  research, art of teaching and   144,
    155–62
  sociology of   4, 20–34
  whole   144, 153–5
  see also general education; Humani-
    ties Curriculum Project

Deciding What to Teach (Fraser)   120
decision-making   87, 88
Democracy and Education (Dewey)   19
Dewey, John   19, 132
dialectics   177–9, 181, 187, 193
  see also discussion-based teaching;
    interaction
differentiation   3, 8, 10, 22–3, 29
  of speech   37–41
discipline   61, 62, 64, 81
disciplines, academic   42–3, 46
  contributory   190–91
discussion-based teaching
  authority in *see* authority, teacher
  balance problem   117, 129–30
  chairman's role   115–19 *passim*,
    124, 126–30
  dialectics   177–9, 181, 187, 193
  effectiveness   136, 138, 151–2
  evidence *see* evidence concept
  experimental framework   78, 79,
    93, 105, 109

  motivation problem   130–31
  reflective   130, 138
  small-group   143, 146–52
  topics   55–60, 62, 91–2, 95–6,
    99–100
  transcript, HCP   145, 169–72
  value positions   120–23
division of labour   8, 9, 13, 15, 29,
  147
dominance rank order   147
Durkheim, Émile   42

economic growth, education and   8
education
  academic   9–10, 16–17, 29–30
  aims concept   47–9, 52–3
  creativity and role of   42–3, 45–6
  cultural, need for   18–19
  as culture transmitter   34–5, 36
  higher   143–4, 148, 178
  for leisure   9, 12, 103
  progressive   17, 18, 51, 132
  as research subject   190–93
  road system   3, 10–12
  social structure and   8–9, 12–14, 31
  sociology of   4, 5, 35–6
  standards *see* standards
  system (changes)   14
  see also comprehensive education;
    general education; secondary
    education; specialization; tech-
    nical education; vocational edu-
    cation
educational
  covenant (contract)   143, 144,
    153–5
  games (small-group)   146
  ideas testing   157–9
  publishing, HCP effect on   70, 94
  research *see* research
  tasks concept   149–50
egocentric speech   37–9
elementary schools   4, 27, 188, 189
élite, educational   18, 28, 188
élitist humanism   145, 166–7, 173,
  176
Elliott, John   144
emancipation   4
  through education   163, 164, 166
    168
  see also independence

English, Cyril 69
environmental studies 103, 111
equality of opportunity 4, 8, 14
ESN pupils 11–12
evaluation unit, HCP 73, 75, 85–8, 103–5
evidence concept 114–16, 175–6
  chairman's role 118–19, 127–8
  effectiveness 136, 138
  interpretation 115–16, 127–8
  pattern of discussion 79, 117, 124
  project archive 96–7
  relevance, nature of 130, 131
  structured collections 97, 99–100, 109, 112–13, 125
  structured materials 90, 93–4, 98–9, 110–11, 124–5
examinations 46, 111
experience
  approach to education 55, 57–65
  'arrests of' 187
  study of human 91, 175–6

factory groups 25, 50
Fantasy and Feeling in Education (Jones) 131
feasibility study (prior to HCP) 90
feed-back, HCP 80, 83, 85, 88
fiction, truth explored in 176, 178
film (teaching aid) 101–2, 111
Floud, Jean 20
Ford Foundation 71
Ford Teaching Project 144
formal geaching 70, 143, 147, 149, 151–2
Fraser, Dorothy 120, 130, 135
free expression 17
Freire, Paulo 137
Fymier, Jack 71

general education 4, 18
  academic education as 9–10, 16–17, 29–30
  interpretation of 12–13
  in public schools 29, 30–31
  in 'road system' 10–12
  specialization and 28–30
  vocational and 9, 14–15
Getzells, Jacob W. 44
graduate teaching 180–81

grammar school 10, 12–13, 16, 31
Gramsci, Antonio 137
group
  culture (shared) 22–3
  dynamics 4, 23–4, 129
  psychology of 151–2
  rules 143, 147, 149, 151–2
  standards 25, 27, 30, 123
  see also discussion-based teaching
Growth of Logical Thinking (Piaget) 44

Halsey, A. H. 20
Hare, Paul 50
Hare, R. M. 133, 135
higher education 143–4, 148, 178
Hirsch, Walter 50
history 175–6, 179–80, 192
Hoffmann, Banesh 20–21
Homans, George 50
Human Group, The (Homans) 50
humanism 137, 163–6
  élitist 145, 166–7, 173, 176
  vernacular 145, 166–77
humanities 6, 55–65
  as creative outlet 26, 167
  definition 69–70
  protective role 57–8, 98–9, 106, 111, 123
Humanities Curriculum Project 6
  administration 73–4
  aim 77, 78, 103–4, 112
  areas of inquiry 91–2, 95–6, 99–100
  aspirations 167–9
  background 89–90
  basic premises 74–8
  central archive 96–7
  central team 94, 96, 99, 111
  classics compared 172–3
  diffusion 103, 105–6
  evaluation unit 73, 75, 85–8, 103–5
  experiment in schools 70–71, 78–9, 83–5, 102–3, 107–15
  follow-up projects 143–5
  induction conference 107–15
  materials *see* materials, teaching
  motivation problem 119–32
  objectives 71, 81–3, 103–5

remit 69–70, 90–92, 110
role definition problems 79–81, 107
tasks 93–4
Hyland, John T. 133–4, 136, 137–8

independence 111–12, 116, 128, 136–7, 143
individual(s) 5, 143, 150
creativity 25–6, 35, 42–6
needs (competitive society) 7–9, 13
indoctrination 58, 98, 106, 111, 123
industrial arts 188
industrial psychology 25, 50
informal teaching 70, 143, 147, 149, 151–2
information
-based study (limitations) 99
coverage 150, 183
see also evidence concept
Inhelder, Bärbel 44
inquiry, research as systematic 185–7
inquiry-based teaching 96–7, 98, 105
instruction and 145, 183–4
teacher's role 106, 108, 185–7
instruction
inquiry interaction 145, 183–4
subject coverage by 150, 183
integrated studies 70, 80–81
intellect 42, 157
intelligence 43, 44, 45
interaction
culture as medium 3, 20–21, 23
social 21, 26, 189
symbolic 4, 5, 23, 36–45
see also communication
interdisciplinary curriculum 95–6, 98

Jackdaw series 70, 83
Jackson, Brian 50
Jackson, Philip W. 44
Johnson, Harry 50
Jones, Richard 131
judgement 163, 164–5, 166, 175–6
Judges, Val 6

Klohr, Paul 71
knowledge
access 145, 166, 181, 188–9
art of teaching and 157, 161
authoritative 178–9, 181–2
coverage context 150, 183
inquiry/instruction interaction 145, 183–4
nature of, control and 134, 138, 145, 178–88 *passim*
uncertainty (research tradition) 187–8, 190
Knox, John 165

language 61, 192
creative innovation and 25–6
culture and 6, 15, 21, 22, 36–41
vernacular humanism 145, 166–77
see also communication; interaction; speech; symbolic systems
leadership 147, 148, 151, 182
learning
outcomes, intended 5, 81, 82
symbolic systems model 43–5
transfer of 95
Learning to Teach through Discussion (Rudduck) 71, 144
legitimate influence, teacher 133–4
leisure, education for 9, 12, 103
library access project 143
literacy 10, 12, 28
logic 132, 151–2

MacDonald, Barry 73, 85–8 *passim*
McNair Report (1944) 193
MAN: a course of study 137, 157, 158, 161, 186
Mao Tse Tung 159
Marsden, Dennis 50
Mason, Charlotte 137
materials, teaching (HCP) 70, 79
central archive 96–7
collections, structured 97, 99–100, 109, 112–13, 125
copyright law 97, 102
difficulty level 83–4, 100–101, 113–14, 124, 128
evaluation of 85
structured 90, 93–4, 98–9, 110–11

mathematics standards 28
meanings (element of culture) 21, 22
Merrill, Frances 50
Mill, John Stuart 176
minority time concept 10, 11, 28
Montefiore, Alan 133
moral education 11, 12, 16, 28, 50
  neutrality in 133–8 *passim*
morale, classroom 50
More, Thomas 176
Morrell, Derek 166, 184
motivation 12, 22, 182
  concept (individual action system)
    43, 44, 45
  conference (Ohio) 71, 119
  minority time 10, 11
  problem, HCP 122, 124–32
multilateral schools 3
music (symbolic system) 21

neutrality, procedural 69, 71–2
  controversial issues 77, 79, 98–9,
    121–4, 126, 128, 168–9
  moral issues 133–8 *passim*
New Education Fellowship 50
Newsom Report (1963) 76, 91, 98,
  112
Nisbet, Stanley 151
Nuffield Foundation 73, 90, 108,
  113
numeracy 10, 12, 27–8

Oakeshott, Michael 187
objectives
  behavioural 5, 81–2, 103–4
  HCP lack of 81–3, 86–8, 117, 134
  see also aims (of education)
Ohio State University 191
Owen, Joslyn 69

pacing (discussions) 117, 130
parents 13, 114, 135, 154
perception, social determinants
  38–9
Perry, Ralph 9
Peters, R. S. 47–8, 52–3, 147
Philippa Fawcett College 73
philosophy research 190–91
physical sciences 173–4
Piaget, Jean 37, 44

Plato 27, 164
positivism, alternatives to 145, 175
Potter, Dennis 176
primary schools 17, 18, 27–8, 55
probability/probabilistic laws 174
procedure
  principles of 52–3, 54, 117, 123,
    134, 147
  rules of 143, 147
professional
  schools 9, 190, 191–2, 193
  standards 28 *bis*, 29, 192
progressive education 17, 18, 51,
  132
project teaching 93
psychology 173, 184
  determinism of 35, 44–5
  group 151–2
  industrial 25, 50
  research 174, 190–91
public schools 8, 12, 14, 16, 29–31
punishments 24, 27
pupil(s) 128, 161
  autonomy *see* autonomy, pupil
  change, objective measurement
    88
  participation 117, 129–30, 146–52
  rights (demands) 153–4
  self-criticism 25, 33, 49, 129
  standards *see* standards
  -teacher interaction 76–7, 106,
    109, 119, 167–8
  with learning difficulties 11–12
  see also adolescents; emancipation

qualifications 13
  see also examinations
questions
  eliciting 127–8
  substantive 135

race relations, teaching about 71,
  137–8, 143, 157
rationalism, humanism and 164
reading
  levels 83–4, 124, 128
  materials, interpretation of 116
  skills, autonomy in 119
reality concept 13, 18, 176–7, 182
reflective discussion 130, 138

relationships (between sexes) 58, 60, 92

relevance, nature of 130, 131

Republic (Plato) 27, 164

research
 'accompanying' 87
 based teaching 145, 177–93
 curriculum *see* curriculum
 dialectics 177–9, 181, 187, 193
 educational 190–93

resource kits 70

resources collections, need for 97, 109

respect concept (group work) 137–8

responsibility allowances 12

rewards 24, 27, 127, 132

Richardson, Elizabeth 151

'road system', educational 3, 10–12

role play 146
 simulation 118, 146, 191

Rommetveit, Ragnar 50

ROSLA
 Crowther Report 3–4, 7–20 *passim*, 28, 98
 Humanities Project aimed at 102, 108–9, 119–20
 Schools Council Working Paper 69, 75–6, 89–90, 134, 161, 166–8, 184

Rudduck, Jean 71, 143–4, 151

rules, group 143, 147, 149, 151–2

sanctions 24, 27

Sapir, E. 38–9

Sayers, Dorothy 57

Scandinavian Journal of Educational Research 4

school
 authority structure 119
 leaving age, raising *see* ROSLA
 sociology of 35–6
 see also elementary schools; multi-lateral schools; primary schools; public schools; secondary modern schools; secondary schools

Schools Council 73, 108, 113

Schools Council Working Papers
 Raising the School Leaving Age 69, 75–6, 89–90, 134, 161, 166–8, 184

Society and the Young School Leaver 69, 90

The Whole Curriculum 13 to 16 144, 153–5

sciences 28, 173
 arts and 10, 28
 in curriculum 26–7, 33–4
 mode of creativity 26, 42

Scott, Sir Walter 184

secondary education 32–3, 188

secondary modern schools 8, 10–11, 12, 16

secondary schools 17, 27–8
 humanities in (approaches) 55–65
 standards 32–3
 whole curriculum aim 144, 153–5

Segerstedt, Torgny 4

selection 3–4, 8, 10

self-criticism, pupil 25, 33, 49, 129

self-development, pupil 9

self-monitoring teaching style 144

Sheard, David 143

Sikes, Patricia 143

simulation 118, 146, 191

sixth form studies 10, 11, 143

skill, teaching as 189

skills, application of (task) 150–51

small-group teaching *see* discussion-based teaching

social
 action 13–14, 44
 change, culture patterns and 12–13
 control, education as form 36, 38
 education 15–16, 18–19
 groups (standards) 32, 50
 interaction 21, 26, 189
 mobility 12–13, 15, 35
 norms (classroom) 50, 54
 policy 74, 154
 pressures 25, 27, 30, 52, 123
 reality 13, 18
 speech 37–9

social class
 class culture 12–13, 15–16
 education and 8–9, 12–13, 14, 31

social determinism 5, 34–46
 creativity (conceptual framework) 36–45

Social Science Research Council 143

social sciences 26, 35, 173–6
social structure, education and 8–9, 35
socialization (education role) 35
society (demands on school) 154–5
sociology
  conceptual scheme 36–45
  of curriculum 4, 20–34
  determinism of 35, 44–5
  of education 4, 5, 35–6
  research (in education) 190–91
Sociology of Teaching (Waller) 36
specialization 8, 9–10, 14–15, 18
  general education and 28–30
speech
  differentiation of 37–41
  egocentric 37–9
  inner 38, 39–40
  social 37–9
standards
  classroom practice 5, 49–54, 155
  cultural education 18–19
  culture patterns and 12–13
  general education 28–9
  group (social pressures) 25, 27, 30, 52, 123
  humanities curriculum 93, 110–11
  public school 31
  pupil 49–51, 52
  secondary school 32–3
status 29, 31, 106
Stenhouse, Lawrence 76, 81, 143
Stevens, Frances 50
Stewart, Dame Muriel 69
streaming 8, 10
style (self-expression in) 165–6
subject
  areas of inquiry 95–6, 99–100
  boundaries 91–2, 106
  coverage 150, 183
  logic 132
symbolic interaction 4, 5, 36–45
symbolic systems
  creativity and 25–6, 43–4
  culture and 21, 22–3, 36–7, 38
  dynamic symbolic field 44–5

tasks (educational) 149–51
Tavistock Institute 192

teacher
  accountability 135, 136
  authority *see* authority, teacher
  bias 58, 98, 106, 111, 123
  as chairman 115–19, 124, 126–30, 136, 143, 168–9
  development 157–62
  diaries (HCP task) 88
  neutrality *see* neutrality, procedural
  -pupil interaction 76–7, 106, 109, 119, 167–8, 184–5
  as researcher 70, 74–9, 107–15, 157–62, 185–7
  roles, task logic in terms of 151–2
  standards *see* standards
  training 103, 162, 193
  see also teaching
teachers' centres 97
teaching 88, 104
  action research in 34, 35, 58, 74–5, 191–2
  art of 144, 155–62, 189
  creative function 25–7
  group process 23–5
  research as basis 145, 177–93
  standards *see* standards
'Teaching and Legitimate Influence in Moral Education' (Hyland) 133–8 *passim*
technical education 7, 10–11, 12
technology 8
television 101–2, 176–7
thematic study 58–60, 96
  experimental approach 61–5
theology, humanism and 163–5, 179
thought
  creative 43–4
  language of 39–41
  reflective 42–3
Times Higher Educational Supplement 178
'tone', classroom 50
Toynbee, Arnold 18–19
trades union education 71
tradition 12, 26–7, 45, 50, 96, 132
  academic 42
  role of, in humanities 93, 111
traditionalist standards 51–2
transfer of learning 95